Conflicting Communication Interests in America

The Case of National Public Radio

Tom McCourt

Westport, Connecticut
London

Library of Congress Cataloging-in-Publication Data

McCourt, Tom, 1958–
    Conflicting communication interests in America : the case of
National Public Radio / Tom McCourt.
        p.   cm.
    Includes bibliographical references and index.
    ISBN 0–275–96358–6 (alk. paper)
    1. National Public Radio (U.S.)   2. Public radio—United States.
3. Public broadcasting—United States.   I. Title.
    HE8697.95.U6 M363 1999
    384.54'06'573—dc21   99–22136

British Library Cataloguing in Publication Data is available.

Library of Congress Catalog Card Number: 99–22136
ISBN: 0–275–96358–6

First published in 1999

Praeger Publishers, 88 Post Road West, Westport, CT 06881
An imprint of Greenwood Publishing Group, Inc.
www.praeger.com

Printed in the United States of America

The paper used in this book complies with the
Permanent Paper Standard issued by the National
Information Standards Organization (Z39.48–1984).

10 9 8 7 6 5 4 3 2 1

LATE 1960's +

Contents

Tables

Acknowledgments

Sharon Strover, John Peters, and David Bywaters provided detailed critiques of successive drafts of this work, and I am greatly in their debt. Of course, I am responsible for any errors in fact or logic. Sharon's assistance, suggestions, and unflagging support were invaluable while I was a student at the University of Texas and beyond. John's seminars at the University of Iowa triggered my interest in the complexities and contradictions of public life; later, whenever I thought I had embarked onto new terrain, I soon discovered his restless footprints. David has helped me in innumerable ways over the years. In addition to his talents as a writer and scholar, his droll insights into the vagaries of human nature have been a constant source of delight.

Cynthia Meyers, Eric Rothenbuhler, Larry Smith, and Nabeel Zuberi offered many helpful comments on all or parts of the manuscript. They are generous colleagues and good friends. Heather Feeny of Wyoming Public Radio gave encouragement as well as a much-needed perspective from the trenches. Tom Connors and Karen King of the National Public Broadcasting Archive provided a pleasant and accommodating environment for research. Steve Behrens of *Current* was always ready to answer questions and provide contacts. Norman Bemelmans of Peach State Public Radio, Peter Fetzek in Minnesota, and Heidi Graatsch of the Corporation for Public Broadcasting provided materials and information. I particularly appreciate the efforts of Mildred Vasan in placing the manuscript. Research was funded by a Houston Endowment Fellowship from the University of Texas and a series of research grants from Shell Oil.

KOOP in Austin, KDHX in St. Louis, and the wonderful Mr. A at Chicago's WNIB provided the soundtrack while I wrote this book. They are public broadcasters in the true sense of the word.

Many colleagues have helped shape this book in tangible and intangible ways, including Glenda Balas, Gene Bernofsky, Barbara Welch Breder, Patrick Burkart, Richard DeLaurell, Said Graioud, Craig Klein, Larry Mullen, David Riddle, America Rodriguez, Nikhil Sinha, Laura Stein, Olivier Tchouaffe, and Willard Uncapher. My deepest appreciation goes to Darren Campeau, Sandra Gayle Carter, Ash Corea, John Downing, Jen Evans, Shuchi Kothari, Jane Martin, Floyd Meadows, Craig O'Connell, Michael "Big Man" Shirk, and Dan Thornbury. I could count on their friendship, generosity, and humor through high times and hard times alike. Bill Bethea, John Boyer, and John Liebrand are keenly missed, and their memory lives on.

My parents, George and Helen McCourt, have been supportive of all my endeavors; they have been a rock upon which I could always depend. Catherine McCourt's delight in her young world remains a source of great joy and inspiration. Finally, Julie McCourt has inspired me in countless ways. Her many acts of courage as a community organizer continue to leave me in awe. Her quick, pointed wit always brought me back to earth whenever I took myself too seriously. Her indefatigable energy has sustained me, and her unwavering trust indulged me, through times when I otherwise would have been consumed by despair. Most of all, her abiding compassion and faith in the essential goodness of people have provided a light that has illuminated my way. This work is dedicated to her.

Abbreviations

ACNO	Advisory Council of National Organizations
ACUBS	Association of College and University Broadcasting Stations
AFTRA	American Federation of Television and Radio Artists
APB	Alliance for Public Broadcasting
APR	American Public Radio (later PRI)
APRS	Association of Public Radio Stations
AQH	Average-quarter-hour
BBC	British Broadcasting Corporation
CPB	Corporation for Public Broadcasting
CSG	Community Service Grant
EEN	Eastern Educational Network
ERN	Educational Radio Network
ETS	Educational Television Stations
FCC	Federal Communications Commission
FRC	Federal Radio Commission
HEW	Department of Health, Education, and Welfare
MPR	Minnesota Public Radio
NACRE	National Advisory Council on Radio in Education
NAEB	National Association of Educational Broadcasters (formerly ACUBS)
NCER	National Committee on Education by Radio

NER   National Educational Radio
NET   National Educational Television
NETRC   National Educational Television and Radio Center (formerly ETRC)
NFCB   National Federation of Community Broadcasters
NPPAG   National Program Production and Acquisition Grants
NPR   National Public Radio
NTIA   National Telecommunications and Information Administration
PBS   Public Broadcasting Service
PRAP   Public Radio Audience Profile
PRI   Public Radio International (formerly American Public Radio)
PRPD   Public Radio Program Directors
PTFP   Public Telecommunications Facility Program
RAC   Radio Advisory Council
SPDF   Satellite Program Development Fund
SRG   Station Resource Group
TCAF   Temporary Commission on Alternative Financing for Public Telecommunications

1

Introduction

What glorious show! Yet but a show, alas!

—Goethe, *Faust*[1]

Public broadcasting's brief history in the United States appears to be a drama punctuated by triumph. On closer inspection, it more often than not resembles a tragedy leavened with farce. The system has been riven from the outset by a contradictory mission: to create a single national identity while giving voice to those excluded by the marketplace. It has been further desiccated by the long-standing hegemony of commercial broadcasting, the vagaries of government regulation and jurisprudence, and an often apathetic public. Dissension within its own ranks worsens these problems. The embers of self-immolation smolder constantly, fanned by those anxious to use the system for their advantage. When fueled by public officials seeking ideological vengeance and self-aggrandizement, these tensions ignite into conflagrations that threaten to consume the system; public broadcasters then cease their internecine warfare only long enough to link themselves into a halting and hesitant firewall. Their "reforms" narrowly averted a calamity in 1972, when Richard Nixon vetoed funding for the Corporation for Public Broadcasting in an effort to squelch dissent; and again in 1980, when Ronald Reagan wanted to phase out public broadcasting's paltry federal support as part of a campaign to reinforce marketplace ideology in the public sector. However, recent attacks on continued funding for public broadcasting have been much more savage and promise to be much more destructive, as a growing number of public broadcasters have come to disavow the legitimacy of public goods in general. Their capitulation bodes ill for the continued viability of public services in the United States.

Public broadcasting increasingly suffered from incessant hectoring by right-wing ideologues in the early 1990s. In 1992, Senate majority leader Bob Dole (R.-Kansas) accused public broadcasting of "unrelenting liberal cheerleading," and Sen. Jesse Helms (R.-North Carolina) wrongly claimed that the PBS documentary "Tongues Untied" had shown "homosexual men dancing around naked" and thus "blatantly promoted homosexuality as an acceptable lifestyle."[2] In October 1994, a House-Senate conference committee sliced $7 million from CPB's 1995 appropriation of $292.6 million. While not as drastic as the $21.1 million cut approved by the House (final funding represented an increase of nearly 4 percent over the previous year), the cut marked the end of a nearly twenty-year policy of "forward funding," in which Congress would earmark CPB funds two years ahead of regular appropriations in order to insulate public broadcasting from overt political pressures. Conservative critics were not mollified; as James Ledbetter notes, "a television and radio system funded with Congressionally controlled money provides the ultimate hot-button issue, a grandstander's dream."[3]

House speaker Newt Gingrich (R.-Georgia) led the pounding of doom drums against public broadcasting. When asked about funding for arts and cultural organizations on the November 13, 1994, broadcast of ABC's *This Week with David Brinkley*, Gingrich retorted, "I personally would privatize them all." In a December 30 C-Span interview, Gingrich belittled public broadcasting as "a little sandbox for the rich." Shortly thereafter, he told a meeting of Republicans that "I don't understand why they call it public broadcasting. As far as I'm concerned, there's nothing public about it. Rush Limbaugh is public broadcasting."[4] Despite Gingrich's seeming antipathy toward public broadcasting, however, his attacks appeared to be somewhat offhand, a way to score easy points with conservative fundraising groups. Gingrich apparently had been inspired to target public broadcasting by Rep. Robert Livingston (R.-Louisiana), whom Gingrich jumped over four senior Republicans to chair the House Appropriations Committee. At a confirmation hearing, Livingston stated that if Congress couldn't "zero out" the Corporation for Public Broadcasting, the National Endowment for the Arts, and the National Endowment for the Humanities, the Republicans might as well abandon their intentions to cut spending. Livingston told journalist Fred Barnes that this statement "was just off the top of my head," but within days Gingrich called for "zeroing out" all three agencies.[5]

The pounding grew louder and louder. In a November 29, 1994, interview on the PBS series *TechnoPolitics*, Sen. Larry Pressler (R.-South Dakota), head of the Senate Commerce Committee, which oversees CPB funding, carped about "the political twist that I believe public TV constantly puts on things. For example, I was watching this nice baseball series and, God, every night I'd have to listen to Mario Cuomo tell about his boyhood. It just seems . . . that all their favorite people are from the American left."[6] On January 27, 1995, Pressler forwarded to CPB board chairman Henry Cauthen a sixteen-page questionnaire that requested, among other things, a list of political contributions by public broadcasting employees; the gender, age and ethnicity of NPR personnel; and the number of NPR staff members who had worked for Pacifica radio, as opposed to "evangelical Christian stations." The questionnaire also included transparently leading questions, including, "Have John Dinges at NPR and Mary Jane McKiven at PBS done a good job at assuring balance and objectivity in programming? If so, why are there so many complaints?" Pressler dropped five of the questions after howls of protest from public broadcasters, who nevertheless dutifully completed and returned the questionnaires; a CPB official estimated that their completion required 1,800 staff hours and $92,000.[7]

Other attacks veiled ideology in pragmatism. Livingston stated that "the issue . . . isn't the merits or demerits of public broadcasting. The issue is that over the last 25 years we've accumulated a $5 trillion debt." Pressler told the *Washington Times*, "Now we have the Internet, cable TV, satellite broadcasting. Should all of these be given public support?" He also claimed that private entrepreneurs were raking in billions of dollars from showcasing their wares on public television, alleging that *Sesame Street* earned $800 million per year and *Barney and Friends* had generated more than $1 billion in profits.[8] The truth was somewhat more prosaic: Children's Television Workshop (the producers of *Sesame Street*) received less than $20 million annually in product licensing royalties. Twelve million dollars were used to fund production costs for the series, and the remainder was applied to children's literacy programs. Income for the privately held Lyons Group, producer of *Barney and Friends*, was estimated to be slightly more than $20 million.[9] Some inside the public broadcasting system joined the chorus. CPB board member Vic Gold snorted, "Hell, let the cultural things go on their own!" Even former NPR president Frank Mankiewicz chimed in: "Public television keeps putting a lot of money into experimental programming and independent production. They could do away with all of that."[10] The salaries of public broadcasting officers provided more ammunition for critics, although these were capped by Congress at less than $150,000 at the time. Critics complained also of public television station overlap, though a 1989 PBS study found that of eight metropolitan areas with more than one public television station, only 15 percent of programming on average was duplicated in any single week.[11]

The 1995 attacks on public broadcasting combined Nixon's ideological vendettas and Reagan's bottom-line reductionism, yet they outdid both in venality and brutishness. Extensive congressional hearings gave conservative groups valuable TV hours and column inches, but the furor, for all its heat and hyperbole, did not result in a "zeroing out" of public broadcast funding. The CPB eventually was funded at $275 million for fiscal year 1996, $260 million for 1997 and $250 million for 1998 and 1999. Though hobbled, public broadcasting survived, for several reasons. Some politicians may have been cowed by public support for the system (although one representative claimed that calls and letters from constituents had been "fairly steady" but not overwhelming).[12] The government also hopes that public broadcasters will create demand for digital television. A public television lobbyist claimed,

If public television is given financial support to make the transition . . . it would lead the entire terrestrial broadcasting industry, as it has in the past with satellite interconnection. This would accelerate by years the establishment of the ATV market and the day when the government could recover and auction the analog spectrum.[13]

Finally, many public broadcasters, eager to rid themselves of the albatross of federal funding, willingly complied with critics. In a meeting about CPB funding with public radio station managers from his state, House Budget Committee chairman John Kasich (R.-Ohio) insisted, "The number is zero!" To Kasich's astonishment, John Perry of WKSU shrugged and said "OK," and Dale Ouzts of WOSU added, "Our problem's never been with zero, it's how we *get* to zero."[14]

These comments illustrate how dramatically public broadcasting has changed since its founding in 1967. Charged by the Carnegie Commission to "provide a voice for groups in the community that may otherwise be unheard," public broadcasting increasingly has embraced the marketplace through programming, sponsorship, and entrepreneurial activities that undermine its very *raison d'être*. Though never given the consistent government support of comparable systems in other countries and therefore always obsessed with money, it lately has concerned itself with little else. Both critics and supporters argue that public broadcasting must be driven down the road of cost-efficiency and competitiveness. Rather than providing a public service, the Public Broadcasting Service and National Public Radio increasingly are bent on "leveraging the brand" to increase subsidies. Even the most ardent defenders of public broadcasting are obsessed with money. Responding to rumors of a deal between NPR and Telecommunications, Incorporated, subsidiary Liberty Media, an independent radio producer stated, "If NPR is seen as just another media company, why should listeners make a donation in their end of the 'moral contract'?" Long-time independent public radio producer Larry Josephson added, "If the perception of NPR changes from that of an independent public-service radio network, to that of a merchandiser not much different from QVC, we could lose the affection that our listener-contributors have for us, and . . . weaken their willingness to send us checks (and to write to Congress)."[15] The pursuit of money deforms the purpose of public radio, which now wants its audience not, say, to deliberate on public issues but simply to consume more public radio.

THE INTERNATIONAL CRISIS OF PUBLIC BROADCASTING

Public broadcasting increasingly is viewed as anachronistic in an age of expanding transnational capitalism, myriad media delivery systems, and sociocultural fragmentation. Yet the privatization of public media is no inevitable by-product of the neoliberal ideology that dominates contemporary life in the West. Instead, it is driven by the corporations that stand to profit from privatization of formerly public goods and services. Technological advancements in communications, the steady migration of jobs to Third World countries, and the search for new means of disseminating products across national borders have led to the growth of transnational media corporations. Nations preoccupied with their shrinking economies have anxiously cooperated with these industries in hopes of garnering a slice of the international market in high technology. This collusion has led many nations to surrender much of their sovereignty over telecommunications, and control now often rests with transnational corporations, removed from any single government or policy authority. More and more nations have come to view communications as a source of money rather than of culture and to question the appropriateness of government subsidies for broadcasting.[16] The distinctions between private and public broadcasters grow ever more blurry as the latter are forced to consider not social utility but cost efficiency and audience maximization.

These economic processes have been supported by ideological rationalizations from both the Right and, paradoxically, the Left. Neoliberal economists and pundits argue that the scarcity rationale that used to justify government control and financing of broadcasting has been rendered obsolete by multichannel media delivery systems. New "technologies of freedom," they claim, will single-handedly create a flowering of pluralism and diversity in an equitable marketplace of ideas.[17] Although based in a facile technological determinism, this belief is brandished as a self-evident truth to buttress claims that new channel capacities should be devoted to market-based broadcasting, in which "the public's interest, then, defines the public interest."[18] However, the essentially political nature of broadcasting is underscored by the government's ability to ease marketplace pressures by lifting restrictions on telecommunications ownership. The 1996 Telecommunications Act started a frenzy of speculation in broadcast properties; from 1995 to 1996, the total value of sales of radio stations skyrocketed from $5.3 billion to $16 billion. Between January 1996 and September 1997, more than a quarter of the nearly eleven thousand radio stations in the United States changed hands.[19] The deregulation represented by the 1996 Telecommunications Act actually is a de facto re-regulation, raising barriers to entry and allowing players with the deepest pockets to snatch up the airwaves without having to account to anyone for their use.

As control of national media increasingly rests in private hands, the very idea of "public" goods per se has come into question. The growing equation of marketplace efficiency with the public interest and the conflation of consumerism with citizenship undermine the value of collective approaches to public needs. People have come to define themselves by their economic, social, or ethnic interests and to mobilize solely on behalf of those interests.[20] Diminishing participation in public affairs is matched by growing private control of formerly public goods such as roads, schools, and security. This process culminates in what Jurgen Habermas terms the "refeudalization" of society, in which people retreat into privately guarded gated communities, withdraw their children from public schools, and then vote down taxes that support local police departments and school districts.[21] In consequence, public goods come to seem slipshod and second-rate. In public housing, public transportation, and public education, "public" means "poor." As it undermines the value of public goods, marketplace ideology at best addresses the public strictly as apolitical consumers. It fosters a withdrawal into a private and apolitical life, redefining citizenship so that "it becomes less a collective, political activity than an individual, economic activity—the right to pursue one's interests, without hindrance, in the marketplace."[22] At worst, by limiting collective approaches to social problems, it walks hand in hand with "a deeply neo-conservative attachment to political and cultural authoritarianism."[23]

Many on the Left also find fault with the idea of universal public goods. Public broadcasters traditionally have held a priori notions of what is best for the public; however, the paternalistic conception of a single (or, as it often has been labeled, "mass") public may be irrelevant, as myths of singular national identities shatter into shards of personal and social difference. Political and cultural discourse increasingly is beset by fragmentation, and challenges by counterdiscourses in racism, nationalism, and fundamentalism.[24] These counterdiscourses form the basis of an emerging politics of "difference" that, while meant to empower those who historically have been shut out of public debate, reinforces a view of public life as built on conflicts between interest groups. Although some of the players are new, the rules of the game are unchanged. The exercise of power, rather than the process of public debate, remains the ultimate arbiter of social relations. Accordingly, group rights alone are important; the collective interest is an illusion. Most significantly (and ominously), a politics grounded in ideals of cultural authenticity attributes an essential character to group identity—which may result in exclusivity and oppression as readily as it does in collective discovery and liberation. While ostensibly engendering democratic participation, the politics of "difference" ultimately may serve reactionary rather than progressive ends. The cultural segmentation of society heightens ethnic tensions and minimizes class issues, and so it plays directly into the hands of those who seek to suppress substantive social change.

The politics of difference have perhaps benefited the expansion of transnational capitalism by helping it convert cultural differences into marketing ploys. Cultural movements are seen as means to advance not social justice but the value of consumer goods, to which they lend an aura of exoticism. As telecommunications industries create transnational markets for news and entertainment, they simultaneously fragment the public, along lines of income, ethnicity, and gender, into a series of taste cultures based on preferences for consumption. In many ways, the politics of difference colludes unwittingly with target marketing and trivializes cultural movements for social justice. As David Rieff notes, the catch phrases of multiculturalism—"cultural diversity," "difference," the need to "do away with boundaries"—"resemble the stock phrases of the modern corporation: 'product diversification,' 'the global marketplace,' and 'the boundary-less company.' "[25]

THE CONTRADICTIONS OF PUBLIC BROADCASTING

If public broadcasting indeed is structurally crippled, moribund, and irrelevant, then why is it subject to such intense ideological assaults? Public broadcasting certainly is no great burden on American taxpayers. In 1995, it accounted for less than two one-hundredths of 1 percent of the federal budget. Nor is there evidence of an overarching conspiracy on the part of public broadcasters to subvert traditional American ideals. Domestic public broadcasting was purposely decentralized to minimize its political role; the service's organization (or lack thereof) precludes any notion of a "controlling" consciousness animating public broadcasters' actions, aside from their desire to draw more revenues. In a stinging critique published in 1993, Lewis Lapham decried public broadcasting's "medieval" structure and finances: "If the system were to be represented on a geopolitical map, it would resemble the Holy Roman Empire during the last years of its decaying hegemony—351 petty states and dukedoms, each with its own flag, court chamberlain, and trumpet fanfare."[26] Nor does public broadcasting necessarily represent, as some claim, a continuing threat to "a complete victory of market ideology in the public sphere."[27] Such wishful thinking ignores the variety of alternative media in place, as well as the fact that public broadcasters have engaged in overt and tacit marketing activities for decades.

Public broadcasting in the United States has been subjected to intense scrutiny from critics across the political spectrum for a number of reasons. First, its scale distinguishes it from other cultural endeavors. It reaches most of the U.S. population, through its affiliate radio and television stations, and its products are exposed to immediate public evaluation. Second, since its production is highly organized and collaborative, public broadcasting is more industrialized than many other cultural realms. It receives public funding to serve constituencies often ignored by commercial broadcasters, yet the industrial structure of public broadcasting on the local and national levels ensures that these constituencies often have minimal input to the system. Third, the effectiveness of public broadcasting is virtually impossible to determine. Commercial broadcasters can easily quantify success in terms of profits, but the services offered by public broadcasters are intangible or ends in themselves.[28] Raymond Ho, the executive director for Maryland Public Television, described the difficulty of establishing normative standards of success for public broadcasting:

If we turn to the traditional criteria of ratings and revenues of commercial broadcasting, we are criticized for selling our souls. If we appeal to small audiences, some say we're elitist. If we try to broaden the base, we are hungry for ratings. If we ask for more federal funds, we are told to look to the private sector. If we try to accommodate corporate interests, we are accused of commercializing.[29]

One the most common criticisms leveled at public broadcasting is that unlike commercial media, its practitioners lack a common agenda. A number of analysts have suggested various goals, modeled vaguely on the BBC's charter, such as universal service; public accountability and editorial independence from government and private interests; programming that caters "to all tastes and interests," particularly those of minorities and the disadvantaged; education and reinforcement of national, regional, and local identity via "cultural enrichment"; creation of an informed electorate; and ethical purpose and commitment to "quality."[30] Nevertheless, these goals may be contradictory and mutually exclusive. "Quality" may be defined as innovative content or as a canonical approach to culture that is the antithesis of innovation. Similarly, it may imply sophisticated production values or rough-hewn authenticity. Public broadcasting also has often been criticized for articulating and perpetuating ruling interests. To Stuart Hall, the BBC's representations of public life are intended to produce social consensus, by equating consumption with political participation, in which "the democratic enfranchisement of all citizens within political society, and the economic enfranchisement of all consumers within the free-enterprise economy, would rapidly be paralleled by the cultural absorption of all groups into the culture of the center." In contrast, Paddy Scannell argues that Hall's critique "collapses any difference or contradiction in the work of broadcasting. As such, broadcasting has no history, no development."[31] Scannell claims that public broadcasting serves democratic principles, by "resocializing" private life and allowing unprecedented access to public life through political and cultural media events, but his analysis overlooks the fact that professionals, rather than the public themselves, frame this public discourse.

We think of a "public" broadcasting system as open rather than closed, freely available rather than privately owned and accessed, and held collectively rather than individually.[32] However, the Corporation for Public Broadcasting, National Public Radio, and the Public Broadcasting Service are *privately* owned, not-for-profit organizations. Many "public" radio and television stations also are operated by private organizations. Public broadcasting received no federal aid until 1962; many stations were founded by high-profile individuals, whose successors remain hostile to what they view as government and public meddling.[33] This proprietary attitude also reflects the nature of the arts in the United States: unlike in other industrialized countries, they are supported almost exclusively by private funding from corporations, foundations, and philanthropists. While this privatization may partially insulate the arts from politics, it nevertheless subjects them to the marketplace, the standards of which outweigh aesthetic, moral, and ethical concerns. The market distribution system operates most efficiently when the tastes and desires of consumers are known and controllable. In order to meet the demands of the distribution system and avoid jeopardizing their subsidies, public broadcasters must concentrate on "the safe, cheap and known."[34] Paradoxically, personnel in arts and cultural organizations tend to be motivated primarily by ideological purposes of creative freedom and cultural uplift, not money. They believe that their work therefore is intrinsically public spirited; in the late 1970s an independent producer breathlessly hailed public radio as "a monastery of liberal humanism in the dark age of mercantilism."[35] In a discussion of the BBC's Channel Four, which was designed specifically to enhance public broadcasting's diversity by commissioning programs from independent producers, Nicholas Garnham argues that the producer's campaign for "freedom" is based on the nineteenth century artisanal mode of cultural and intellectual work, which has long been obsolete in a market-based economy.[36] While intended to justify continuing subsidies, this ideology inherently limits public broadcasters' awareness of their relationship to the public.

The domestic public broadcasting system is also caught between convergence and decentralization. Unlike the BBC's model of public broadcasting, which is based on a centralized administrative and production bureaucracy and a nationwide network of transmitters, the Public Broadcasting Act of 1967 cobbled the American public broadcasting service together from disparate, preexisting elements. Congress and commercial broadcasters were strongly opposed to a publicly subsidized national network controlled from a single base of operations; the former feared such a system's influence on the electorate, the latter potential competition for audiences. Educators also desired to avoid the perceived abuses of centralized control by the three commercial networks. Indeed, one can make a compelling argument that the domestic public broadcasting system is a "system" in name only. Former CPB administrator James Fellows states that public broadcasting "from a managerial or operational perspective . . . is not one system, but many."[37] Station licenses are held by public universities and private colleges, state governments, private community organizations, and public schools. In addition to wide variations in revenue, administration, and funding, their agendas often differ (for instance, general audiences as opposed to specialized audiences, education as opposed to entertainment). The imposition of new organizational forms on this decentralized system created tensions between licensees and national agencies over distribution of federal funds and programming responsibilities. For example, NPR is allowed to produce programming, but PBS is not. Since public broadcasting is constituted by so many differing organizations and agendas, decision making requires a slow and difficult consensus; former National Educational Television executive James Day once referred to public broadcasting as "a long series of meetings occasionally interrupted by a program."[38] Countless task force reports and endless bureaucratic restructuring produce minimal results. Reviewing public broadcasting's history, John Macy (the first president and chief executive officer of CPB) complained that

it is unhappily the cultural tendency of public service institutions to assume a life of their own, without adequate reference to those for whom they were established to serve. Decisions tend to be formed more to serve those within the institution or to strengthen some feature of the institution without relation to its service goals.[39]

Despite their claims to public service, public broadcasters cannot completely distance themselves from their commercial counterparts, who set the general level of production costs directly by supplying equipment and programs and indirectly by establishing benchmarks for labor costs.[40] Public broadcasters are locked into competition for talent, but they cannot pass on cost increases by raising the price of their services. Nor can they cut production costs, which they regard as tied to the "quality" that differentiates them from commercial broadcasters. Media deregulation was partially rationalized by the claim that public broadcasters would assume the mantle of news and public affairs service to their communities. In 1980, then-FCC chairman Charles Ferris told the Public Radio Conference that placing public radio outlets in every community "helps reduce the rationale for federal regulation of certain aspects of radio service" and would assure the delivery of specialized entertainment formats such as classical, folk music, and jazz.[41] Ferris's vision for public broadcasting was partially realized; the service's emphasis on "quality" was used to justify the pandering to mass tastes by commercial broadcasters. An anonymous representative of a commercial network stated that "PBS does the kind of programming which relieves us of any supposed obligation to put on similar kinds of things."[42]

A final contradiction involves popularity versus diversity. Willard Rowland, Jr., notes, "As noncommercial broadcasting began to call itself 'public' in order to justify calls for greater funding, it was expected to achieve greater and more frequent audience reach."[43] Moreover, public broadcasting also was supposed to represent political and social diversity, and higher tax-based appropriations led to proportionally greater insistence by groups for representation and participation in the system, as well as to greater government oversight and political interference. Historically, public broadcasters (particularly on the local level) avoid programs that might offend a segment of the public broadcasting community (that is, underwriters, station managers, board members, subscribers and politicians). Given the costs and uncertainties of program production, public broadcasters readily accept programs produced under corporate subsidies, yet the fear that innovative programming will alienate viewers and listeners is countered by equal fear that a lack of innovative programming will alienate them. The inability to resolve these issues has led public broadcasters to respond to public scrutiny with a siege mentality and institutional torpor. In August, 1989, a *Newsweek* columnist dismissed federal funding for public broadcasting as "highbrow pork barrel."[44] No one from the public broadcasting industry responded to the charge, leading Rowland to claim that public broadcasters have

expectations [that] are now mundane and short-term. The refrain goes something like this: "The cuts of the early Reagan years have been restored; be happy. The general revenue trend is still upward; be content. Listeners and viewers still seem to be so grateful for any alternative to commercial television that they readily turn out to help with pledge weeks and auctions; be satisfied."[45]

Because of external pressures and internal conflicts, public broadcasters are unable to present a coherent agenda comparable to the profit motive that drives the actions of commercial broadcasters. Nevertheless, local and national public broadcasting organizations seeking to legitimate their activities make a fetish of mission statements. According to Donald Mullally, the manager of public radio station WILL and former vice president of National Public Radio, "The mission statement is the touchstone against which every activity of the station is tested. . . . [I]t is, in a sense, the tablet of commandments handed down by the licensee." However, these mission statements largely consist of strings of platitudes purposely selected for their vagueness and calculated inoffensiveness. Mullally cites the mission statement crafted by his station as a model for public licensees: the station will "inform citizens of the significant issues facing society[;] . . . convey the diverse cultural past[;] . . . entertain the public by presenting the significant in the fields of music, the arts, and ideas in an appealing way."[46] The equivocal nature of these goals is intended to appease conflicting divisions and individuals within the station as well as head off potential conflicts between stations and their licensing institutions. For example, Mullally's failure to mention economically marginal audiences may be attributed to the "high culture" focus of a station licensed to a major university.

Ambiguous goals serve to bind disparate elements within public broadcasting, including government entities responsible for regulation, funders, programming creators and distributors, pressure groups, audiences, and other sociocultural institutions.[47] However, their very ambiguity hampers the ability of public broadcasting to define itself and demonstrate its difference as the vagaries of its service ethos are confronted by the culture of the economic marketplace. William Hoynes finds that the "mission" soon gives way to exclusive concern with raising funds, building audiences, and boosting prestige.[48] The system also appeases its most vocal elements and important constituencies by periodically redefining its goals, redistributing its budget, and restructing its form. This process accounts for the continuing acquiescence of public broadcasters to primary funders, whether federal or state governments or private corporations, and their relative indifference to the concerns of independent producers or public interest groups, who, while overtly involved in public broadcasting's mission of diversity, deliver the content rather than the money required to maintain the system.

As other media divert its audience, and as spiraling production and distribution costs erode its finances, public broadcasting must justify additional subsidies by demonstrating its cost-effectiveness. One strategy is to consolidate operations between stations or eliminate stations altogether. As James Ledbetter notes, "Beginning with a Boston Consulting Group study in 1991, many national public broadcasters seized on 'station overlap' as one of the system's villainous efficiencies."[49] A second strategy involves aggressive merchandising, promotions, and commercial tie-ins. A third is to "unbundle" goods and services, offering them individually with the intent of winnowing out those that are uneconomical or have limited demand. NPR began to unbundle its programming in the late 1980s under pressure from its member stations, with drastic consequences for the public radio system. A fourth tactic, related to unbundling, involves constructing a consistent "product image" to enhance predictability for consumers and minimize risk for producers. This trend is clearly exemplified by the growing number of public radio stations that adopt commercial radio programming structures in hopes of attracting a stable "core" audience that will contribute financially to the organization and, in turn, attract business underwriters. Finally, public broadcasters increasingly seek to quantify their audiences through commercial audience research methodologies. According to Ien Ang, such research has an aura of scientific "objectivity" and serves to rationalize and reinforce institutional decisions. Results from ratings surveys also reinforce public broadcasters' claims of representing popular will by providing empirical proof of audience demographics for existing and potential funding sources.[50] While proclaiming that their concern with education and cultural uplift differentiates them from commercial broadcasting, public broadcasters increasingly belie that difference by following the path of least resistance and reifying the public through the divide and conquer strategies of commercial broadcasting.

Public broadcasters now speak of their constituencies as "customers" rather than a self-aware public. The irrelevance of the actual public was starkly illustrated by 1995 congressional hearings over federal funding for the Corporation for Public Broadcasting. Testimony in support of continued funding was presented almost exclusively by people affiliated with public broadcasting organizations or by groups who benefited from specific ancillary services, such as the American Council for the Blind. The public was conspicuously absent from both sides of the debate, as it had been in 1987 hearings held by the Senate Commerce Committee's telecommunications subcommittee to commemorate the Public Broadcasting Act's twentieth anniversary. Asked why no members of the public were invited to participate at the 1987 hearings, Sen. Daniel Inouye replied that "about a month ago this committee advised the public of the oversight hearings to be held at this time. None of the consumer groups indicated an interest."[51] Such statements limn the fundamental irrationality of public broadcasting in the United States. Although "public," its organizational structure and practices on the local and national levels largely have been determined by private groups and individuals, and its efforts at increasing "popularity" have been based on practices adopted from commercial broadcasters. These practices fragment the public into a series of discrete and passive taste cultures, distracting them from any common interest grounded in active participation in politics and culture. They ultimately deprive public broadcasting of any clear purpose, and the system continues to stumble through an identity crisis.

PUBLIC RADIO AND PUBLIC LIFE

National Public Radio has grown dramatically since its incorporation in 1970. The May 1971 debut of *All Things Considered* was carried by 104 stations in thirty-four states and Puerto Rico; by 1992, more than 450 stations in forty-eight states were NPR affiliates. In 1973, the first detailed estimate of public radio's listenership revealed an audience of 2.2 million persons per week; by 1992, this number had grown to ten million.[52] The number of individuals contributing financially to National Public Radio and its affiliate stations soared from forty thousand in 1971 to nearly one and a half million by 1992, and the average contribution in that period more than doubled. These increases were reflected in the range and scope of NPR's news programming. Although National Public Radio's early programming could be strikingly adventurous and innovative, more often it reflected the amateurish efforts of a struggling and marginal operation. By 1992, in contrast, NPR had come of age: *Newsweek* was hailing NPR as "the *New Yorker* of the airwaves."[53] Three years later, at the height of the CPB funding controversy, NPR's status as a player in contemporary political and social life was underscored by President Bill Clinton's comment to a fundraising banquet for the NPR Foundation: "What can I tell you? I'm just an NPR kind of president."[54] Throughout its history, NPR's news and public affairs programming has been showered with accolades and awards. Its affiliate stations provide the sole outlet for noncommercial radio programming in most American communities. To the majority of the American public, National Public Radio *is* public radio.

Despite the high profile of public radio and television, research about public broadcasting in the United States has been conspicuous largely by its absence until relatively recently. Several reasons account for this absence. Audiences for public broadcasting were relatively small, which supposedly minimized its social impact (although corporate underwriters would beg to differ). Public broadcasting targeted educated audiences, who were likely to analyze it less critically than they would commercial broadcasting, and scholarly research, which emphasized the market forces that shape commercial radio and television, regarded public broadcasting as an inscrutable anomaly, if it considered it at all. Analyses of public broadcasting characterized audiences in the passive terms used by commercial broadcasting, or they focused on the ways in which corporate subsidies shaped public broadcasting's agenda. However, a recent renewal of scholarly interest in citizenship has begun to redress this neglect. One of the primary catalysts for this interest was the 1989 publication of Jurgen Habermas's seminal *The Structural Transformation of the Public Sphere* in an English translation.[55] Revisionist accounts of early broadcasting by Susan Douglas (1987), Robert McChesney (1993), and Susan Smulyan (1994) have undermined many of the assumptions regarding the development of electronic media in the United States. In addition, global transformations in public service broadcasting have stimulated interest in domestic public broadcasting. Within this decade, several noteworthy books have been published on public broadcasting in the United States, including scholarly works by Marilyn Lashley (1992), William Hoynes (1994), Ralph Engelman (1996), and James Ledbetter (1997), as well as popular accounts by Mary Collins (1993), James Day (1995), and Thomas Looker (1995).

Nevertheless, scholarly research about radio broadcasting (particularly critical research) has been quite rare since the dissolution of the Columbia radio research project following World War II, and research on public radio is almost nonexistent. With a handful of exceptions, public radio has been consigned to occasional chapters, fleeting addenda, and footnotes. The report that led to radio's last-minute inclusion in the Public Broadcasting Act of 1967 referred to it as "The Hidden Medium," and one of the few academic journal articles examining public radio's structure and practices referred to it as "The Other Public Medium." Three major policy statements have been issued on public broadcasting in the last thirty years: two reports commissioned by the Carnegie Foundation (published in 1967 and 1979, respectively) and a 1993 report from the Twentieth Century Task Force on Public Television. Of the three, only the second Carnegie report specifically mentions public radio. Recent popular press books on National Public Radio are encomiums for the most part and provide virtually no analysis of NPR's relationship with the public. In both academic texts and the popular press, radio usually is depicted as an anachronism whose cultural heyday ended more than half a century ago, although one that remains a substantial component of the American economy. According to Bob Edwards, the host of NPR's *Morning Edition*, "Radio is pretty much a cash register now. It's not even a jukebox anymore. It's simply a vehicle for making the station manager wealthy."[56]

Two primary factors account for radio's neglect by scholars. As television's political, economic, cultural, and social implications became manifest in the 1950s, it attracted economists and sociologists who previously had devoted their attentions to radio institutions and audiences. Second, and most important, radio was transformed in the 1950s. The number of radio stations in the United States nearly quadrupled between 1950 and 1960, and the diffusion of transistor radios allowed increased portability. At the same time, television began to siphon off network programming, and radio's overall audience shares fell during the all-important prime-time evening hours. In response to these developments, radio programmers turned their attention to reconstructing the broadcast day. Morning and afternoon "drive times" became the most valuable commercial periods as car radios proliferated, and isolated listening by individuals, rather than the group listening patterns of prewar radio, led programmers to seek increased listener identification with stations rather than programs. Station programmers began to focus on music selection as a means to define specific audiences, which could then be sold to advertisers. Radio's subsequent status as an ambient medium is based in the need for programmers and advertisers to encourage passive listening and reinforce industrial control of the audience.

Yet radio remains a vital, if overlooked, medium. One can make the case that its very ubiquity has rendered it invisible. Radio's portability and relatively low production costs make it unrivaled in immediacy and flexibility. Despite industrial trends toward syndication (abetted by deregulation), radio programming often is highly localized. The popularity of interactive talk radio belies the received view of radio as an exclusively passive medium, although its potential often remains unrealized; in the case of talk radio, the talk show host remains an omniscient gatekeeper. Although radio was developed as what Harold Innis termed a space-binding medium, conquering the constraints of geography in order to disseminate short-lived messages, the medium maintains, Jody Berland claims, a link to the time-binding traditions of oral culture: Radio is "aural, vernacular, immediate, transitory; its composite stream of music and speech, including local (if usually one-way) communication, has the capacity to nourish local identity and oral history."[57] Finally, since radio was the first broadcasting medium, government regulation and commercial exploitation created a template into which all subsequent electronic media were placed. Despite past and present panegyrics to the presumed inevitability of a "wired nation," radio broadcasting will remain a vital element in the matrix of electronic communication, and the electromagnetic spectrum will continue to be a primary, finite, and contentious physical resource. An analysis of radio's development may provide insight into the development, structure, and control of the future technologies that promise vast menus of information and possibilities for interaction.

The Federal Communications Commission now licenses approximately 1,700 noncommercial radio stations in the United States, including community-access and religious stations as well as part-time or low-wattage educational stations.[58] For the purposes of this book, "public" radio refers to the stations that receive tax-based funding from the Corporation for Public Broadcasting and are affiliated with National

Public Radio. This focus is not intended to denigrate or marginalize the efforts of Pacifica Radio or the stations affiliated with the National Federation of Community Broadcasters; their turbulent and often glorious histories, however, await the efforts of future chroniclers. Although Public Radio International (formerly American Public Radio) distributes more programming to public radio stations, NPR also *produces* programming and serves as a membership organization for its affiliate stations. Because it represents public radio to the government for lobbying and funding purposes, National Public Radio plays an instrumental role in setting the agenda of public radio in the United States.

I believe we must examine public broadcasting as a *process*, or practice, rather than a *product*, or collection of symbolic works. Indeed, I argue that the service's emphasis on "product" accounts for public broadcasting's growing irrelevance to the participatory processes essential to public life. This point has been largely ignored by many critics of public broadcasting, who argue that public broadcasting programs are ideologically distorted. I argue that public broadcasting is *structurally* distorted. Hence, I examine not the content of NPR's programming but the processes of cultural production embodied in public radio's organization and practices. I will attempt to show that efforts to enact marketplace economics have led public radio to come into conflict with its basic principles; that to ensure institutional stability, public radio chose structures and activities that abetted the commodification of public life; and that public radio has transformed social activities into property and put them up for sale.

This book is not intended as an exhaustive history of National Public Radio. I did not interview the principal figures involved in NPR's development and its contemporary operations; their past comments are matters of public record, extensively documented in the trade press and elsewhere. In any case, it has been my experience that recollections may be distorted by selective recall, a desire to settle old scores, or clouded by an elegiac haze of memory. Ledbetter has characterized NPR's Washington offices as a "site of internal squabbling, personnel struggles, and wars waged by memoranda," but my purpose is not to catalogue the clashes between NPR personnel, although a certain amount of background is necessary to place events and processes in context. This book instead is intended as a critique, based on the following issues: How has National Public Radio historically defined the public in response to changing economic, regulatory, and institutional factors? What roles has the public (or such de facto publics as advisory boards, program underwriters, and independent producers) played in formulating National Public Radio's policies and programming?

Because of the complex interrelationships involved in these questions, this work is structured thematically rather than chronologically, with each issue treated chronologically within its chapter. The next chapter, "The Development of National Public Radio," describes legislative and organizational events that led to the creation of NPR and surveys key events in the service's history. Chapter 3, "The Localized Public: The Federalist Conundrum," discusses the relationship between National Public Radio and its affiliate stations, and the ways in which struggles for control of funding and programming have affected public radio's agenda. Chapter 4, "The Surrogate Public: Boards, Funders, and Producers," examines how public radio incorporates public representatives (governing and community advisory boards, foundations, corporate funders and independent producers) into its operations. Chapter 5, "The Reified Public: From Ascertainment to Ratings," discusses the methods by which National Public Radio and its affiliates determine the needs and interests of the public, and how these methods have changed across the system's history. In particular, this chapter shows how the efforts of audience researchers to institutionalize themselves in the system led to the use of quantitative and qualitative methodologies inimical to purposes of public discourse. The epilogue reviews the structure of public radio and proposes a public radio service based on public ownership and community participation.

Public radio exemplifies the prospects and problems of contemporary public life—which, for better or worse, increasingly operates in a mediated context. The social, political, and economic pressures exerted on National Public Radio are manifest in all areas of American cultural life. The paradoxes contained within NPR reflect many of the contradictions of modern life—the tensions between homogeneity and diversity, localism and nationalism, public and private space, culture and the marketplace. The history of public radio should be written as one part of a larger conversation about the fate of democracy in America. Why has American democracy been largely hostile to public broadcasting? As public institutions grow and mature, do they necessarily move away from a public dimension? Although many observers believe that the diversity of radio broadcast programming adequately reflects the pluralism of American life, few would claim that the commercial broadcast industry serves all audiences equally. Public radio was intended to serve listeners who are otherwise ignored by commercial media on economic, cultural, or aesthetic grounds, yet it is debatable whether it has engendered a participatory democracy. This book examines the ways in which American public broadcasters, as represented by National Public Radio and its affiliate stations, have succeeded or failed in serving the public.

NOTES

1. Johann Wolfgang von Goethe, *Faust*, trans. Walter Arndt (New York: W. W. Norton, 1976), p. 12.

2. J. Wilner, "CPB Funding Debated on Senate Floor," *Current*, March 16, 1992, pp. 1, 7.

3. J. Ledbetter, *Made Possible by . . . the Death of Public Broadcasting in the United States* (New York: Verso, 1997), p. 10.

4. S. Behrens, "Gingrich Wants to 'Zero-Out' Federal Funding of CPB," *Current*, December 12, 1994, p. 1; S. Behrens, "Stations Call for Grassroots Support While Strategists Seek to Broaden Image," *Current*, January 16, 1995, p. 12; T. Edsall, "Defunding Public Broadcasting: Conservative Goal Gains Audience," *Washington Post*, April 15, 1995, p. A-4.

5. F. Barnes, "Revenge of the Squares," *New Republic*, March 13, 1995, p. 28.

6. Behrens, "Gingrich Wants to 'Zero-Out' Federal Funding of CPB," p. 17. In contrast, a critic for the *Village Voice* cited *Baseball* as "rich in sentiment, light on conviction, and generically boring. Just what you'd expect when you ask *both* George Will and Mario Cuomo to talk sports" (T. Goetz, "Reasons to Be Fearful," *Village Voice*, January 24, 1995, p. 45).

7. E. Rathbun, "PBS Overhauls Itself amid Criticism," *Broadcasting and Cable*, February 6, 1995, p. 16; K. Bedford, "Pressler Stocking Up on Ammunition," *Current*, February 6, 1995, p. 10; E. Edwards, "The $92,000 Questions: CPB's Exhaustive Reply to Pressler's Query," *Washington Post*, February 14, 1995, p. B-2.

8. J. Gray, "House Committee Discusses Public Broadcasting Budget," *New York Times*, January 20, 1995, p. A-22; Goetz, "Reasons to Be Fearful," p. 45; B. Rosewicz, "GOP's Targeting of Public Television's Subsidy Creates Fuzzy Image of What's behind the Scenes," *Wall Street Journal*, February 22, 1995, p. A-18.

9. Rosewicz, "GOP's Targeting of Public Television's Subsidy Creates Fuzzy Image of What's behind the Scenes," p. A-18.

10. Behrens, "Stations Call For Grassroots Support While Strategists Seek to Broaden Image," p. 13.

11. T. Goetz, "57 Channels (and *Nova*'s On)," *Village Voice*, February 21, 1995, p. 42.

12. J. Conciatore, "House Panel Backs '98 Aid to CPB," *Current*, July 31, 1995, p. 24.

13. S. Behrens, "Congress to Hear Custom-Made Pleas," *Current*, September 11, 1995, p. 30. Though routinely castigated for "needless" interference in the marketplace, government often benefits private interests, while taxpayers shoulder the risk. Noncommercial broadcasting helped establish the viability of FM radio and UHF television. According to Robert McChesney, "The major function of nonprofit broadcasting in the United States from 1920 to 1960 was, in fact, to pioneer new sections of the electromagnetic spectrum when commercial interests did not yet find them profitable" (R. McChesney, "Public Broadcasting in the Age of Communication Revolution," *Monthly Review*, December 1995, p. 9).

14. S. Behrens, "Ripples of Optimism Felt on Hill," *Current*, July 3, 1995, p. 18.

15. S. Tolan, "What Do You Do When TCI Comes Courting Your Reputation?" *Current*, July 8, 1996, p. 17; J. Conciatore, "Turned Down for the PRC Schedule, Josephson Rents Space for Debate," *Current*, April 28, 1997, p. 3.

16. N. Garnham, "Public Service Versus the Market," *Screen* 24(1), January/February 1983, pp. 10–11; W. Rowland, Jr., and M. Tracy, "Worldwide Challenges to Public Service Broadcasting," *Journal of Communication* 40 (2), Spring

1990, pp. 14–15; R. Avery, "Introduction," in *Public Service Broadcasting in a Multichannel Environment: The History and Survival of an Ideal*, R. Avery, ed. (New York: Longman, 1993), p. xiii.

17. See I. de Sola Pool, *Technologies of Freedom* (Cambridge, MA: Harvard University Press, 1983); also W. Dizard, Jr., *The Coming Information Age: An Overview of Technology, Economics and Politics*, Third Edition (New York: Longman, 1989).

18. M. Fowler and D. Brenner, "A Marketplace Approach to Broadcast Regulation," *Texas Law Review* 60, 1982, p. 210. This perspective also enjoys domestic juridical support. In *FCC vs. WNCN Listener's Guild* (1981), the U.S. Supreme Court upheld the FCC's position that the public interest is best served through the competitive market (see T. Glasser, "Competition and Diversity among Radio Formats: Legal and Structural Issues," *Journal of Broadcasting* 28 (2), Spring 1984.

19. J. Goldsmith, "Radio Concerns Set to Broadcast Strong Results," *Wall Street Journal*, April 21, 1997, p. A-8; E. Shapiro, "A Wave of Buyouts Has Radio Industry Beaming with Success," *Wall Street Journal*, September 18, 1997, p. A-1.

20. J. Habermas, *The Structural Transformation of the Public Sphere: An Inquiry into a Category of Bourgeois Society* (Cambridge, MA: MIT Press, 1989 [1961]), p. 134.

21. M. Lind, *The Next American Nation: The New Nationalism and the Fourth American Revolution* (New York: The Free Press, 1995), p. 183. Also see M. Davis, *City of Quartz: Excavating the Future in Los Angeles* (New York: Verso, 1990).

22. M. Dietz, "Context is All: Feminism and Theories of Citizenship," *Daedalus*, Fall 1987, p. 5.

23. J. Keane, *The Media and Democracy* (Cambridge, UK: Polity Press, 1991), p. 112.

24. See A. Appadurai, "Disjuncture and Difference in the Global Cultural Economy," in *Global Culture*, M. Featherstone, ed. (Newbury Park, CA: Sage, 1990).

25. D. Rieff, "Multiculturalism's Silent Partner," *Harper's*, August 1993, p. 67.

26. L. Lapham, "Adieu, Big Bird," *Harper's*, December 1993, p. 38.

27. L. Friedland, "Public Television as Public Sphere: The Case of the Wisconsin Collaborative Project," *Journal of Broadcasting and Electronic Media* 39 (2), Spring 1995, p. 173.

28. D. Campbell and J. Campbell, "Public Television as a Public Good," *Journal of Communication* 28 (1), Winter 1978, p. 60.

29. "What They Said on Capitol Hill," *Current*, December 8, 1987, p. 13.

30. See Avery, "Introduction"; S. Barnett and D. Docherty, "Purity or Pragmatism: Principles and Practice of Public Service Broadcasting," and J. Blumler, "Television in the United States: Funding Sources and Programming Consequences," both in *Broadcast Finance in Transition: A Comparative Handbook*, J. Blumler and T. J. Nossiter, eds. (New York: Oxford University Press, 1991); J. Day, *The Vanishing Vision: The Inside Story of Public Television* (Berkeley, CA: University of California Press, 1995); D. McQuail, *Media Performance: Mass Communication and the Public Interest* (London: Sage, 1992).

31. S. Hall, "The Rediscovery of 'Ideology'. Return of the Repressed in Media Studies," in *Culture, Society and the Media*, M. Gurevitch, T. Bennett, J. Curran, and J. Woolacott, eds. (New York: Methuen, 1982), p. 60; P. Scannell, "Public

Service Broadcasting and Modern Public Life," *Media, Culture and Society* 11 (2), April 1989, p. 157.

32. This definition of public goods is provided by McQuail, *Media Performance*, p. 2.

33. Day, *The Vanishing Vision*, p. 41.

34. See M. Reeves and T. Hoffer, "The Safe, Cheap and Known: A Content Analysis of the First (1974) PBS Program Cooperative," *Journal of Broadcasting* 20 (4), Fall 1976.

35. L. Josephson, "Why Radio?" *Public Telecommunication Review*, March/April 1979, p. 9.

36. See N. Garnham, "Public Service versus the Market," *Screen* 24 (1), January/February 1983, p. 25.

37. J. Fellows, "The Truth about Public Broadcasting," *Current*, July 7, 1987, p. 2.

38. J. Witherspoon and R. Kovitz, *The History of Public Broadcasting* (Washington, D.C.: Current, 1987), p. 25.

39. J. Macy, *To Irrigate a Wasteland: The Struggle to Shape a Public Television System in the United States* (Berkeley: University of California Press, 1974), p. 116.

40. G. Murdock, "Large Corporations and the Control of the Communications Industries," in *Culture, Society and the Media*, M. Gurevitch, T. Bennet, J. Curran, and J. Woolacott, eds. (London: Metheun, 1982), p. 121.

41. "NPR Voices Qualms about Deregulation," *Current*, March 31, 1980, p. 1.

42. J. Blumler, "Meshing Money with Mission: Purity Versus Pragmatism in Public Broadcasting," *European Journal of Communication* 8 (4), December 1993, p. 82.

43. W. Rowland, Jr., "Continuing Crisis in Public Broadcasting: A History of Disenfranchisement," *Journal of Broadcasting and Electronic Media* 30 (3), Summer 1986, p. 263.

44. R. Samuelson, "Highbrow Pork Barrel," *Newsweek*, August 21, 1989, p. 44.

45. W. Rowland, Jr., "A Failure of Leadership," *Newsweek*, February 5, 1990, p. 8.

46. D. Mullally, "Long-Range Planning and the Local Station," *Public Telecommunications Review*, March/April 1979, pp. 42, 43.

47. See J. Turow, *Media Industry Systems* (New York: Longman, 1992); McQuail, *Media Performance*; M. Lashley, *Public Television: Panacea, Pork Barrel or Public Trust?* (Westport, CT: Greenwood Press, 1992).

48. W. Hoynes, *Public Television for Sale* (Boulder, CO: Westview Press, 1994), p. 60.

49. Ledbetter, *Made Possible By . . .*, p. 216.

50. See I. Ang, *Desperately Seeking the Audience* (New York: Routledge, 1991).

51. "What They Said on Capitol Hill," p. 17.

52. "NPR Scrutinizes Ratings Gain," *Current*, November 4, 1991, p. 14.

53. "The *Newsweek* 100," *Newsweek*, October 5, 1992, p. 38.

54. R. Roberts, "At the White House, Radio Free America," *Washington Post*, March 4, 1995, p. C-9.

55. R. Avery, "Contemporary Public Telecommunications Research: Navigating the Sparsely Settled Terrain," *Journal of Broadcasting and Electronic Media* 40 (1), Winter 1996, p. 133.

56. T. Looker, *The Sound and the Story: NPR and the Art of Radio* (New York: Houghton Mifflin, 1995), p. 48.

57. J. Berland, "Radio Space and Industrial Time: The Case of Music Formats," in *Rock and Popular Music*, T. Bennett, S. Frith, L. Grossberg, J. Shepherd, and G. Turner, eds. (London: Routledge, 1993), p. 112.

58. A. Stavitsky and T. Gleason, "Alternative Things Considered: A Comparison of National Public Radio and Pacifica Radio News Coverage," *Journalism Quarterly* 71 (4), Winter 1994, p. 783.

2

The Development of National Public Radio

National Public Radio will serve the individual; it will promote personal growth; it will regard the individual differences among men with respect and joy rather than derision and hate; it will celebrate the human experience as infinitely varied rather than vacuous and banal; it will encourage a sense of active constructive participation, rather than apathetic helplessness.

—William Siemering, "National Public Radio Purposes," p. 1[1]

While recent efforts to eliminate federal funding have increased pressures on public broadcasters to consolidate and commercialize their operations, the 1995 crisis was only the latest link in a chain of policy disputes that runs through the history of domestic public broadcasting. Uncertainty and instability are not unique to public broadcasting in the United States. Although the BBC enjoys substantially greater funding than the American system, it must undergo review by committee at regular intervals and whenever there are real or perceived threats to state security. Yet critics argue that U.S. public broadcasting, unlike that in most Western democracies, has operated largely on the periphery of society, as a "palliative" or "a broadcaster of gaps—providing those services which are uneconomic for commercial broadcasters."[2] Though some of this marginality is due to its haphazard evolution, public broadcasting in the United States has been impeded by the deeply ingrained American belief that private enterprise will fulfill public needs. Liberal individualism, which presumes that the unimpeded actions of private entrepreneurs will result in an equitable marketplace and adequate provision of public services, has never resolved the glaring contradiction between an ideology of speech freedom and the reality of structural inequalities of power. A vital democracy requires a "public sphere," a neutral and freely accessible arena for dialogue among equals, but broadcasting is restricted to those with the money to buy stations. Raymond Williams argues that the "marketplace" ethos of commercial broadcasting has led to a system in which "anything can be said, provided that you can afford to say it and that you can say it profitably."[3]

The historical dominance of commercial broadcasting has caused the public system to be torn between accommodation with and resistance to the commercial model. Public broadcasting's marginality also is due to the fact that the institutions that provided its initial support often defined it in narrow educational terms. In addition, a "progressive" belief in the professional as arbiter of public discourse has relegated the public to an ancillary role in the system. Finally, American paternalism has been historically defined by private interests rather than state interests; the public broadcasting system's goals have almost invariably been set by foundation and corporate elites, with negligible popular input. Public broadcasting's structure and practices are determined by a shifting coalition of actors whose influences grow or wane according to the convergence of political ideology, economics, and social and cultural circumstances at specific historical moments. These actors include government entities responsible for regulation (Congress, the president, and the FCC, who frequently are in conflict with each other); funders (the Corporation for Public Broadcasting, corporate underwriters, and stations); programming creators and suppliers (stations, independent producers, and distributors); pressure groups and information sources; and audiences and other sociocultural institutions. This chapter traces their respective ebbs and flows in the development of public radio in the United States. In addition to providing an overview of National Public Radio's history and operations, it discusses how internal and external pressures have led NPR to define the public in utilitarian terms of marketplace ideology rather than in discursive terms of public participation.

THE PROCESS OF DEFINING RADIO

Private control of radio followed the precedents of the railroad and telegraph industries. The American judiciary granted exclusive franchises to private developers; once this infrastructure was in place, the judiciary favored entrepreneurial risk taking for further development. By the mid-19th century, the economy was established as a sphere beyond direct political intervention, though the burden of entrepreneurial risk frequently was taken on by government subsidies.[4] As advances in transportation and communication intensified competition, the large industries of the 19th century became obsessed with staking out and maintaining the boundaries of their operations. Guglielmo Marconi, who from the outset followed a monopolistic strategy to control radio, clearly modeled his organizational practices on these precedents.[5] Marconi envisioned wireless as a point-to-point, coded medium and had no conception of "broadcasting." He managed total control over his industrial system by selling service, rather than equipment; his clients paid for access. Yet radio's domination by commerce was not inevitable. The amateur radio movement before World War I had great value: it was perhaps the closest approximation of a participatory public sphere in the history of American broadcasting. Amateurs were not passive broadcast consumers but active participants in transmission. Thomas Streeter elaborates:

For the amateurs, the radio spectrum . . . was a realm free of hierarchy. They saw the formless, wide-open character of the spectrum as a fascinating and enjoyable potentiality, as something to be played with and explored and as the source of an alternative community.[6]

Radio clubs promoted community in an increasingly depersonalized society, yet it is debatable whether even the amateur use of the spectrum truly represented a "public" medium. Access to transmission and reception were the province of those with the technical knowledge to construct wireless apparatus. The amateur radio public, although decentralized, was largely exclusive.

This radio community, though sentimentally appealing in many ways, was potentially disruptive. The U.S. military initiated a move toward regulation on grounds that amateur activities compromised national security. The Radio Act of 1912 gave government the power to assign property rights in the spectrum. Many critics have noted that the issue of spectrum scarcity, which served as the cornerstone of broadcast regulation, is fundamentally specious. While the amount of usable spectrum is finite, no natural "scarcity" exists; channel boundaries have been drawn for social and economic, rather than technical, reasons. Broadcasting regulation primarily was designed to alleviate technical chaos and market instability. The 1912 Act assigned the bulk of frequencies to military and commercial use; the government asserted influence after the *technical* consequences of radio expansion (particularly indiscriminate access and reception) had become chaotic.[7] The Alexander Bill of 1916, which would have enabled the government to acquire radio stations and become a potential competitor to commercial wireless, was defeated only after intense lobbying by Marconi and other commercial interests. After the war, Secretary of the Navy Josephus Daniel proposed that the U.S. Navy's wartime technical advances made it the natural candidate to control radio, and a bill supported by the army and the state department was introduced in Congress in 1918. Congress, however, viewed such control as inherently anti-individualistic: Congressman William Greene claimed that "having just won a fight against autocracy, we would start an autocratic movement with this bill."[8] The press also whipped up popular opposition to regulation that would ostensibly transfer "private" activities to the state. The bill died in committee, ending overt attempts at government control of broadcasting.

Although state control was quickly dismissed, nationalist ideology continued to play a central role in the development of domestic broadcasting. The navy responded to its defeat by forming a private monopoly that would be sympathetic to its interests while undermining the hegemony of British-controlled Marconi. Closed-door negotiations between the navy and General Electric led to the 1919 creation of a patent pool that would advance corporate and government collaboration in the control of wireless communications. Nationalistic motives were embodied in the very name and structure of the new organization: the officers and directors of the Radio Corporation of America had to be American citizens, and no more than 20 percent of RCA stock could be held by foreigners.[9] RCA's partners included GE, Westinghouse, American Telephone and Telegraph, and the United Fruit Company. Although the patent pool was formally dissolved in 1926, it served to legitimate corporate control of radio.

In contrast, the structure of the British Broadcasting Corporation was a model for other European nations. The BBC was formed in 1926 and financed by license fees on radio ownership (which was anathema to manufacturers of radios in the United States). The BBC was overseen by a board appointed by the government but remained independent enough to formulate operational goals and programming policies. According to Graham Murdock, easy passage of this model was achieved in England due to the successful public management of resources during World War I.[10] Also, the British government viewed radio from the outset as an explicitly cultural force, rather than drawing on the American transportation or transmission–system precedent.[11]

The number of radio stations in the United States grew exponentially following World War I, giving the appearance of localism, pluralism, and competition in broadcasting, but networks predominated by the end of the 1920s, because their low distribution costs compensated for the high costs of production. As the networks grew in power and reach, they learned to control costs through uniform scheduling. In a key development, networks began turning programming over to advertising agencies, which sought to convince the public of the "naturalness" of ads: they pointed to the "rich variety of entertainment at the expense of the advertiser, instead of the anemic flow as in England at the expense of the set owner."[12] Ad agencies demystified radio for advertisers by establishing broadcast "markets" (for instance, daytime programs targeted toward women) and touted the consistency and professionalism of their programming, based on new techniques of audience measurement. As a result of these actions, radio listeners were formalized into an "audience," or what Ien Ang terms a "taxonomic collective": "[an] entity of serialized, in principle unrelated individuals who form a group solely because each member has a characteristic—in our case, spectatorship—that is like that of each other member."[13]

Ang claims that both commercial and public service broadcasters define their audiences as taxonomic collectives. The former view audiences as anonymous consumers grouped around objectified variables or demographics, while the latter see them as collectives of citizens bound together by national or political culture. However, "public" broadcasting (at least normatively) has a commitment not only to serving citizens as broadly defined groups but also to including them in the functioning of the system. In addition, until relatively recently American public broadcasting defined itself through the activities of diffuse educational licensees.

THE PREHISTORY OF PUBLIC RADIO

Although public broadcasting was established in the United States as a formal entity only in 1967, its roots lie in the civic education movements of the 19th century. By 1837 John Holbrook's Lyceum movement had established adult learning centers in an estimated three thousand towns; and after the Civil War, the Chatauqua Movement included fifteen thousand "home study circles" for lectures, performances, and discussions of public affairs.[14] These movements provided the momentum for the development of land grant universities in the waning years of the 19th century. Proposing that American colleges should provide community resources as well as liberal arts training, Justin Morril imported the principle of university extension programs from England in the 1880s. Much as the Settlement House movement targeted the urban poor and immigrant communities, these university programs were designed to improve rural productivity and citizenship. Morril has been hailed as "the father of educational broadcasting," as Midwestern land grant colleges used radio to supplement their extension programs.[15] The activities of land grant universities were also a reflection of the growing Progressive movement in the United States, and it is the Progressive movement, with all of its positive and negative implications, that shaped the development of domestic public broadcasting.

The Progressive movement gathered momentum at the close of the

Spanish-American War, peaked around 1913, and continued in diminished form until the end of the 1920s. Driven by a rhetoric of national crisis and failure, a sense that society was splitting at the seams, the Progressives' chief concerns were economic concentration, government corruption, and degraded working and living conditions among the urban poor. The Progressive movement was an uneasy coalition of two conflicting groups. Rural activists, or Populists, were alarmed by the growing consolidation of economic power and sought to recover an idealized American state through a return to small-scale capitalism, prohibition, and anti-immigration laws. In contrast, the foremost intention of urban middle-class professionals such as doctors, lawyers, academicians, journalists, and social workers was to institutionalize their standing in the social hierarchy. Although the former group drew the most popular attention, the latter group had the most significant and lasting effect on American society. Their efforts at increasing social efficiency through "rational" administration led to the growth of government agencies whose broad regulatory powers ensured social order and stability rather than substantial reform.

To "good government" Progressives, an increasingly abstracted and distended society demanded precise and specialized administration. They embraced the metaphors of science to reform public life. "Scientific" solutions to social problems were considered to have universal applications; as John Peters states, "The social scientist could read chains of causation that ordinary folks were blind to."[16] Knowledge and policy no longer were grounded in local public deliberation; instead, they were compartmentalized through the development of elites who carefully screened admission into professional and academic communities. To James Carey, the urban progressives "were joined to one common desire: a desire to escape the merely local and contingent, an enthusiasm for everything that was distant and remote, a love of the national over the provincial."[17] The Progressive moment would be long passed by 1967, but the desire of educational broadcasting professionals to transcend the local and parochial was to lead directly to the formation of a national public broadcasting system. In their eyes, a national service could more efficiently serve the public than localized entities—while it simultaneously relegated public participation to the margins.

Wisconsin was a focal point for Progressives. It is no surprise, then, that domestic public broadcasting can be traced to the University of Wisconsin, where experimental station 9XM was established in 1914 (the station later was formally licensed as WHA). Before World War I, stations at state universities in Wisconsin, Nebraska, and North Dakota as well as the private Nebraska Wesleyan were sporadically broadcasting news bulletins, weather forecasts, and market reports. After the war, noncommercial broadcasting was almost exclusively the province of educational stations. By 1925, 171 educational organizations had stations on the air, accounting for almost one-third of all operating stations. Yet non-commercial radio was hardly framed in exclusively educational terms. In the early 1930s, a survey of land grant university stations revealed that nearly half of their schedules were devoted to entertainment programming, 43 percent to farm, home, and general information, and only 8 percent to formal instruction.[18]

The attrition rate for educational stations initially was lower than that for commercial stations, but only thirty-eight educational stations remained on the air by 1936. They were often operated by departments of electrical engineering and of little concern to administrators, since they had few listeners and little effect on enrollments.[19] As the novelty of radio wore off by the late 1920s, many colleges and universities sold their licenses to commercial broadcasters, a trend accelerated by Depression-era cutbacks in educational funding. In addition, many private institutions did not embrace the land grant philosophy of community service. Columbia University is alleged to have rejected the gift of a station that later became the key NBC affiliate in New York City.[20]

The four Radio Conferences held from 1922 to 1925 further undermined educational broadcasters. These conferences were organized by Secretary of Commerce Herbert Hoover, who had been given the power (largely by default) to assign wavelengths. A firm believer in the free market, Hoover advocated industry self-regulation rather than overt state intervention and so gave broadcasting insiders, who monopolized information, the right to determine public policy. The March 1923 conference created a "Class C" designation, in which stations with less than five hundred watts of power (primarily religious and educational broadcasters) were forced to share frequencies, while Class A and B stations (representing larger, established commercial interests) enjoyed exclusive frequencies.

In 1924, Hoover stopped issuing broadcast licenses, on grounds that the usable frequencies were filled; however, since licenses were applied to broadcast apparatus rather than operators, commercial interests were free to enter the marketplace by purchasing broadcast equipment. By permitting the sale of stations and their assigned wavelengths, Hoover "in effect made a radio channel private property."[21] In an attempt to address many of the regulatory shortfalls stemming from the Radio Conferences, Congress passed the Dill-White Radio Act on February 23, 1927. The Act defined the electromagnetic spectrum as a natural, or public, resource and created the Federal Radio Commission (staffed largely by private industry) as a temporary, but sole, agency to license broadcast stations. Although intended to exist only as a stopgap measure for one year, the FRC ruled for six. Its staff of "experts" represented the legacy of Progressivism, in that its efforts to create social efficiency ultimately served the interests of industry. Commercial broadcasters preferred that federal administrators rather than legislators establish and enforce licensing standards, as the latter were theoretically more accountable to the public than the former.[22]

According to the 1927 act (and the 1934 Communications Act), licenses would be granted to individuals and organizations serving the "public interest, convenience and necessity." In 1903 Marconi had used the word "public" as a synonym for "commercial purposes"; it was written into law with the Transportation Act of 1920.[23] The phrase "public interest" had originated in utility regulation; the broadcast regulatory model was clearly based on precedent, not sui generis. The "public interest" label also served to validate the nascent medium by defining the audience as a "public," thus enveloping commercial purposes with an aura of high-mindedness that suited the instrumental purposes of the FRC's businessmen. The Act stated that the "public interest" meant "serving" the public within the station's reception area; what such "service" included, aside from avoiding interference with other stations, was not defined. Broadcasters had no specific property rights, yet they enjoyed complete editorial discretion over programming. Judging the public interest was left to commercial owners and operators, freedom of speech was equated with the decisions of entrepreneurs in the marketplace, and the "public" was conflated with the broadcasting market. No channels were reserved for education, and the growing stature of broadcast networks was ignored. The language of the 1927 Act implicitly endorsed the view that commercial advertising was the only legitimate form of financial support for broadcasting, but advertising was mentioned only as a peripheral topic and was left to industry self-regulation via the Code of the National Association of Broadcasters. In sum, the 1927 Act was written by commercial broadcasters to serve the single purpose of profit.

By 1934, noncommercial broadcasters accounted for only 2 percent of the total broadcasting time in the United States.[24] Nine years earlier, several Midwestern land grant radio stations had formed the Association of College and University Broadcasting Stations (ACUBS). At its first national convention, held in 1930, ACUBS called for the establishment of a noncommercial network; later it lobbied Congress unsuccessfully for a block of spectrum for use by land grant radio. On February 26, 1934, Franklin Roosevelt went before Congress to propose a new agency that would consolidate the FRC with the communications interests of the Interstate Commerce Commission. Bills were introduced by Sen. Clarence Dill (D.-Washington) and Rep. Sam Rayburn (D.-Texas) that resulted in the Communications Act of 1934. The 1934 act was in many ways a formalized revision of the 1927 act, yet Robert McChesney argues that debate over the 1934 legislation represented "the sole instance in which the structure and control of a major mass medium were subject to anything close to legitimate political debate."[25]

Believing that the spread of broadcast advertising had debased American culture, a number of educators, labor organizations, religious groups, and intellectuals viewed the decline of educational radio with alarm. A resulting broadcast reform movement was headed by two organizations with significantly conflicting agendas and support. The National Committee on Education by Radio (NCER) was established in 1930 as an umbrella organization for a number of groups, including the National Educational Association, the National Catholic Educational Association, and the Association of Land Grant Colleges and Universities. Supported by the Payne Fund, which also sponsored a number of media effects studies, NCER advocated channel reservations for educational broadcasters. In contrast, the National Advisory Council on Radio in Education (NACRE), founded in 1930, was funded by the Carnegie Corporation and stressed cooperation with commercial broadcasters rather than systemwide reform. Ralph Engelman finds that NACRE and NCER represent

the twin poles of the American media reform movement from the 1920s to the present. The emphasis of the former was on *public access*—civic use of electronic media operated by commercial or governmental entities. The goal of the latter was *public control*—a greater degree of popular dominion over electronic channels of communication.[26]

The reformers failed because of counterattacks from the commercial broadcasting industry (who also controlled the channels of public discussion), a lack of political savvy and coordination, and their own inherent elitism. While the reformers have been portrayed as egalitarian and enjoying broad popular support, with the exception of organized labor's WCFL, the movement was populated almost exclusively by the upper middle class. The reform movement largely was based in paternalistic notions of cultural uplift (the reformers frequently cited the benefits of the explicitly paternal BBC system); yet save for the ACLU, they did not completely denounce privatization, on the grounds that free market ideology was too deeply ingrained in the American consciousness to allow for discussion of alternatives. They also regarded listeners as an "audience," which casts doubts on their pluralist intentions. The last gasp of the reformers was the Wagner-Hatfield Amendment, which would have reserved one-quarter of all radio frequencies for educational stations. The Amendment also proposed a category of nonprofit stations that would be allowed to meet costs by selling limited amounts of airtime. Commercial broadcasters countered that they already provided educational programs, and the reformers had little support from politicians increasingly aware of the nascent medium's power. The Wagner-Hatfield Amendment was defeated by a vote of forty-two to twenty-three; however, Congress included a section in the 1934 act requiring the FCC to study assigning channels to nonprofit organizations. Following the defeat, ACUBS changed its name to the National Association of Educational Broadcasters (NAEB) and devoted itself exclusively to representing the narrow interests of educators. NCER folded in 1941, and thereafter noncommercial radio broadcasting receded into a wilderness of uncertainty from which it would not reemerge for nearly three decades.

PICKING UP THE PIECES: THE FCC AND THE NAEB

Only thirty-eight noncommercial AM stations were broadcasting by 1936, and the majority of these were licensed to land grant colleges. Despite the broadcast reform movement's failure, continued lobbying led the FCC to establish a "noncommercial educational" class of stations between 41 and 42 MHz (megahertz) in January 1938. This reservation was problematic in both access (it could not be received by existing radios) and nomenclature: Rowland notes that "the name [noncommercial educational] evoked something far less popular and universal than the concept of public service broadcasting being developed abroad."[27] The issue was complicated further by the FCC's tendency to shift frequencies seemingly at whim. In 1940, the FCC's Report and Order 67 established the layout of FM radio and allocated five channels between 42 and 43 MHz for "noncommercial educational" purposes. The FCC reallocated the FM spectrum to 88–108 MHz in June 1945, and set aside twenty FM channels (88–92 MHz) for "noncommercial educational" use. This action was supported by commercial broadcasters, who anticipated that FM's restricted range would not pose a serious challenge to AM's hegemony and saw the reservation as a way to avoid compulsory educational programming. By the end of 1945, the FCC had granted twelve "noncommercial educational" FM licenses, and a handful of these stations were on the air. Struggling community organizations were ill equipped to purchase the hardware needed to use spectrum reallocations; only such larger entities as colleges and universities were easily able to take advantage of them. This policy set the stage for their later domination of public radio.

To encourage use of the noncommercial spectrum, the FCC ruled that effective September 27, 1948, educational FM stations could operate at ten watts of power, far lower than the previous minimum of 250 watts. Although the range of these stations seldom exceeded three to five miles, the lower threshold was intended to reduce equipment costs to a few hundred dollars. The first ten-watt license was awarded to WGRE at Depauw University, and forty-eight noncommercial FM stations were broadcasting by December 1949.[28] This number had risen to seventy-three a year later, but the FCC pressured more noncommercial broadcasters to use these frequencies or risk being banished from FM altogether. By 1951, approximately 40 percent of all educational FM stations were low-power operations. Though the FCC hoped that these stations would serve a wider public, universities used them solely as student training laboratories. Programming was marginal at best. The more powerful educational radio stations served as little more than "the faculty's 'classical music jukebox' " when they were not airing lectures, symposiums, or panel discussions. Others recycled old commercial shows as "nostalgia" programs.[29]

After channel reservations were implemented, educational broadcasters began turning their attention to interconnection. The first approximation of an educational radio network resulted from efforts of the NAEB (formerly ACUBS) in the early 1950s. At the NAEB's behest, the Allerton House Seminars were convened at the University of Illinois in 1949 and 1950 to discuss the status of educational radio. With a five-year grant of nearly a quarter of a million dollars from the Kellogg Foundation, a tape exchange for educational radio stations was created in 1950 in Urbana, Illinois. Two-thirds of the educational radio station managers surveyed in 1968 found the content of the resulting programming satisfactory, but a majority also claimed they were technically substandard.[30] In the late 1950s, WGBH-TV president Hartford Gunn founded the first regional educational television network, the Eastern Educational Network (EEN), to increase production of programs. Gunn also brought in Donald Quayle, the manager of WOSU of Columbus, Ohio, to develop a radio counterpart to EEN: the result was the Educational Radio Network (ERN), founded in 1961. By 1962, seven noncommercial stations on the East Coast were interconnected through ERN, whose major production was *Kaleidoscope*, a daily newsmagazine produced from Boston, New York, Philadelphia, and Washington, D.C.

However, the major power behind the growth of educational broadcasting in the 1950s and '60s was the Ford Foundation, which awarded over $268 million to noncommercial broadcasting between 1951 and 1974.[31] Although the Carnegie and Payne Foundations had supported noncommercial broadcasting in the 1930s, the duration and stability of Ford Foundation support almost single-handedly defined pre–Carnegie Commission public broadcasting. James Day finds that "whenever an idea's paternity was in doubt, fingers generally pointed to the brass-and-glass headquarters of the Ford Foundation."[32] Ford's educational broadcasting activities from 1951 to 1963 focused on construction of television facilities and on exploring possibilities for cultural and informational programming for general audiences after the failure of its *Omnibus* arts and cultural program on CBS in 1952. The Ford Foundation provided a grant to the NAEB for its tape exchange network, but radio was a secondary concern. In late 1952, Ford financed the Educational Television and Radio Center (ETRC; later National Educational Television and Radio Center, or NETRC), which was created to support the production of programming in humanities, national and international affairs, and economics. Still, Robert Blakely reports, the Center's "operating objective was almost solely to give program service to educational television stations."[33]

In 1963, NETRC dropped its radio service altogether and changed its name to National Educational Television (NET). The Ford Foundation awarded ERN $150,000 to merge with NET concomitant with EEN, and Quayle was named NET's director of radio (he later became the first president of NPR). However, ERN ceased programming when Ford withdrew its funds to concentrate exclusively on television; the radio network's last live broadcast covered Martin Luther King's March on Washington in August 1963. Radio continued to be overshadowed by television; Quayle stated that the "glamour wasn't there, attention wasn't there, the audience wasn't there."[34] Between 1951 and 1972, 90.7 percent of overall foundation monies for public broadcasting were poured into television, 8.8 percent were allocated to program-related activities, and a miserly 0.5 percent went to radio projects.[35] The same held true for federal funding. The first direct federal support for educational broadcasting (the 1958 National Defense Act) earmarked money for formal instructional uses, and the Educational Facilities Act of 1962 completely omitted any funding for radio. By 1963, even the NAEB regarded radio as a marginal concern. That year, the NAEB split into two semi-autonomous divisions, Educational Television Stations (ETS) and National Educational Radio (NER). The latter relocated to Washington, D.C., and combined the tape network with the NAEB's Radio Station Division, a mentoring and representation organization for its approximately 275 member stations. Although dwarfed in stature and influence by ETS, NER made a brief splash in September 1965 by interconnecting seventy educational radio stations for live coverage of the German national elections. The success of NER's coverage led a columnist for *Saturday Review* to call for "a permanent, national, live, educational radio network."[36] Costs for the three-hour special were picked up by the German government. Briefly bringing noncommercial radio to national attention, the program established a trend in which funding sources determined programming—a trend that haunts public radio to the present.

CARNEGIE I AND ITS AFTERMATH

C. Scott Fletcher (a former Ford Foundation executive and the head of ETS) organized the First National Conference on Long-Range Financing of Educational Television in December 1964. The conference's keynote speech was delivered by WGBH founder Ralph Lowell, who proposed the formation of a presidential commission to study the financial needs of educational television and make recommendations for a cohesive national policy. Lyndon Johnson's administration, which had close ties to the commercial broadcast industry, refused to fund the study directly. Yet the media-savvy Johnson realized the cultural and political significance of a public broadcasting system and approved the creation of a privately funded commission to examine the matter. The Kennedy and Johnson administrations frequently used commissions and task forces to defuse potential conflicts with Congress; as Rowland states, "These task forces had seemed to become useful for reviewing problematic social issues and providing at least the image of serious governmental concern, while also securing more time to gauge and perhaps influence the then current mix of political forces before deciding what, if any, steps to take."[37] The Ford Foundation was the logical choice for funding, but Hartford Gunn argued that "if the President were to take us up on this, it would look like Ford was trying to buy its way out [of supporting educational television]. . . . Carnegie was the next largest foundation that I knew of."[38] A commission was convened in November 1965, under Carnegie's auspices. Its findings led to the creation of the public broadcasting system that survives today.

Although ostensibly independent of the White House, politics played a major role in the selection of the Carnegie Commission's members. James Killian, Jr., the retiring president of MIT and a former science advisor to President Eisenhower, chaired the commission. According to Engelman, "Killian was a prominent representative of the Cambridge-Washington axis which fed high-level personnel back and forth between MIT and Harvard and the federal government."[39] Killian tapped several of Johnson's cronies for membership, including J. C. Kellam, who managed Johnson's broadcast properties; John Hayes, the head of the *Washington Post* group of stations; and Oveta Culp Hobby, the publisher of the *Houston Post* and a longtime Johnson ally. The commission's other members were drawn from educational, business, and cultural elites. They included author Ralph Ellison; the former president of Harvard, James Conant; UAW vice president Leonard Woodcock; David Henry, Franklin Patterson, and Lee DuBridge, the presidents of the University of Illinois, Hampshire College, and Caltech, respectively (DuBridge also served on the board of NET); former North Carolina governor Terry Sanford; TV producer Robert Saudek; Joseph McConnell, former president of NBC, now employed by Reynolds Aluminum; Edwin Land of the Polaroid Corporation; and pianist Rudolph Serkin.

Rather than suggesting significant reform, the Carnegie Commission's report (published in 1967 as *Public Television: A Program for Action*) substantially accommodated the existing order. The Commission did not propose to replace "educational television"; instead, "public" programming for general audiences would supplement formal instruction. Since the existing educational broadcasting system was based upon independent licensees, the report envisioned a decentralized public broadcasting system that would allow for local and regional diversity and prevent political manipulation on the federal level. Yet the Commission never *explicitly* stated that the stations should be in overall control of the system. The report stated, "There must be a means of performing services, as in the development of experimental programs and the recruitment of manpower, which are likely to be more efficiently carried out by an organization that can act for Public Television."[40] As a compromise between local autonomy and national control, the Carnegie Commission proposed the creation of an independent, nonprofit Corporation for Public Television (CPT) to disburse federal and private funds for programming, establish two national production centers (rather than relying solely on NET), and create an interconnection system.

However, the creation of a "Fourth Network" was not Carnegie's intent. To defuse objections from commercial broadcasters, the Corporation for Public Television would be barred from producing programs, and no provision was made for simultaneous transmission to affiliates. Instead, the production centers and interconnect service would facilitate exchanges between autonomous stations, and the Corporation would serve local stations as a conduit for federal funds. The Carnegie Commission avoided calling for direct federal appropriations to the CPT; according to commission member Lee DuBridge, "One person who talked to us . . . gave an impassioned plea: Don't go to the federal government, you'll be a captive and slave to the federal government if you let them in on this."[41] Instead, as a "least objectionable" compromise, the Corporation for Public Television would be partially funded by an excise tax on the sale of televisions, beginning at 2 percent and rising to a ceiling of 5 percent.

Instead of attempting to explicitly define "public" broadcasting, the Carnegie Commission offered a shopping list of generalizations. Among other things, the system would

provide a voice for groups in the community that may otherwise be unheard[;] . . . help us see America whole in all of its diversity[;] . . . open a wide door to greater public expression and cultural richness for creative individuals and important audiences[;] . . . seek out able people whose talents might otherwise not be known or shared[;] . . . give a stage to experimental drama[;] . . . carry the best of knowledge and wisdom directly into the home.[42]

Critics have charged that the Carnegie Commission employed the word "public" chiefly to attract broader funding support from government, individuals, corporations, and foundations.[43] All broadcasting stations could be considered "public," since they are licensed as public trustees that operate in the public interest. The Carnegie Commission's suggestions were intended to bolster support for institutional educational licensees, but the interests of these licensees (as with commercial broadcasters) are not necessarily the same as the public's interests. The report also states:

If we were to sum up our proposal with all the brevity at our command we would say that what we recommend is freedom. . . . We seek for the public servant freedom to create, freedom to innovate, freedom to be heard in this most far-reaching medium. We seek for the citizen freedom to view, to see programs that the present system, by its incompleteness, denies him.[44]

"Freedom" is always a fine thing to recommend, but Robert Blakely finds a significant omission in the Carnegie Commission's report: "The producer, the educator and the 'public servant' are all considered. But missing is the explicit inclusion of the citizen's freedom to do more than 'to view, to see programs.' "[45] The Carnegie Commission aspired to bind the nation into what Benedict Anderson calls an "imagined community," a "deep, horizontal comradeship" whose members cannot know each other but are aware of each other's existence.[46] Yet the report's technological utopianism assumed this effect miraculously would follow from the nature of the medium itself. The report refused to challenge the institutional view of a passive audience; the "public" continued to be seen as vague and amorphous. Finally, the report made no mention of radio. According to John Witherspoon and Robert Kovitz, the Commission avoided radio out of fear that "the radio system's long history of weakness would drag the entire Carnegie effort into oblivion."[47]

The Public Broadcasting Act of 1967, which drew on the findings of the Carnegie Commission, originated with Lyndon Johnson's "Message on Education and Health in America" on February 28, 1967. On March 5, Sen. Warren Magnuson (D.-Washington) introduced a bill that would formally establish public radio and television systems in the United States. The bill passed Congress in only seven months. Token opposition was offered by a few Republicans and conservative Democrats, who feared the prospect of federally controlled broadcasts, and by the National Association of Broadcasters, who were reacting to the first tentative stirrings of the broadcast reform movement and worried that public broadcasting offered potential competition for audiences. The most contentious issue among the bill's proponents was whether to include radio in the Act. Jerrold Sandler, the executive director of NAEB's radio division (NER), was the primary advocate for its inclusion. In September 1966, nearly a year after the Carnegie Commission convened, Sandler and NER organized a seminar called "Educational Radio as a National Resource" at Wingspread, the headquarters of the Johnson Foundation in Racine, Wisconsin. The Wingspread conference called for increased funding on the federal, state, and local levels; greater research into community needs; and the establishment of citizens' councils on the national and local levels "to help formulate educational radio station policies, in the true spirit of 'public radio,' " as well an HEW-funded pilot project to upgrade station equipment.[48]

With a $38,000 grant from the Ford Foundation, NER conducted a comprehensive study of educational radio in the winter of 1966–1967. It mailed questionnaires to 320 of the 346 educational radio stations in the United States. Reflecting the chaos and neglect of educational radio, only 135 were returned. A report, *The Hidden Medium: A Status Report on Educational Radio in the United States*, was hurriedly drafted from the study by broadcast consultant Herman Land and published in April 1967, more than a month after the original bill was introduced. It was created as a lobbying document and included no template for national organization, aside from calls for a programming production center and a Washington-based news and public affairs bureau. Sandler and Ed Burrows, the manager of the University of Michigan's radio stations, then lobbied Michigan Sen. Robert Griffin, who was working on the committee drafting legislation, to add "and radio" after each mention of "public television" in the bill. Griffin later simplified the language to "public broadcasting" and also suggested that the proposed CPT should be more appropriately dubbed the Corporation for Public Broadcasting.[49]

The Public Broadcasting Act of 1967 was signed into law on November 7, creating the Corporation for Public Broadcasting to distribute federal money to stations. Ironically, all three commercial television networks supported the bill. CBS's Frank Stanton (who had led the fight against channel reservations for educational broadcasting in 1952) pledged a million dollars to the CPB. Stanton's actions were not entirely altruistic: commercial broadcasters believed that public radio and television would serve small, special-interest audiences that fell outside the realms of commercially viable markets. Public broadcast programming also would reduce demands that commercial broadcasters air public-service programs, and public stations would limit the number of television channels that otherwise would be used for commercial purposes. More significantly, the public was virtually shut out of deliberation over the 1967 Act. Educational interests had dominated noncommercial broadcasting since the 1934 Communication Act, and they feared that prolonged debate would threaten the bill's passage. In their haste to pass the bill, educational broadcasters failed to resolve many thorny issues or ignored them altogether. Consequently, the language of the Act created problems that have plagued public broadcasting to the present.

A primary problem concerned the CPB's institutional status. Section 396 (b) of the Act authorized the Corporation for Public Broadcasting to operate as a private nonprofit corporation, independent of the U.S. government, to shield it from political influence. Yet was the CPB to serve as an integral part of public broadcasting, or was it to stand apart? While the CPB was intended to set policy, it was given no regulatory powers and was prohibited from system operation. Secondly, Section 396 (g) (1) (d) of the 1967 act required the CPB to develop programming with "strict adherence to objectivity and balance." This provision was designed to ensure that CPB, which was not subject to FCC jurisdiction, would use public funding to promote programming that was consistent with the Fairness Doctrine.[50] Yet the Act included no guidelines for judging "objectivity and balance." In addition, the provision could refer to a single program or an entire season's schedule. Similarly, Section 399 (a) forbade editorializing by public broadcasters even if they did not receive CPB funding. This provision, which excluded public broadcasters from exercising the First Amendment rights of commercial broadcasters, remained law until 1982, when a California judge ruled in favor of a petition by the League of Women Voters and the Pacifica Foundation that public broadcasters had the right to editorialize.[51]

Third, the Carnegie Commission had recommended twelve directors for CPB. Six would be appointed by the president and confirmed by the Senate, and six by previous CPB appointees. This process theoretically would remove at least half the board from direct presidential influence. Instead, the 1967 act called for a CPB board that consisted of fifteen directors, all of whom would be appointed by the president and approved by the Senate. To defuse political concerns, not more than eight could be from the same party. Section 396 (c) (2) of the Act called for CPB board members to be selected on grounds of "various kinds of talent and experience appropriate to the functions and responsibilities of the corporation," but the fact that all were presidential appointees meant that board openings would serve as political patronage plums and opened the CPB to direct political meddling. Since its inception, CPB board seats have been doled out as political favors to major political campaign contributors and relatives of Cabinet members and congressional staff. In 1997, David Stewart (the former director of international activities for CPB) summed up the CPB Board's main focus:

They have been almost exclusively preoccupied by process and politics. There are reasons for this—it is what they know best. . . . [A CPB] president-elect was introduced to the CPB staff by a proud board chairman who said that the new man's chief attribute was that in his previous position he had handled much more money than CPB's current budget.[52]

Fourth, although long-term funding was seen as a prerequisite to insulate public broadcasting from both government and private pressures, Congress failed to implement any of the Carnegie Commission's proposals for funding. President Johnson had removed excise taxes of 10 percent or more on consumer goods two years earlier, so the Commission's proposal for funding through an excise tax on television receivers was stillborn. Although the CPB was established as an *independent* agency, it was given an annual appropriation, as if it were a government agency. Long-term funding would have set an appropriations precedent, and it was dropped in the face of likely opposition by Wilbur Mills, then chairman of the House Ways and Means Committee. The Corporation for Public Broadcasting initially was appropriated $9 million, rather than the $50 million recommended by Congress. According to John Carey, this appropriation "was intended to establish a start-up level of federal funding, not a funding baseline for long-term operations. However, it became a de facto baseline from which year-to-year funding modifications were made."[53] This amount was insufficient for both programming and operations; after interconnection and programming for evening hours, almost no money was left over for local stations.

CPB appropriations followed a byzantine process. The 1967 Act established CPB under HEW's Office of Education for accounting and supervision, and funds for establishing and maintaining facilities were channeled directly to stations through the Public Telecommunications Facility Program (PTFP). The PTFP in turn was administered by National Telecommunications and Information Administration (NTIA). Thus public broadcasting was funded and overseen by three federal agencies: NTIA, HEW, and CPB. Under the Carter administration, CPB appropriations were transferred from HEW to the House Committee on Communications Subcommittee on Telecommunications, Consumer Protection, and Finance, creating even more direct opportunities for political influence.

Finally, the Act heightened tensions between local stations and national entities, by implicitly favoring the latter. The Carnegie report's "bedrock of localism" was based on encouraging locally produced programs, asserting the rights of individual stations to make programming decisions, and protecting the system from central political manipulation. However, interconnection improved technical efficiency and offered the potential for same-time national coverage. As a result, programs were designed to heighten the system's profile, by drawing large audiences, rather than to serve regional or local communities. This programming policy encouraged more private and corporate support for national programs, yet the trend toward national service exacerbated conflicts between licensees and national agencies over program production and distribution of federal funds. Rather than engendering localism, the de-

Table 2.1
CPB-Funded Radio Stations by Type of License, 1988

Colleges and Universities	173	(58%)
Community Organizations	93	(31%)
Local Schools and Governments	20	(7%)
State Governments	13	(4%)
	299	

Source: Adapted from John Carey. "Public Broadcasting and Federal Policy." In *New Directions in Telecommunications Policy*, vol. 1, P. Newbury, ed. Durham, NC: Duke University Press, 1989.

velopment of a centralized system forced local stations to implement decisions made by a distant administration with an often differing agenda. The Public Broadcasting Act of 1967 failed to resolve a host of questions regarding funding, structure, and accountability. Rather than serving as a forum for public debate, public broadcasting was quickly defined as a battleground for competing interests and political pressures.

NPR'S FORMATION AND EARLY YEARS

Internecine warfare, based on oft-conflicting goals and funding uncertainty, has determined much of domestic public broadcasting's agenda throughout its history. However, one significant factor distinguishes NPR from the Public Broadcasting Service: unlike PBS, NPR was chartered to produce and distribute programming. Whereas PBS largely was a creation of public TV stations themselves, the CPB took the lead in establishing NPR.[54] As a result, the CPB initially had more control over NPR as a national programming source, which lessened some of the friction that characterized the relationship between CPB and PBS. While NPR functioned more like a traditional network than did PBS, it was spared much of the overt political meddling endured by public television, because of what Robert Avery and Robert Pepper term its "low profile—some would say invisibility."[55] Public radio stations also were less dependent on national programming and more flexible in their scheduling than PBS affiliates, because radio production costs were lower. These stations also were less subject to outside political intervention, since most were licensed to colleges and universities, whereas the majority of public television licenses were held by state and local governments (see Table 2.1).

Although public radio largely had been ignored by the foundations that poured money into educational television, the number of educational FM radio stations swelled from twenty-nine in 1948 to 326 in 1967. Despite this impressive growth, *The Hidden Medium* summarized the medium's mid-decade status gloomily: "Educational radio, for the most part, is underfinanced, understaffed, underequipped, underpromoted and underresearched."[56] Almost 50 percent of the reporting stations were budgeted at less than $25,000 per year, and approximately one-third scraped by on less than ten thousand dollars. The report pinned the blame for educational radio's malaise squarely on the stations themselves. By restricting their programming to instruction and coverage of campus affairs, the stations had failed to cultivate interest and support in their surrounding communities. The 1966 Wingspread Conference made no specific proposal for interconnection among stations, but it implicitly recommended the formation of a national network, by calling for NER to establish a Washington-based news and public affairs bureau as well as a national production center for programming and training. In its summary, *The Hidden Medium* offered that

a striking feature of the new educational radio scene is its movement in almost direct opposition to the current development of commercial radio. Where, to meet the inexorable competition of television, commercial radio has transformed itself into a *local* medium, with a steady diminution of network service educational radio is moving impatiently toward the day of full live network operations.[57]

With funding from the CPB and the Ford Foundation, former WGBH station manager Samuel Holt completed *The Public Radio Study* in March 1969. Holt's report reiterated many of *The Hidden Medium*'s findings. He cited the root of educational radio's malaise in its academic affiliations, claiming that the "academic organization is itself traditionally imprecise and flexible, and broadcasting exposed to this situation has only tended to adapt itself to this structure and its strictures." He concluded that "the [CPB] should seek to lend its influence to efforts to upgrade the value placed on their stations by the upper administrators of these license-holding institutions."[58] However, Holt recommended that CPB first focus on building regional networks, which would in turn be linked to a Washington-based public affairs service. Holt also called for establishing a CPB radio division, with an advisory board of experienced noncommercial radio broadcasters. At the 1969 NAEB convention, the CPB established a Radio Advisory Council of twelve station managers to pursue possibilities for building a noncommercial radio network. RAC's director was Al Hulsen, who previously had been station manager at WFCR in Amherst, Massachusetts, and chairman of the board at EERN. The RAC was hardly representative of educational radio at large: all RAC members were from well-established stations in the Northeast, Midwest, and West Coast.[59] Hulsen and the RAC pressed for the creation of a new organization rather than a remodeled NER, in order to make a clean break with educational radio's impoverished past. In December 1969, after discussions with the seventy-three noncommercial radio stations that had qualified for federal funding, the CPB created a National Public Radio Planning Board.

A board meeting was held in January, and National Public Radio was formally incorporated on March 3, 1970. The board consisted of fourteen directors, of whom nine represented stations, two the CPB and NPR, and three the "general public."[60] As was the case with the Carnegie Commission, the 1967 act, and the RAC, the public was conspicuously absent from any substantial involvement; instead, a closed circle of well-connected insiders made far-reaching decisions for the public radio system. Several NPR board members had served on the RAC and NER Boards and were well acquainted with leaders at CPB.[61] NPR's early executives came from public television, thus heightening the insularity of public broadcasting's decisionmakers. In late June, Donald Quayle was selected as NPR's first president, replacing interim head John Macy of CPB. Quayle (who held office from 1970 to 1973) was a former NET administrator who began his career at WOSU. Joseph Kirkish describes Quayle as a consensus candidate, selected after a struggle between "visionaries" (who favored NER's executive director Robert Mott) and "pragmatists" (who supported media critic and former CBS producer Robert Shayon). Kirkish claims the struggle "suggested on a microscopic level the kind of conflict that would affect the organization on a grand scale in the future—between NPR staff members and, later, between the entire NPR staff and various member stations."[62]

William Siemering, the former general manager of Buffalo's WBFQ-FM, was hired as NPR's program director, and the NPR Board adopted his "National Public Radio Purposes" as the system's mission statement. Under his leadership, WBFO (licensed to SUNY-Buffalo) established a satellite station operated by Buffalo's minority community that broadcast twenty-five hours of programming a week. Like the Carnegie Report, "National Public Radio Purposes" was long on rhetoric; the loftiness of its intentions becomes all the more poignant in the light of subsequent developments at NPR. Among other things, "National Public Radio Purposes" called on the new service to

encourage a sense of active constructive participation, rather than apathetic helplessness[;] . . . provide listeners with an aural esthetic experience which enriches and gives meaning to the human spirit[;] . . . speak with many voices and dialects[;] . . . not only call attention to a problem, but be an active agent in seeking solutions. . . . National Public Radio should not only improve the quality of public radio, but should lead in revitalizing the medium of radio so that it may become a first class citizen in the media community.[63]

Siemering cited sources as diverse as Susan Sontag and the British journal *Anarch*, but perhaps the primary, although unstated, inspiration for NPR's mission statement was John Dewey. In writings such as *The Public and Its Problems*, Dewey had emphasized the dissemination of information to the public as a necessary component of modern democratic life and viewed the media as performing a vital educative function within society. Dewey had advocated public activism and thought media should be used to encourage and improve public participation in society and politics. To Dewey, the liberal ideology of individualism was insufficient to cope with the mechanical forces and vast impersonal organizations that had created an "inchoate and unorganized" public.[64] As individuals were absorbed into a dominant, institutionalized association, their perceived powerlessness had led to alienation. This alienation in turn had bred disenfranchisement, and, Dewey argued, the "Great Society created by steam and electricity may be a society, but it is no community."[65] Dewey believed individuals could exist only in context of a "Great Community" and that "culture" consists of participation. Like Dewey, "National Public Radio Purposes" holds that the challenge to democracy lies in drawing people into the life of the community, although its vision of democracy is impervious to obstacles of scale or class. Engelman states:

Siemering envisaged a decentralized system reflecting the diversity of the nation: a system of local audio laboratories to train radio producers, submissions of programs to the network by affiliates, and reciprocal trade of material among stations. By fulfilling this mission, Siemering believed that NPR would revitalize the medium of radio.[66]

Siemering's manifesto set the tenor for early NPR programming. Former NPR executive Joe Gwathmey recalled that "in part, NPR was a missionary enterprise whose role was to broadcast programs which would *not* be commercially viable." NPR's first distribution to stations was a tape of twenty concerts by the Los Angeles Philharmonic.[67] The network created public radio's first full-time, national, live interconnection system with coverage of the Senate Foreign Relations Committee hearings on Vietnam in April 1971. Most importantly, NPR's mission statement called for "an identifiable daily product . . . [that] may contain some hard news, but the primary emphasis would be on interpretation, investigative reporting on public affairs, the world of ideas and the arts. The program would be well-paced, flexible, and a service primarily for the general audience."[68] At its January 1970 meeting, the NPR board agreed that its first effort would be a public affairs program service featuring contributions by member stations; NPR's flagship program, the newsmagazine *All Things Considered*, made its debut on May 3, 1971. The newsmagazine format had been previously used by NBC on the *Monitor* radio program. Al Hulsen had produced a daily local magazine at WOSU in the 1950s and later had been responsible for ERN's *Kaleidoscope*, which aired from 1961 to 1963; *All Things Considered*'s major model, however, was the Canadian Broadcasting Company's *This Country in the Morning*, whose "long-form" reports of narratives interspersed with "actualities" (taped interviews and ambient sound) marked a significant departure from the sixty-second news spots that were standard fare on commercial network radio. Siemering stated that *All Things Considered* "really came out of a reaction against the superficiality of commercial radio, and also the grayness and lack of timeliness of educational radio."[69] He sought a return to the folksiness of the land grant radio of his youth; senior NPR producer Art Silverman averred that "as much as people need to hear two more reports about Eastern Europe or the Third World, they also need to hear about how to pick rhubarb for a pie."[70]

Nevertheless, professionalism was an integral part of *All Things Considered* from the outset. Siemering (undoubtedly conscious of NPR's chief funding source) avoided the confrontational stance of the era's "alternative" media; looking back on his tenure at NPR, he later stated, "We did not regard NPR as an experimental alternative to commercial broadcasting"[71] NPR president Quayle staffed NPR with experienced reporters drawn from the newspaper industry; according to James Haney, "Quayle believed it was easier to teach a journalist how to be a broadcaster than it was to teach a broadcaster how to be a journalist."[72] Cleve Mathews from the *New York Times* became NPR's first news director, and the *Times'* Robert Conley was tapped as the first host of *All Things Considered*.[73] The NPR board originally proposed that the program air in the morning; it began instead at 5 P.M., because many educational stations did not sign on before noon. An afternoon program also would make an overnight staff unnecessary and allow for direct competition with commercial "drive time" news programs.[74] Board members debated whether *All Things Considered* should air for one or two hours; the program's ninety-minute length was a compromise. The program's focus on news rather than the arts also was partially due to the fact that NPR's live programming would be distributed on AT&T landlines, which had limited frequency response. The first broadcast, on May 3, 1971, included nearly half an hour of excerpts from May Day protests by Vietnam veterans, a sixteen-minute story about a heroin-addicted nurse, a CBC piece about war, and a contribution from WOI in Ames, Iowa, about waning business for barbers. It concluded with a conversation between poet Allen Ginsberg and his father. Conley, expected to ad lib for the final six minutes, failed to do so, and stations were left with five and a half minutes of dead air.

Early station reactions to *All Things Considered* were uniformly negative. NPR board member Karl Schmidt complained, "Our child has been born and it is ugly"; Gwathmey claimed "no one was satisfied with it."[75] Conley was removed as host in July 1971 and replaced by cohosts Mike Waters and Jim Russell. Jack Mitchell (formerly of WHA), became the producer of *All Things Considered* in March 1972 and immediately replaced Russell with Susan Stamberg as Waters' cohost. Mitchell also formalized the program's structure. *All Things Considered* would begin with a billboard listing of stories, followed by five minutes of hard news and then by shorter news and feature stories as time permitted. Reporters also developed NPR's "acts and tracks" formula, in which a story begins with an actuality (usually a "full-up" ambient sound that fades under the announcer's script) and concludes with a brief interview segment.[76] While nearly everyone associated with NPR lauded Siemering for his conceptual skills, his day-to-day abilities as NPR program director were frequently questioned by Quayle and others, and he resigned in December 1972.

All Things Considered won a Peabody award for excellence in radio journalism the following year, yet the program remained a flashpoint for national-local tensions within the public radio system. Siemering had intended for station submissions to account for one-third of *All Things Considered*'s content in order to enhance the show's pluralism and defuse criticism that NPR focused on its Washington base of operations at the expense of its member stations. However, relatively few station submissions were aired on the program. NPR's Washington staff complained that local stories were often of poor quality and lacked universally interesting subject matter, while stations charged that their stories were judged by inconsistent standards and that their tapes became dated while awaiting decisions or were lost altogether. The stations' arguments were buttressed by the fact that empty airtime was filled with ad-libbed pieces by Stamberg and her cohosts, such as a four-minute discussion of Fig Newtons. Neil Conan, NPR's acting managing editor, acknowledged that "what was considered 'a marvelous sense of spontaneity' was really programming put on the air out of pure desperation to fill airtime."[77] In addition, NPR reporters would suddenly appear to cover an event in a local affiliate's coverage area without giving the station prior notice, and NPR's afternoon program afforded few opportunities for local cut-ins. The biggest complaint, however, was that much of NPR's self-consciously "populist" programming was at odds with the high-culture agenda of university stations. While these stations may have welcomed the heightened profile and prestige afforded by national programming, many chafed at carrying programs that were not tailored exclusively to elite audiences or did not fit into precise categories. Mary Collins found that "the station managers just couldn't adjust to this new animal. Clearly it wasn't commercial radio. It certainly wasn't land-grant educational radio. NPR had become some kind of unrecognizable hybrid. They didn't know what to do with it."[78]

Such conflicts are inevitable whenever new structures are overlaid on older organizational forms, and station representation has been a particular source of conflict within the public radio system. NPR represented both its own agendas and those of its stations before the CPB and Congress, and stations frequently argued that their interests were shortchanged or ignored. No structure for regular communication between NPR and member stations existed after the NAEB changed from a representative organization to a professional group, before folding altogether in 1981.[79] NPR also moved quickly to sever its roots in educational radio. It absorbed NER's tape network in July 1972 but three years later stopped distributing the Instructional Radio Series and announced that it would no longer solicit new educational series, despite its statements to the contrary before absorbing the tape library.[80] The NER board voted to disband the organization in April 1973, recommending that a new representational organization for public radio be formed for lobbying activities and interaction with the FCC, CPB, Congress, and other public and private groups. NPR's assumption of these roles would involve a possible conflict of interest, since it also was a programming service, and its effectiveness as a lobbying organization was compromised by the fact that it received virtually all its funding from the CPB.

The Association of Public Radio Stations (APRS) was formed on May 24, 1973, after vote at the Public Radio Conference. Former NER chair Hugh Cordier was elected chairman of the new organization, with Minnesota Public Radio's William Kling serving as vice chairman (shortly thereafter, he would head the organization). APRS aggressively pushed for decentralized programming sources, and Kling in particular hoped to build a radio production center comparable to those of the leading PBS stations. NPR general counsel Ernest Sanchez recalled in 1981: "Bill has a special vision of what destiny holds for Minnesota Public Radio. It takes a lot of money to finance that vision."[81] APRS served primarily as a mouthpiece for the larger stations in the public radio system, and the organization never counted more than 60 percent of NPR's affiliates in its membership. NPR provided programming to its station members, but APRS's lobbying and representation activities offered intangible benefits. The division between public radio's operational (NPR) and representational (APRS) arms also led to interorganizational competition and confusion over their respective roles. While public television was united under PBS, public radio's divided organization had difficulties representing the interests of public radio broadcasters to the CPB. By the summer of 1975, relations between APRS and NPR had degenerated into open hostility. The key event was a series of CPB hearings over how money would be divided between public radio and television. Since fiscal year 1973, radio had received less than 17 percent of CPB's allotment for public broadcasting. PBS could present a united front to the CPB, while NPR and APRS could not. Beginning in August 1975, representatives of NPR and APRS began hashing out their differences in a series of meetings. Robert Avery and Robert Pepper find that "APRS brought to the merger emotion, theory, philosophy and responsibility, while NPR brought mostly money and function. . . . [A]s one observer described it, the negotiations were between 'the big fat slow one [NPR] and the lean, mean, quick one [APRS].' "[82]

One proposal floated in the talks suggested that a "buy-back" provision, in which stations would pay directly for specific functions such as programming and representation, would make a merged organization more accountable to member stations. Further discussion led to a program-by-program buy-back proposal, similar to PBS's Station Programming Cooperative.[83] However, some participants quickly grasped the implications of this proposal. NPR programming costs would rise, and resources for production would be cut, as large producing stations such as Minnesota Public Radio did more of their own programming. These stations also would exert a disproportionate amount of leverage over national policies and programming. In a compromise, NPR acknowledged that representation and programming functions would have parity in the new organization. APRS, in turn, backed off from its buyback proposal. The merger was approved at the 1977 Public Radio Conference by a vote of 146 to sixteen. The new organization kept the name NPR, since it "was one of the few things in the public radio system with any name recognition at all."[84] Like PBS, the new NPR provided interconnection for member stations and was responsible for systemwide planning and representation.

Several public radio figures believe that the merger was essentially a takeover of NPR by a group of powerful station managers, namely Kling and Ron Bornstein of WHA, to draw more CPB money to their stations.[85] The merger also was driven by a wish to oust top NPR management, owing to station dissatisfaction with the network's programming and operations. After a somewhat stormy tenure marked by a penchant for cronyism, Quayle had resigned as NPR president in June 1973 to become senior vice president for programming at CPB. He was replaced by his lieutenant, Lee Frischknecht, in July. Like Quayle, Frischknecht was a long-term industry insider, having been head of station relations at NET and NPR's vice president for administration and planning. Stations quickly pressured Frischknecht to increase NPR's cultural programming. In efforts to heighten its Washington profile, NPR had allocated only 23 percent of its 1974 budget to cultural programming; most of the money went to news and public affairs. Yet stations were nearly as likely to air cultural programming as news: A 1975 survey of stations indicated that 95 percent of NPR's affiliates aired *All Things Considered*, while 80 percent aired NPR's Arts information package. Despite station complaints, NPR also continued to ignore specialized audiences. Out of two thousand hours of programming produced in fiscal year 1976, less than ten hours targeted senior citizens and minorities.[86] Responding to station concerns, the NPR board hired a consultant in 1976 to reorganize NPR's programming production. Frischknecht proposed to merge the news division with the cultural affairs department and to fold public information, station relations, and development into a new "corporate relations" division. News staffers, already peeved at low salaries and Frischknecht's formal managerial style, saw the reorganization as an attempt to discourage controversial public affairs programming and squelch union organizing efforts at the news bureau. Frischknecht countered that the NPR news bureau, headed by Robert Zelnick, "doesn't share the goals of public radio" and "is too oriented towards Washington concerns like international news and national politics."[87]

The reorganization went through, with Jim Russell, executive producer of *All Things Considered*, replacing Zelnick as head of the combined news and cultural division. The thirty-one-member NPR programming staff responded in June 1976 with a vote to organize with the American Federation of Radio and Television Artists (AFTRA). Frishknecht resigned in June 1977, and Edward Elson served as an interim president of the new NPR until a permanent replacement could be found. NPR's board wanted a strong leader to settle ongoing internal disputes and increase federal support. After reviewing more than three hundred candidates, it unanimously chose Frank Mankiewicz, who assumed NPR's presidency in July 1977.[88] A former director of the Peace Corps in South America and a lawyer specializing in representing entertainment and real estate interests, Mankiewicz had served as Robert Kennedy's press secretary and had managed George McGovern's disastrous presidential bid in 1972. His broadcasting experience was limited to a short stint with U.S. Armed Forces Radio; he had been unaware of NPR's existence before being selected to head the organization.[89] Though bound to inflame conservative opponents of public broadcasting, his reputation as a consummate "Washington guy" attracted NPR's board. In early 1979, Mankiewicz told the *Washington Post* he had been hired "to get more money, but mostly to get more recognition" for NPR. A long-time NPR staffer agreed, saying "Mankiewicz presents a complete turnaround in NPR's management philosophy. Formerly, the idea seemed to be that if we were very quiet and nobody noticed what we were doing, perhaps a lot of people would be able to hang on long enough to collect their pensions."[90]

Mankiewicz proved to be remarkably proficient at turning the tap for federal money. In the early 1970s, public radio had received 10 percent of the money dispersed by the CPB; by 1979, Mankiewicz had expanded this to 25 percent, for a total of $20 million. However, the overall funding picture for public broadcasting had remained consistently bleak since the initial federal appropriation in 1967. Virtually no one inside or outside of public broadcasting was satisfied with the system in its present form, and a second Carnegie Commission was convened in June 1977 to reappraise it. Carnegie II was chaired by William McGill, the president of Columbia University. Like those of the first Carnegie Commission, its seventeen members were mainly representatives of public and commercial broadcasting, with a sprinkling of high-profile corporate heads and celebrities to lend business and cultural cachet. Nevertheless, the Commission's report (*A Public Trust: The Report of the Carnegie Commission on the Future of Public Broadcasting*) was highly critical of the existing state of public broadcasting in the United States. The report's summary found "public broadcasting's financial, organizational and creative structure fundamentally flawed."[91]

A Public Trust called for a major overhaul of public broadcasting's structure, beginning with the CPB's replacement by an independent, nonprofit Public Telecommunications Trust. The Trust's nine directors would be nominated by a panel "chaired by the Librarian of Congress, drawn from governmental institutions devoted to the arts, the sciences, the humanities, and the preservation of our heritage" and serve nonrenewable nine-year terms.[92] The Trust would plan and lead but it would not fund programming. That would be the work of a semiautonomous Program Service Endowment, whose fifteen-member board would be appointed by the new Trust. *A Public Trust* also advocated a quantum leap in federal support, from $163 million to more than $600 million annually by 1985. This funding would come from general revenues and a fee on spectrum use by commercial broadcasters. Unlike Carnegie I, *A Public Trust* addressed the public radio system at length and in detail. It found that significant sections of the country were excluded from public radio service and that existing stations consistently lacked variety in programming. To address the problem of limited geographical coverage, the commission suggested activating 250 to 300 additional public radio stations and increasing the range of existing ones. These expansion efforts were to be accomplished through regulatory reform, financial assistance for existing stations, and the purchase of additional stations from commercial concerns. Carnegie II also challenged NPR's status as the system's focal point:

Our plan does not include the assured, lump-sum support that has been NPR's mainstay since its inception. Instead, NPR and others face a more open, competitive environment in which it will be necessary to plan for, seek, and justify support from several quarters: first and foremost, the audiences being served, and secondarily, the Endowment and the Trust.[93]

The report also called for heightened public participation in public radio and television through equal opportunity employment practices and greater access by minorities via ownership, as well as "public involvement in station governance." The guidelines for expanding public participation were purposely vague: *A Public Trust* merely suggested that "each community and its licensees must decide precisely what mix of public participation tools seems appropriate and effective."[94]

A Public Trust met with a largely negative reception upon its publication on January 30, 1979. NPR chair Edward Elson declared that the Carnegie Commission had produced a report that, if enacted "would endanger the existence of the very public radio system it praises," while a *Broadcasting* editorial argued that "the worst features of the existing system would be preserved, if by other names, at three times the existing expense."[95] More significantly, Carnegie II failed to address the issue of long-range financing in sufficient detail and largely ignored programming issues. Its specific recommendations were highly problematic. The commission suggested that one means to increase the number of public stations "would be for the FCC to grant the right of first refusal to qualified public groups at the negotiated price for the transfer of any license." Aside from failing to define criteria for "qualified" public groups, the report's proposal to offer stations at the "negotiated-price" did not address the financial barriers to entry that often have precluded public groups from gaining control of broadcast facilities in the first place. The report also displayed a lack of imagination by advocating the creation of multiple stations in large markets on the grounds that listeners are "conditioned" to expect formats: "A single public radio station in a major market is inhibited from developing a 'sound' or a format that can be promoted and can attract audiences and general listener support." Ironically, while calling for public stations to expand their coverage areas, the commission criticized commercial broadcasters for downgrading local service: "With more stations to divide the audience, a commercial operator must be able to turn a profit with smaller and smaller audiences. The only way is to cut operating costs."[96]

The report also was plagued by a lack of consensus among participating parties. A national organization for public broadcasting was already in place, and the system of local stations was much larger and wealthier than it had been in 1967. These forces were intrinsically resistant to significant structural change.[97] The federal, corporate, and public indifference to *A Public Trust* also was due to the changed political environment of the 1970s. The first Carnegie report, written amid the ferment of Lyndon Johnson's "Great Society," had been the product of close cooperation between the Carnegie Commission, the White House, Congress, and educational broadcasters. In contrast, the 1970s were a time of social, political, and economic retrenchment. The Johnson administration's guns and butter economic policy had created an overheated, inflationary economy that began to contract after the 1973 oil embargo, and a burgeoning deregulation movement had little use for more active federal intervention in broadcasting. Despite the high profile of its members and the clout of the Carnegie imprimatur, virtually none of *A Public Trust*'s suggestions were implemented.

CRISIS AND CHANGE

If the 1970s were a time of retrenchment, the Republican resurgence of 1980 plunged public broadcasting into crisis. A headline in the January 26, 1981, issue of *Broadcasting* described the incoming administration's attitude toward public broadcasting: "Reagan Transition's Verdict on CPB: Terminate with Extreme Prejudice." The first Reagan budget, drawn up by David Stockman, had no public broadcasting funds whatsoever. Sharon Rockefeller describes how public broadcasting narrowly escaped from being "zeroed out":

When I was chairman of CPB, David Stockman was being confirmed as director of the Office of Management and Budget. . . . Stockman's hearing was at 10 a.m. We met outside my father's [Sen. Charles Percy's] office at ten of ten. [Percy] said to Stockman, "My daughter's here. She wants to ask you some questions about public broadcasting and what kind of cuts . . . are you considering for CPB?" Stockman said, "Well, let's see. We have an A, a B, a C, and a D list. They're on our D list. That's a 50 percent cut." We said, "No, that really won't be acceptable." So Stockman said, "Well, I can move you back to the B list. That's a 25 percent cut." That's how arbitrarily it happened.[98]

Congress eventually rescinded $35 million of $172 million it already had appropriated for fiscal year 1983. Also, Reagan packed the CPB board with right-wing ideologues and sympathizers throughout the course of his administration. They included M. Stanton Evans and Richard Brookhiser (who at the time of their appointments were respectively former and current editors of the *National Review*); Helen Taylor, a long-time Reagan supporter who contributed to the campaigns of Jesse Helms and others; and Karl Eller, president of Columbia Pictures Communications, who told a Tucson audience in 1981:

It makes no sense at all to have our society insisting on a "democracy of judgment"—a group decision; because a group decision is nothing more than a compromise of mostly mediocre minds. . . . The phrase "elitist" is usually invoked by those who have uncritically embraced the average or ordinary pieties of the new populist morality in today's America.[99]

The proportion of NPR's funding coming from CPB had declined from 95 percent in 1980 to 70 percent in 1982. Its program hours had grown by 62 percent between 1977 and 1982, but expenses in this period nearly quadrupled, from $7.3 million to $26.7 million. With the intention of making NPR "the *New York Times* of radio," Frank Mankiewicz had steered NPR further in a "hard news" direction. He also sought to raise the service's profile through expensive (and derivative) radio adaptations of *Star Wars* and *The Empire Strikes Back* in 1981 and 1983. Facing deep cuts from the Reagan administration and growing antagonism from CPB, Mankiewicz and the NPR board formulated plans to wean NPR from all federal funding. Announcing that "we will go into every profession except the oldest one," on April 21, 1982, Mankiewicz unveiled "Operation Independence" to station representatives at NPR's annual membership meeting. The plan would replace NPR's projected $30 million in federal support with $15 million in underwriting from corporations and foundations, with the remainder to come from various commercial ventures, by fiscal year 1987.[100] Despite the fact that NPR already had lost two million dollars in CPB money for fiscal year 1983 as a result of the Reagan recisions, NPR executive vice president Tom Warnock stated that Operation Independence "could be considered a no-risk situation. In every case, our greatest risk is that we won't make any money. We're not putting our assets in jeopardy."[101]

Operation independence was based on increased underwriting, a new program service called *NPR Plus*, and NPR Ventures, which would develop for-profit partnerships with private companies. The NPR board formally approved the plan on July 30, 1982. To raise underwriting support the NPR board created the position of Vice President of Development to sell "shares" in NPR programs, in which funding credits would be announced throughout NPR's schedule. This position, however, was filled only six weeks before the start of fiscal year 1983, which was to be heavily funded by grants and contributions.[102] Emblematic of the confusion at NPR, the newly hired fundraiser was informed that the target was $5.3 million, while CPB had been told that the goal was $7.2 million. NPR banked on its belief that the $7.2 million goal would be met by two large grants, yet as of September 1982 one potential grantor had bailed out, and NPR had not even begun negotiations with the other. *NPR Plus* was intended as a twenty-four-hour-a-day classical music feed available to NPR member stations, at a cost to them in excess of five thousand dollars per year. The service was originally budgeted at $700,000, but the promise of more station fees and grant support led NPR to add hourly newscasts, a news analysis program called *Dateline*, and a thirty-six-hour-a week corollary service based on *Jazz Alive*. Though the program's budget quickly swelled to $1.7 million, and by March 1983 only 101 out of a projected 150 stations had signed up, the project was approved. Beginning in October, an attenuated *NPR Plus* offered 103 hours of classical and twenty-one hours of jazz each week; the price was raised to $5,700 per station, and the service shed the public affairs reporting that initially had attracted many stations.[103] The program was phased out of production and scheduling by the end of 1984, two and a half years after its introduction.

The third arm of Operation Independence, NPR Ventures, was to use the spare capacity of NPR's satellite transponders. NPR had begun satellite transmission in October 1979 on Westar I, commencing stereo broadcasts the following January. To boost the system's growth, NPR paid for affiliates' satellite receivers; 120 of 203 CPB-qualified stations were hooked up by early March of 1980, and the remainder by late April.[104] The Public Radio Act of 1981 authorized commercial use of NPR's satellite transponders as long as public service was not threatened. NPR Ventures formally negotiated five projects. *Cellular Radio* was a paging system aimed at small to medium-sized markets; the project was announced at the 1983 Public Radio Conference as NPR's financial problems were deepening, and it failed for lack of partners. *Codart*, a form of "pay radio" developed by San Francisco's KQED and a commercial engineering firm, would allow listeners to record specialized programming broadcast overnight. The project was abandoned in March 1983 because development costs proved prohibitive. *Dataspeed* was contingent on the FCC's deregulation of FM subcarriers. Dataspeed, Inc., would manufacture and market portable receivers that would receive nonbroadcast information like stock quotes, sports scores, and airline schedules from NPR's satellite. The project failed because of FCC delays in deregulating subcarrier frequencies, which were used by radio reading services for the visually impaired. The *Information Network Corporation* was formed as a joint venture between NPR and National Information Utilities Corporation to transmit point to multipoint data (for instance, price changes from a supermarket chain's headquarters to local stores). Although it was not expected to turn a profit for two or three years, INC was projected to provide five million dollars to NPR by 1987, and stations were expected to reap $6,000 to $75,000 annually, depending on market size and coverage area. Like the Dataspeed project, INC required FCC approval for NPR to use subcarriers for commercial purposes. *National Satellite Paging* was a co-venture with Mobile Communications Corporation of America to use NPR's transponders to send paging signals across the country. Sixty percent of the revenues would go to MCCA, the remainder to NPR and participating stations. The venture was joined by Western Union in September 1983; by the end 1984, it was the only part of NPR Ventures that remained active. NPR Ventures was formally dissolved in October 1985.[105]

NPR sank more than $865,000 into venture startup costs for fiscal year 1983—before the FCC deregulated subcarriers. The network also neglected to hire a vice president for NPR Ventures until August 1982, which resulted in a lack of oversight and accountability for its projects. Budget problems were compounded by a new computer system installed by the NPR finance department in June 1982. The old system stopped issuing reports comparing actual operational costs to budgets, and new reports were not generated until the second quarter of fiscal year 1983, due to bugs in the replacement system. In November, $320,000 in bills remained unsent. NPR also hired sixty-four full-time and seventeen part-time employees and gave 5 to 12 percent raises to 250 staffers, at a time when Vice President Tom Warnock had received a written note from NPR financial officers that "now may not be the time for increases."[106] By December 1982, NPR officers had begun to realize that the system was hemorrhaging money, but they believed these problems would be redressed by collections. Departments were overspending wildly. A hundred and ten American Express cards were handed out to NPR staff, who rang up $800,000 in travel and entertainment expenses in the six months before April 1983. A Coopers and Lybrand audit released in June 1983 found that "not only were charges *not* itemized; in some cases it wasn't even known who had used the card."[107] Most damagingly, the audit found that NPR used $650,000 in payroll taxes to finance operations between January and April 1983, although Mankiewicz claimed all but $100,000 had been repaid by mid-June.[108]

Piecing together information, Warnock reported an estimated deficit of $2.8 million to Mankiewicz on February 26, 1983. Mankiewicz responded, "Hell, we're only talking about a few million dollars. The United States government is going to have a deficit of $250 billion, and their president's not resigning."[109] The board was less sanguine, and NPR began laying off employees and canceling programs. Forty-seven of NPR's four hundred employees were axed in March 1983, and the *Sunday Show* and *Jazz Alive!* were dropped. The News and Information department lost 8 percent of its budget and seventeen staff positions. The Performance Programming division was particularly hard hit, losing a dozen employees and a quarter of its budget.[110] NPR deferred $250,000 in payments to the Satellite Program Development Fund from June to October 1983, alienating many independent producers in the process, but the deficit still climbed, to $5.8 million in mid-April. Informed of the loss on April 18 at the Public Radio Conference, member stations passed a resolution asking the board to maintain *Morning Edition* and *All Things Considered* as "the number-one programming priority."[111]

Mankiewicz resigned as NPR president May 10, 1983. Minimizing his role in the financial debacle, he stated, "I'm not a bad financial manager, but that's not what I was hired to do. . . . [W]e had a system going for five-and-a-half years where I didn't have to look at a printout." He also told reporters, "We ran a goddamn tight ship," and he defiantly declared, "If our major preoccupation is to balance the budget, we will not serve our major purpose. It must not be our only objective. I don't want it said on my epitaph: 'He balanced the budget.' " In a parting shot, he added, "I didn't think I was going to stay on forever and this focused it a bit. It was a good year to leave."[112] After a few months as an NPR consultant, in July 1983 Mankiewicz joined the lobbying and public relations firm of Gray and Company (later Hill and Knowlton Public Affairs Worldwide). Ten years later, a *Wall Street Journal* story on former Robert Kennedy staffers found Mankiewicz ensconced as vice chairman at Hill and Knowlton, which it characterized as symbolizing "special interest entrenchment."[113] The article made no reference to Mankiewicz's tenure at NPR. That same year, William Siemering was awarded a MacArthur Foundation "genius" grant for his contributions to public radio.

Ronald Bornstein, one of the station managers instrumental in the merger of NPR and APRS, was named interim NPR president following Mankiewicz's resignation. Bornstein immediately imposed a hiring freeze, a hold on all financial records, and demanded that all checks over five thousand dollars bear his signature.[114] He also ordered the Coopers and Lybrand audit, which found that NPR had a working-capital deficit of $6.5 million as of June 1983. Even if its assets were liquidated, NPR would still be $1.2 million in debt. The audit report stated that NPR "may be unable to continue."[115] By late June, board chairman Myron Jones had resigned, as had chief financial officer Art Roberts, membership committee chair Wallace Smith, and finance committee chair Steve Meuche. Bornstein laid off 154 staffers but the estimated deficit soared to $9.1 million. The July 4 issue of *Business Week* stated, "Right now, NPR's survival seems an even-money bet."[116] After twelve hours of negotiations and pressure from Rep. Tim Wirth (D.-Colorado, chairman of the House Subcommittee for communication) and Sen. William Proxmire (R.-Wisconsin), the CPB advanced NPR $500,000 to meet its July 29 payroll. The agreement was concluded at 3:15 A.M., one day before the network would have gone off the air.

The major point of contention concerned who would control NPR's satellite transponders. CPB wanted the title to NPR's satellite uplink equipment, but NPR refused to relinquish control of its primary asset. After what was termed a "game of chicken," the system was placed in the hands of an independent trust, overseen by former U.S. attorney general Elliot Richardson, NTIA head Henry Geller, and Virginia Duncan, a former CPB board member employed by Bechtel.[117] To meet the projected $9.1 million deficit, CPB gave NPR a line of credit up to $8.5 million, with the remainder to come from a $600,000 loan from CPB. The latter loan was forgiven in exchange for transfer of the titles of NPR's transmitting equipment to the group of trustees, who then leased it back to NPR.[118] CPB community service grants from member stations served as collateral, and a systemwide on-air fundraising appeal, the "Drive to Survive," netted NPR approximately $650,000. Although NPR was the main program supplier for most CPB-qualified public radio stations, only one-third of NPR's member stations carried the appeal, out of fear that this would cut into their own fundraising.

Friction between the national organization and its affiliates was heightened by the financial crisis. Reports on the May 16, 17, and 18 broadcasts of *Morning Edition* and *All Things Considered* discussed subscriber contributions and possible on-air and direct-mail fundraising for NPR. Stations were aghast that NPR would even imply that it might trespass onto the sacred territory of their own pledge drives. The broadcasts were decried by station manager and former NPR finance committee chair Steve Meuche as "a bunch of people whining about how they're not allowed to do fundraising on network programs." Others believed that the pleas were "self-serving" in informing listeners that their contributions were used for local station expenses rather than national programs. Gary Shivers of WUNC in Chapel Hill, North Carolina, claimed that the network's on-air reports "totally neglected the presence and talents of independents and station-based producers. It assumed that the programming must come from NPR staff."[119] Nevertheless, seeing an opportunity to gain a significant amount of leverage over the public radio system, the stations agreed to cover NPR's debt. Following a unanimous vote of the NPR board of directors on July 17, 1984, NPR's affiliates assumed full responsibility for NPR's debt (which amounted to a final figure of $6.9 million) and levied an additional $1.5 million dues assessment on the stations for fiscal years 1985 and 1986.[120] Smaller stations were allowed to stretch out their payments, yet the financial burden forced many of these stations to trim other services in order to bail out NPR.

Between March and September 1983, the NPR staff was reduced by more than one-third, from more than 442 employees to 285.[121] *Morning Edition, All Things Considered*, and *Weekend ATC* were saved, but overall spending was slashed 30 percent from 1983's $26.6 million. Administration funding was cut 27 percent, News and Information funding 15 percent. Production personnel were spared, NPR agreeing not to reduce the length of these programs following pleas from stations, but several reporting positions were eliminated. This reduction hurt NPR's ability to cover breaking stories, and it led to a greater emphasis on telephone interviews and "canned" features. The Performance Programming division lost 79 percent of its funding, which virtually eliminated the division; it largely stopped producing regular programming and became an acquisition service. The Satellite Program Development Fund (the major funding source for independent producers) lost 29 percent of its funding.[122] NPR's arts programming never fully recovered from these cutbacks. Summarizing the financial debacle, former NAEB president James Fellows wrote:

The NPR experience can teach all elements of public broadcasting about the practical difficulties and opportunities of managing organizational growth and complexity. It has all the typical ingredients: executive attention to promising new business opportunities, diversion from the basic mission of the organization, unwillingness to deal with difficult personnel issues that need attention, simplistic management control processes, financial reporting and analysis problems, and the tendency to believe the corporate press releases about rosy futures and prospects.[123]

The crisis also provided ammunition to NPR's congressional foes, Rep. William Dannemeyer (R.-California) argued that NPR should be "terminate[d] . . . at least as per public tax dollars" and denounced the NPR staff as "a Washington-based nest of trendies and leftists," while Rep. Dan Coats (R.-Indiana) fumed at "the arrogant abuse of federal dollars." Even NPR's supporters chastised the system for mismanagement. In a June 1983 House hearing over CPB appropriations, Rep. David Obey (D.-Wisconsin) told Bornstein, "I sit here listening to what you are telling me this morning, and I have to regretfully conclude that the enemies of public broadcasting could not have done as much damage to the system as its friends over the last year or so."[124] While it had been FCC footdragging over subcarrier deregulation that helped cripple NPR Ventures, NPR did not enjoy the resources needed to behave like a venture capitalist in any case—its lack of deep pockets precluded absorbing major losses. Mankiewicz's backslapping bonhomie may have made him a popular figure at NPR, but his managerial acumen had been suspect even before he became NPR's president. Most importantly, the fallout from the debacle forever changed the balance of power at NPR. Stations assumed a greater role in managing the system, which led to program "unbundling" later in the decade and spread the growth of marketplace economics in the public radio system. Cultural and performance programming would continue as only a shadow of its former self, and National Public Radio would stake its reputation on news and public affairs programming. NPR repaid the CPB loan and showed a $250,000 profit by 1985, but the days of innovation at the network were over.

Douglas Bennet was elected to succeed Bornstein by a unanimous vote of the NPR board on October 27, 1983. Like Mankiewicz, Bennet had no prior public radio experience. Described as a "political apparatchik" and "a high-level political operative for Democratic politicians since the days of Chester Bowles," Bennet was a former administrator of the U.S. Agency for International Development and had served as an assistant to Senators Hubert Humphrey, Ed Muskie, Tom Eagleton, and Abraham Ribicoff.[125] In his first press conference as NPR president, Bennet stated his differences with Mankiewicz's "independence" strategy for NPR: "Clearly understood, I believe there should be public money in public radio. I do not believe it would be well served by being independent of public resources." Nevertheless, Bennet shared Mankiewicz's goal of minimizing direct CPB influence on the organization. Three months later, he announced that NPR would actively seek corporate and foundation support for specific areas of news coverage, such as a $250,000 grant from Hewlett-Packard targeted for science coverage.[126] This process would have profound implications for NPR's future. While NPR would become a more sleek, efficient, and comprehensive news machine, the dollars needed to feed this machine would lead critics to find the network's integrity increasingly compromised.

Another shift in funding sources would dramatically impact National Public Radio. At Bennet's behest, the NPR board unanimously agreed in 1985 that CPB should redirect all appropriated radio funds to stations rather than NPR. The stations then would pay NPR for representation and programming, through a fee structure based on each station's annual revenue. NPR's member stations adopted the plan on May 22, 1985, by a vote of 159 to five, and the CPB approved the plan on November 22. The plan would take effect at the beginning of fiscal year 1987. While intended to insulate NPR from an increasingly ideologically driven CPB, the plan meant that NPR's success would be linked to station support of its programming. The plan left "the stations NPR [had] served since 1970 in firm control of the network—not vice versa."[127] Emboldened by the increase in direct funding from the CPB, many larger stations also wanted a greater say in program production. Claiming that NPR's "all or nothing" strategies posed a significant barrier to entry for outside programming sources, NPR's chief competitor, American Public Radio (now Public Radio International), threatened to bring an antitrust suit against NPR. In late 1987, in response to these pressures, NPR unbundled its programming into separate packages, or streams. This development placed larger producing stations on a more competitive footing with NPR, but NPR's previous comprehensive programming package had enabled the network to protect developing shows as well as those appealing to smaller audiences by allowing them to run higher budgets than station carriage (or the number of stations airing a program) dictated. In addition, massive subsidies no longer were available from CPB and

NPR for programming development. In 1991 Peter Pennekamp, NPR's vice president for cultural programming, stated, "Only during a very short period [did] financing of public radio allow the large-scale development of major projects. We're beyond that now."[128]

Programming now would be driven by stations. Acting on the claims of public radio consultants, these stations would pressure NPR to develop salable "strip" shows that would retain audiences between morning and evening "tent pole" programs like *Morning Edition* and *All Things Considered*. To Collins, unbundling created "a market-driven mentality that fundamentally altered the mission of NPR. . . . If the stations felt that something wouldn't draw an audience in their area, they just wouldn't buy it."[129] Independent producers were forced to peddle their programs to individual stations to stimulate demand; NPR would distribute a program only if enough markets showed interest.

Cultural programming is now largely the province of NPR's competitors, such as Public Radio International. NPR's remaining cultural programming is increasingly niche oriented, in order to increase crossover listenership from news programs. According to NPR's Bob Ferrante:

What confuses people is that National Public Radio is a news service. We don't own a station. We're in the marketplace now. If they don't think we're doing a good job, they can buy something else. I don't want to risk sounding too commercial, but we do have to be sought after or we'll become insular. We'll begin to think that what we're doing is God's work. We're not doing God's work. We're doing the news.[130]

Throughout the 1980s, Arbitron ratings revealed that NPR was becoming the primary radio news provider in large markets. NPR's weekly cumulative listenership rose from 3.1 million in 1976 to 12.1 million in 1991, but more and more stations and listeners were claiming that NPR was becoming "mundane and dull, very traditional, very predictable." A former NPR correspondent, William Drummond, complained that programming is "rarely inspired. . . . Maybe we're just burned out and don't want to fight anymore."[131] The turmoil following NPR's near bankruptcy had exacted a toll on morale, and new producers and correspondents often found their paths blocked by the growing power of longtime NPR insiders, particularly correspondents Nina Totenberg, Cokie Roberts, and Linda Wertheimer, to determine story assignments and hires. A former NPR executive claimed that before NPR hired Bennet as president, the trio called him in for an unofficial interview.[132] Stories increasingly emphasized Washington politics, affirming NPR's status as a media player and helping ensure continued federal support for public radio, yet NPR News vice president Adam Clayton Powell III often focused on media events like the 1988 Reagan-Gorbachev summit. Ten reporters were dispatched to Moscow to cover the largely symbolic meeting, and coverage costs amounted to $70,000. Faced with increasing dissension within his staff, Powell resigned in early 1990, less than three years after he was hired.

NPR's news operations rebounded in early 1991, when its coverage of the Persian Gulf War resulted in a 30 percent rise in its listening audience. NPR dispatched seven reporters to assist its sole Middle East correspondent, increased its number of five-minute newscasts from eighteen to twenty-four each day, and added an afternoon talk show to its lineup. The Gulf War brought increased public attention to NPR, but despite the increase in listenership (and a 20 percent rise in listener donations to stations), Gulf War coverage severely strained NPR's finances. By May, NPR had spent over $1.4 million on it. The system recouped much of its outlay by raising money from stations, corporate underwriters, foundations, and the CPB, but it was forced to reduce its newscasts and cut its overall budget.[133] Member station dues provided 63 percent of NPR's revenues, but these were held down by continuing squabbling between NPR and its stations. Spending at NPR grew approximately 4 percent per year throughout the early '90s; to continue at this rate, NPR would have to raise $60 million by 2000, up from 1993's $40 million. To cover the difference, NPR executive vice president Peter Jablow predicted, underwriting and other sources would have to grow from their 1996 level of 4 percent to 15 percent.[134]

Underwriting announcements are being integrated into NPR programming with greater frequency, and programming also is designed to showcase funders. NPR increasingly emphasizes programs like *Car Talk*, which, in addition to attracting corporate funders, show potential for merchandising spin-offs. As Nicholas Garnham notes, "The quantity of the funding and the nature of the financing source . . . [are] the most fundamental determining constraint on a broadcasting structure."[135]

Frequently criticized for aloofness, Douglas Bennet left NPR in April 1993 for a Clinton appointment as assistant secretary of state for international organizations. Former CBS Radio News vice president Joseph Denbo served as interim president until Delano Lewis joined NPR in January 1994. After a career in the military, Lewis had served as president of C&P Telephone (later swallowed by Bell Atlantic) and also in a paid capacity on the boards of Chase Manhattan, Colgate Palmolive, and Gelco insurance. Like Bennet, Lewis had no background in broadcasting or journalism. He was hired as NPR president for his management and fundraising abilities; he would use "his corporate skills to build NPR into a corporate team" and bring big-money deals to the system.[136] Eyeing the success of arch-rival Public Radio International (a privately owned program distributor), Lewis and the NPR board began exploring ways to turn NPR's cultural capital into more lucrative commodities. In

July 1996, the NPR board passed a resolution urging the service to "move forward with new enterprises in the spirit of public service and without adversely affecting NPR's fundamental mission."[137] NPR allocated $600,000 to venture projects, including compact disks compiled from NPR's *Performance Today*, and direct marketing of audio tapes. "NPR Town Square" kiosks were placed in Borders bookstores to display books and music produced by NPR or featured on the network. A video pilot of *Morning Edition* also was produced; in it host Bob Edwards did not look at the camera: "It wouldn't be radio" if he had, said executive producer Bob Ferrante.[138]

These efforts failed to produce significant revenues, so NPR followed up with another typically '90s strategy: finding a corporate partner. TCI's Liberty Media subsidiary picked up the $50,000 tab for NPR's twenty-fifth anniversary gala in 1996, in which "logos of the Discovery Channel, BET and other famous-brand channels owned or part-owned by the TCI subsidiary glowed in spotlights alongside hastily added banners bearing NPR's own famous brands." Peter Barton, the president and chief executive officer of Liberty Media, delivered the keynote address at the 1996 Public Radio conference, and NPR president Delano Lewis later suggested that NPR "stay close" to Liberty and TCl, because their futures "may be intertwined."[139] Paralleling Mobil's support of PBS in the 1970s and 1980s, such an arrangement would give TCl much-needed public-interest credibility and temper its image as one of the most rapacious communication conglomerates. TCl also would receive badly needed content for its delivery systems as well as access to an exclusive, upscale market, while NPR would have access to the deep pockets that had been lacking in the network's early 1980s venture projects.

The rumored joint ventures between NPR and Liberty Media came to naught, but an even more astonishing proposal surfaced in late 1997: NPR would merge with its archrival, Public Radio International. Four years earlier PRI and NPR had begun collaboration on international programming, through a joint satellite service, America One. In 1996, however, PRI began producing as well as distributing programming with *The World*, a newsmagazine produced in conjunction with WGBH and the BBC.[140] Rivalries between PRI and NPR had always been fierce, but they accelerated further in 1997 when *The World* squared off against an expanded version of *All Things Considered* between 4 and 5 P.M. Both programs consumed substantial portions of NPR's and PRI's respective budgets. Lewis approached PRI's president Steven Salyer to discuss possibilities to fuse the organizations, believing that a merger would attract more underwriting funds to public radio, help position public radio against commercial competitors through greater economies of scale, and also allow public radio to act quickly on entrepreneurial ventures. The proposed NPR/PRI merger would create a single program distributor for public radio. Spinoff organizations would handle representation and lobbying, and Salyer would replace Lewis as head of the combined organization.[141] In October 1997, a merger plan was presented to the NPR and PRI boards. The plan quickly died. While NPR is controlled by stations (its board includes ten station representatives and five public members), PRI was not interested in station representation. Ruth Seymour, president of KCRW, stated, "Del Lewis knew that NPR member stations would never tolerate a move toward the PRI structure."[142] An NPR/PRI merger would have reduced entry points for program distribution and also diminish variety. As one observer asserted, the merger would lead to "fewer gatekeepers, fewer opportunities, less diversity."[143] After successfully defending NPR during the 1995 funding debate yet failing to reap substantial revenues, Lewis retired as NPR president on August 1, 1998. He was succeeded by Kevin Klose, who had spent twenty-five years as a reporter and editor at the *Washington Post*. Before coming to NPR, he had served as director of the U.S. International Broadcasting Bureau, which supervises overseas broadcasting units, including the Voice of America.

In 1982, former CPB president Ed Pfister remarked that "commercial broadcasting produces programs to make money; public broadcasting raises money to produce programs."[144] Although NPR invokes the "public" to differentiate itself from commercial competitors, the system increasingly behaves like a commercial enterprise. This commercialism did not appear overnight; it has been creeping into NPR since the early 1980s. Frank Mankiewicz may have tried to free NPR of federal funding to reduce interference by an increasingly ideologically driven CPB, but a broader concern lies beneath NPR's actions. Private organizations seek to maximize profits, but nonprofit organizations operating in social service areas, such as public broadcasting, have no easy metric to measure their effectiveness. The closest approximation for these organizations tends to be units serviced within the limits of the budget.[145] Therefore, budget increases ultimately become the yardstick of success. Funding achieves a momentum of its own, overriding all other purposes. The result is abandonment of the "public" in the name of "service."

Public radio consultant David Giovannoni argues that "NPR is here as a public service. Public service is defined—at least in part—by the number of people listening to it. . . . [B]y definition, if nobody hears it, there's no service. So the more people who listen, the better the service."[146] However, the servant chooses the richest master rather than the most deserving: former NPR board member Jack Mitchell says that "you put out good stuff that the people *we want will* want."[147] In the face of an uncertain, competitive environment, public broadcasters on the local and national levels increasingly emulate the practices of commercial format radio. *Morning Edition* host Bob Edwards told *Current*, "This is the big problem I have with this place. They don't know they're in the radio business. . . . I'd market the place. [Commercial broadcasters] sell their programs, and we don't."[148] Greater emphasis is given to programs that pay their own way to venture schemes, and to marketing potential. At the 1998 Public Radio Conference, a consulting firm suggested that the service "use 'NPR' as the primary communicative name . . . [because] the words "National," "Public," and "Radio" perpetuate some of NPR's most common perceptual problems."[149]

In the market-based system of public radio, the search for major audience draws and predictable formats precludes the development of risky and innovative (and publicly valuable) programming. Public radio is unable to describe its difference; rather than providing a grounds for public debate, it divides its audience into a series of taste cultures. The "public" it purports to serve is a public in name only. In this regard, National Public Radio reflects the history of broadcasting in the United States. Successive regulatory actions have dictated that the use of the public airwaves be shaped by the public as a market. The historical tenuousness and marginal status of public radio may be attributed to the fact that its agenda has been determined by private groups and individuals, with minimal public input. When their agendas have clashed with political realities, the public is defined as a paying audience, so that the system can survive. These clashes are exemplified in the history of federal funding, system networking, and tensions between stations, a history that is the subject of the next chapter.

NOTES

1. W. Siemering, "National Public Radio Purposes," National Public Radio, 1970, in J. Haney, *A History of the Merger of National Public Radio and the Association of Public Radio Stations*, unpublished dissertation, Iowa City, University of Iowa, 1981, p. 248.

2. R. Williams, *Television: Technology and Cultural Form* (New York: Schocken Books, 1975), p. 37; S. Barnett and D. Docherty, "Purity or Pragmatism," p. 28.

3. R. Williams, *Culture and Society 1780–1950* (New York: Columbia University Press, 1958), p. 119.

4. R. Horwitz, *The Irony of Regulatory Reform: The Deregulation of American Telecommunications* (New York: Oxford University Press, 1989), pp. 9–12.

5. See S. Douglas, *Inventing American Broadcasting* (Baltimore: The Johns Hopkins Press), 1987.

6. T. Streeter, *Selling the Air: A Critique of Commercial Broadcasting in the United States* (Chicago: University of Chicago Press, 1996), p. 65.

7. N. Garnham, "Public Service versus the Market," *Screen* 24 (1), January/February 1983, p. 13; Streeter, *Selling the Air*, p. 219; Horwitz, *The Irony of Regulatory Reform*, pp. 234–239.

8. R. Engelman, *Public Radio and Television in America: A Political History*

(Thousand Oaks, CA: Sage, 1996), p. 16; J. Witherspoon and R. Kovitz, *The History of Public Broadcasting*, p. 5.

9. See E. Barnouw, *A History of Broadcasting in the United States, Vol. 1: Tower in Babel: To 1933*. (New York: Oxford University Press), 1966.

10. See G. Murdock, "Citizens, Consumers and Public Culture," In *Media Cultures; Reappraising Transnational Media*, M. Skovmand and K. Schroder, eds. (New York: Routledge, 1992).

11. Susan Smulyan cites several reasons why a centralized federally operated broadcasting system failed to develop in the United States. In addition to the long-standing federal preference for influence over, rather than strong regulation of, industry, the business community was familiar with chain organizational structures, and the radio companies were well equipped to protect their interests. Also, a system of radio transmitting stations that appeared decentralized was both politically and otherwise appealing. She argues that another key factor involved the physical geography of the United States. England and Germany could be covered by a relatively few number of broadcasting stations, but the sheer expanse of the nation, as well as its large and evenly distributed population, precluded such coverage (although David Sarnoff proposed the establishment of a few "superpower" stations in the 1920s). The country also was unified linguistically; by comparison, the Soviet Union programmed in sixty-two languages over sixty-four stations (S. Smulyan, *Selling Radio: The Commercialization of American Broadcasting 1920–1934* [Washington, DC: Smithsonian Institution Press, 1994]). Raymond Williams also notes that the social elite in Great Britain was more cohesive than that of the United States, which precluded the possibility of a singular paternalistic system along the lines of the BBC (see Williams, *Television*).

12. Smulyan, *Selling Radio*, p. 77.

13. I. Ang, *Desperately Seeking the Audience* (New York: Routledge, 1991), p. 33.

14. H. Boyte, "Public Opinion as Public Judgment," In *Public Opinion and the Communication of Consent*, T. Glasser and C. Salmon, eds. (New York: Guilford Press, 1995), p. 422.

15. Witherspoon and Kovitz, *The History of Public Broadcasting*, p. 59.

16. J. Peters, "Satan and Savior: Mass Communication in Progressive Thought," *Critical Studies in Mass Communication* 6 (3), September 1989, p. 249.

17. J. Carey, "The Press, Public Opinion and Public Discourse," in *Public Opinion and the Communication of Consent*, Glasser and Salmon, eds., p. 387.

18. Witherspoon and Kovitz, *The History of Public Broadcasting*, p. 60.

19. K. Engar, "ETV a Vast Testland," *NAEB Journal*, July–August 1962, pp. 17–22.

20. Witherspoon and Kovitz, *The History of Public Broadcasting*, p. 61.

21. D. Czitrom, *Media and the American Mind: From Morse to McLuham* (Chapel Hill: University of North Carolina Press, 1982), p. 76.

22. Engelman, *Public Radio and Television in America*, p. 21.

23. Streeter, *Selling the Air*, p. 95. The term "public broadcasting" is attributed to M. S. Novik, the former head of New York City's WNYC-AM, who used the term in a 1942 program bulletin from the station (J. Robertson, "The Public Buys In," *Current*, November 2, 1992, p. 18).

24. R. McChesney, *Telecommunications, Mass Media and Democracy: The Battle for the Control of U.S. Broadcasting, 1928–1935* (New York: Oxford University Press, 1993), p. 31.

25. Ibid, p. 3.

26. Engelman, *Public Radio and Television in America*, p. 272.

27. W. Rowland, Jr., "Public Service Broadcasting in the United States: Its Mandate, Institutions and Conflicts," in *Public Service Broadcasting in a Multichannel Environment: The History and Survival of an Ideal*, R. Avery, ed. (New York: Longman, 1993), p. 159.

28. J. Guy, "Nation's First 10-Watter Increases Power," *NAEB Journal*, September–October 1963, p. 51.

29. G. Crotts and W. Rowland, Jr., "The Prospects for Public Broadcasting," in *Telecommunications in the U.S.: Trends and Policies*, L. Lewin, ed. (Dedham, MA: Artech House, 1981), p. 184.

30. R. Estell, "Profile of the Educational Radio Manager," *Educational Broadcasting Review*, December 1968, p. 44.

31. M. Lashner, "The Role of Foundations in Public Broadcasting, Part 1: Development and Trends," *Journal of Broadcasting* 20 (4), Fall 1976, p. 532.

32. J. Day, *The Vanishing Vision: The Inside Story of Public Television* (Berkeley: University of California Press, 1995), p. 141.

33. R. Blakely, *To Serve the Public Interest: Educational Broadcasting in the U.S.* (Syracuse, NY: Syracuse University Press, 1979), p. 103.

34. Haney, *A History of the Merger of National Public Radio and the Association of Public Radio Stations*, p. 28.

35. M. Lashner, "The Role of Foundations in Public Broadcasting, Part 2: The Ford Foundation," *Journal of Broadcasting* 21 (2), 1977, p. 247.

36. R. Avery and R. Pepper, "Balancing the Equation: Public Radio Comes of Age," *Public Telecommunications Review*, March/April 1979, p. 23: R. Shayon, "Getting Away from It All," *Saturday Review*, October 23, 1965, p. 53.

37. W. Rowland, Jr., "The Illusion of Fulfillment: Problems in the Broadcast Reform Movement and Notes on the Progressive Past," *Journalism Monographs*, no. 79, 1982, p. 23.

38. J. Robertson, "The Public Buys In," *Current*, November 2, 1992, p. 17.

39. Engelman, *Public Radio and Television in America*, p. 156.

40. Carnegie Commission on Educational Television, *Public Television: A Program for Action* (New York: Bantam Books, 1967), p. 36.

41. Robertson, "The Public Buys In," p. 18.

42. Carnegie Commission on Educational Television, *Public Television*, pp. 92–94.

43. See D. Cater, "The Politics of Public TV," *Columbia Journalism Review*, July/August 1972; Blakely, *To Serve the Public Interest*; Rowland, "Continuing Crisis in Public Broadcasting."

44. Carnegie Commission on Educational Television, *Public Television*, pp. 98–99.

45. Blakely, *To Serve the Public Interest*, pp. 178

46. See Benedict Anderson, *Imagined Communities* (New York: Verso, 1983).

47. Witherspoon and Kovitz, *The History of Public Broadcasting*, p. 16.

48. Herman W. Land Associates, *The Hidden Medium: Educational Radio* (New

York: National Educational Radio, National Association of Educational Broadcasters, 1967), p. iv.

49. Scholars are divided over whether tensions between radio and television educators led to sabotage of the bill. Haney (1981, p. 46) claims that radio was not purposely excluded from early legislative proposals, but McCauley (1997, p. 91) cites interviews he conducted to argue that radio was taken out the day before Johnson was to announce the bill and was replaced only at the last minute.

50. A. Branscomb, "A Crisis of Identity: Public Broadcasting and the Law," *Public Telecommunications Review*, February 1975, p. 21.

51. The ruling was upheld by the U.S. Supreme Court by a vote of five to four in July 1984, over objections from the Reagan administration and Mobil Oil. However, the ruling did not challenge the provision that restrained public broadcasters from supporting or opposing political candidates ("Mobil Joins Opponents of Editorializing," *Current*, September 27, 1983, p. 3; "Editorials No Longer off Limits," *Current*, August 20, 1982, p. 1).

52. D. Stewart, "The Emperor's Old Clothes: It's Time to Retailor CPB," *Current*, September 8, 1997, pp. B-8, B-9.

53. J. Carey, "Public Broadcasting and Federal Policy," in *New Directions in Telecommunications Policy*, Vol. 1, P. Newberg, ed. (Durham: Duke University Press, 1989) pp. 220–221.

54. See Crotts and Rowland, Jr., "The Prospects for Public Broadcasting."

55. R. Avery and R. Pepper, "An Institutional History of Public Broadcasting," *Journal of Communication* 30 (3), Summer 1980, p. 132.

56. Herman W. Land Associates, *The Hidden Medium*, p. 1–28.

57. Ibid., p. 1–2.

58. S. Holt, *The Public Radio Study* (Washington, DC: CPB, 1969), pp. 66–67.

59. L. Frischknecht, *The Policy for Public Radio Assistance of the Corporation for Public Broadcasting, 1969–1978* (Washington, DC: CPB, 1978), p. 12.

60. Witherspoon and Kovitz, *The History of Public Broadcasting*, p. 35.

61. See K. Garry, *The History of National Public Radio: 1974–1977*, unpublished dissertation, Carbondale: University of Southern Illinois at Carbondale, 1982.

62. J. Kirkish, *A Descriptive History of America's First National Public Radio Network: National Public Radio, 1970 to 1974*, unpublished dissertation, Ann Arbor: University of Michigan, 1980, p. 25.

63. Siemering, "National Public Radio Purposes," pp. 1, 4, 7, 16.

64. J. Dewey, *The Public and Its Problems*, in *John Dewey: The Later Works, 1925–1953; Volume Two: 1925–1927*, J. A. Boydston, ed. (Carbondale: Southern Illinois University Press 1988 [1927]), p. 303.

65. Ibid., p. 296.

66. Engelman, *Public Radio and Television in America*, p. 91.

67. T. Looker, *The Sound and the Story: NPR and the Art of Radio* (New York: Houghton Mifflin, 1995), p. 113.

68. Siemering, "National Public Radio Purposes," pp. 3–4.

69. S. Behrens, "ATC: Caught in the Act of Thinking," *Current*, April 27, 1981, p. 4.

70. B. Porter, "Has Success Spoiled NPR?" *Columbia Journalism Review*, September/October 1990, p. 26.

71. Engelman, *Public Radio and Television in America*, p. 98.

72. Haney, *A History of the Merger of National Public Radio and the Association of Public Radio Stations*, p. 79.

73. Siemering turned down Edward P. Morgan's offer to serve as host after Morgan left ABC, even though the Ford Foundation offered to subsidize Morgan's salary. *All Things Considered* producer Jack Mitchell told *Current*, "We couldn't really have a conventional, though excellent, journalist" (Behrens, "ATC," p. 5). Nevertheless, NPR's flagship news programs traditionally have emphasized the personalities of the anchors; Mary Collins notes that "NPR fans . . . seem to take an unusually personal interest in the network's stars" (Collins, *National Public Radio*, p. 2).

74. Kirkish, *A Descriptive History of America's First National Public Radio Network*, p. 72.

75. Ibid., p. 92; Haney, *A History of the Merger of National Public Radio and the Association of Public Radio Stations*, p. 81.

76. See D. Amos, "Producing Features," in *Telling the Story: The National Public Radio Guide to Radio Journalism*, L. Josephson, ed. (Dubuque, IA: Kendall/Hunt Publishing, 1983).

77. Porter, "Has Success Spoiled NPR?," p. 28.

78. M. Collins, *National Public Radio: The Cast of Characters* (Washington, DC: Seven Locks Press, 1993), p. 31.

79. As public broadcasting grew in size and scope, specialized institutions assumed the NAEB's functions of programming, research, and representation. However, until its demise the NAEB provided the only common forum for the public broadcasting community. Public broadcasters now engage in a growing number of specialized discussions yet pay little attention to major themes and first principles, aside from concerns over funding (see R. Avery, "Contemporary Public Telecommunications Research: Navigating the Sparsely Settled Terrain," *Journal of Broadcasting and Electronic Media* 40 [1], Winter 1996, p. 132).

80. "Instructional Radio Decries NPR Ruling," *NAEB Newsletter*, January 13, 1975, p. 1.

81. Haney, *A History of the Merger of National Public Radio and the Association of Public Radio Stations*, p. 126.

82. Avery and Pepper, "Balancing the Equation," p. 25.

83. Haney, *A History of the Merger of National Public Radio and the Association of Public Radio Stations*, p. 145; "Public Radio Ponders Switch to One National Organization," *Broadcasting*, March 22, 1976, p. 81.

84. Haney, *A History of the Merger of National Public Radio and the Association of Public Radio Stations*, p. 182.

85. M. McCauley, *From the Margins to the Mainstream: The History of National Public Radio*, unpublished dissertation, Madison: University of Wisconsin, 1997, p. 171.

86. Garry, *The History of National Public Radio*, pp. 76, 96.

87. J. Carmody, "Reorganizing Public Radio," *Washington Post*, April 24, 1976, p. C-2.

88. See A. Sheldon, "Face-to-Face with Frank Mankiewicz," *Public Telecommunications Review*, September/October 1977, pp. 17–29.

89. D. Schribman, "Frank Mankiewicz's New Cause: Saving National Public

Radio," *New York Times* March 4, 1982, p. B-14; also see Avery and Pepper, "Balancing the Equation."

90. J. McLellan and M. Kernan, "National Public Radio's Voice at the Top," *Washington Post*, February 26, 1979, pp. B-1, B-4.

91. Carnegie Commission on the Future of Public Broadcasting, *A Public Trust, The Report of the Carnegie Commission on the Future of Public Broadcasting.* (New York: Bantam Books, 1979), p. 11.

92. Ibid., p. 14.

93. Ibid., pp. 216–217.

94. Ibid., pp. 19, 289.

95. "One-Hand Clapping for Carnegie Commission," *Broadcasting*, February 5, 1979, p. 31; "Editorial," *Broadcasting*, February 5, 1979, p. 106.

96. Carnegie Commission on the Future of Public Broadcasting, *A Public Trust*, pp. 196, 206, 213.

97. See Rowland, "Continuing Crisis in Public Broadcasting."

98. J. Yore, "Public Broadcasting's Favorite Daughter Moves On," *Current*, March 31, 1987, p. 17.

99. B. Gladstone, "Two of Four Nominees Multimillionaires," *Current*, February 11, 1983, p. 8.

100. "NPR Announces Digital Data Delivery Service," *Public Broadcasting Report*, July 2, 1982, p. 7; S. Solovitch, "NPR's Crisis Quarter," *Washington Journalism Review*, June 1983, p. 17.

101. B. Gladstone and S. Behrens, " 'Independence Ventures' on NPR's Agenda," *Current*, April 16, 1982, p. 1.

102. "GAO Auditors Report on NPR," *Current*, February 14, 1984, p. 4.

103. B. Gladstone, "Vertical Service Gets Nod, But Reserved SCA's Don't," *Current*, August 20, 1982, p. 5; I. Molotsky, "What Went Wrong at National Public Radio?" *New York Times*, June 12, 1983, p. B27; B. Gladstone, "NPR Plus Lives; But No Longer 'Round the Clock," *Current*, September 13, 1983, p. 1.

104. " 'Ad Hoc' Radio Networks," *Current*, March 17, 1980, p. 1.

105. B. Gladstone, "Cellular: NPR's Most Adventurous Venture Yet," *Current*, April 5, 1983, p. 1; "NPR Announces Joint Venture with Dataspeed, Inc., to Form Nationwide Portable Paging and Information Service," *Public Broadcasting Report*, November 19, 1982, p. 4; R. Harrington, "National Private Radio?" *Washington Post Magazine*, March 27, 1983, p. 12; "INC: NPR's Partnership in Data," *Current*, April 30, 1982, p. 1; "NPR Announces Plans for National Paging Service with MCCA," *Public Broadcasting Report*, July 16, 1982, p. 4.

106. P. McCombs and J. Truscott, "NPR: Camelot in Crisis," *Washington Post*, August 15, 1983, pp. C-1, C-4.

107. M. Hamilton and J. Truscott, "NPR Said to Use Withheld Taxes for Daily Operations," *Washington Post*, June 15, 1983, p. D-8; "Withheld Taxes Part of NPR's Debt; Finance Aide Quits," *Current*, June 21, 1983, p. 5.

108. Hamilton and Truscott, "NPR Said to Use Withheld Taxes for Daily Operations," p. D-8; "National Public Radio Audit Shows Network Owes $850,000 Taxes," *Wall Street Journal*, June 16, 1983, p. 16.

109. Collins, *National Public Radio*, p. 73.

110. B. Gladstone, "Retrenchment: 'First Phase of Reality,' " *Current*, March 25, 1983, p. 1.

111. "Mankiewicz Steps Down at NPR," *Broadcasting*, April 25, 1983, p. 76.

112. B. Gladstone, "No Villains, Just Miscast Characters in Budget Saga," *Current*, August 9, 1983, pp. 1, 8; P. McCombs and J. Truscott, "NPR: Camelot in Crisis," *Washington Post*, August 15, 1983, p. C-1; J. Fellows, "Lessons for Tomorrow: NPR Went after Growth without Close Controls," *Current*, May 13, 1983, p. 8; S. Solovitch, "NPR's Crisis Quarter," *Washington Journalism Review*, June 1983, p. 16.

113. J. Abramson and G. Seib, "Paths of RFK Aides Reflect the Divisions among the Democrats," *Wall Street Journal*, June 4, 1993, p. A-8.

114. B. Gladstone, "No Bail-Out Til Dust Clears in NPR Probes," *Current*, May 3, 1983, p. 1.

115. "Withheld Taxes Part of NPR's Debt; Finance Aide Quits," *Current*, June 21, 1983, p. 1.

116. I. Molotsky, "Public Radio Chairman Resigns in Fiscal Crisis," *New York Times*, June 22, 1983, p. C20; "NPR's Bad News Gets Worse," *Broadcasting*, June 27, 1983, pp. 36–37; J. Truscott, "NPR Predicts $9.1 Million Deficit," *Washington Post*, June 23, 1983, p. D-12; "The News Turns Worse at National Public Radio," *Business Week*, July 4, 1983, p. 42.

117. B. Gladstone, "NPR Plucked from Brink by 'Creative' Compromise," *Current*, September 27, 1983, p. 5.

118. S. Smith, "Loan is Approved for Public Radio," *New York Times*, July 29, 1983, p. 1; "Loan is Set for Public Radio," *New York Times*, August 4, 1983, p. C19; J. Truscott, "Loan Gives NPR 'Breathing Room,' " *Washington Post*, August 4, 1983, p. D-3.

119. B. Gladstone, "NPR Turns Microphone on Itself," *Current*, May 24, 1983, p. 7.

120. E. Robinson, "Radio Stations to Assume NPR Debt," *Current*, July 17, 1984, p. 1.

121. "Public Radio Board Trims '84 Budget 30 Percent," *New York Times*, September 17, 1983, p. 43.

122. B. Gladstone, "Bornstein Drops the Other Shoe," *Current*, May 24, 1983, pp. 1, 6.

123. Fellows, "Lessons for Tomorrow," p. 8.

124. B. Gladstone, "GAO Probes as Lawmakers Lean on CPB," *Current*, June 12, 1983, p. 8.

125. Engelman, *Public Radio and Television in America*, p. 107; Porter, "Has Success Spoiled NPR?" p. 31.

126. E. Robinson, "Bennet Named to NPR Presidency," *Current*, November 8, 1983, p. 2; I. Molotsky, "New NPR Chief Hails Recent Gains," *New York Times*, February 9, 1984, p. C30.

127. D. McDougal, "Public Radio Mainstays Survive Latest Crisis," *Los Angeles Times*, May 25, 1985, pp. 1, 7; Looker, *The Sound and the Story*, p. 35.

128. J. Robertiello, "Has Public Radio Hit the Wall?" *Current*, May 13, 1991, p. 19.

129. Collins, *National Public Radio*, p. 77.

130. Ibid., p. 96.

131. M. Fisher, "The Soul of a News Machine," *Washington Post Magazine*, October 22, 1989, pp. 19, 42.

132. Ibid., p. 37.

133. S. Bernstein, "NPR Choices: Pass the Hat, Cut Coverage," *Los Angeles Times*, February 7, 1991, pp. F-1, F-3.

134. S. Behrens, "TCI Offers Helping Hand to Pubradio," *Current*, May 27, 1996, p. 9.

135. N. Garnham, *Structures of Television* (London: British Film Institute, 1978), p. 53.

136. "Delano Eugene Lewis," *Broadcasting and Cable*, March 20, 1995, p. 73; S. Behrens, "Delano Lewis Hired to Lead NPR," *Current*, August 23, 1993, p. 1; J. Conciatore, "Lewis Will Retire from Running NPR," *Current*, April 6, 1998, p. 11.

137. J. Conciatore, " 'Don't Worry. I Hug Everyone,' " *Current*, July 22, 1996, p. 1.

138. J. Conciatore, "Board Likely to Give Go-Ahead for NPR Pursuit of Venture," *Current*, July 8, 1996, p. 4.

139. Behrens, "TCI Offers Helping Hand to Pubradio," p. 1.

140. J. Conciatore, "Lewis, Salyer Propose Merger of NPR and PRI," *Current*, November 3, 1997, p. 21.

141. J. Conciatore, "NPR-PRI Merger Talks Are Off, Says Salyer," *Current*, February 2, 1998, pp. 1, 13.

142. I. Peterson, "Rivalry Grows at Low End of Dial," *New York Times*, March 2, 1998, p. C7.

143. S. Behrens and J. Conciatore, "New Chief Moves Ahead on Station Partnerships, Newsroom Relations," *Current*, February 2, 1998, p. 8.

144. A. Van Allen, "Has Audience Building Gone Too Far?" *Current*, January 20, 1987, p. 8.

145. M. Lashley, *Public Television: Panacea, Pork Barrel or Public Trust?* (Westport, CT: Greenwood Press, 1992), p. 5.

146. Looker, *The Sound and the Story*, p. 416.

147. A. Stavitsky, "Listening for Listeners: Educational Radio and Audience Research." *Journalism History* 19 (1), Spring 1993, p. 17.

148. S. Behrens and J. Conciatore, "We've Got the Journalism Down—I've Got Problems with Our Radio," *Current*, May 25, 1998, p. A-7.

149. J. Conciatore, "PRC: Branding, Bypass, the Bird and Goodbye, Del," *Current*, May 25, 1998, pp. A-1; 15.

3

The Localized Public:
The Federalist Conundrum

It would not . . . substitute superficial blandness for genuine diversity of regions, values, and cultural and ethnic minorities which comprise American society; it would speak with many voices and many dialects.
—William Siemering, "National Public Radio Purposes," p. 4.

National programming serves several crucial functions for public radio stations. By spreading development and production costs among stations, it allows them to present "high" cultural and minority programming that they could not produce individually. By transcending exclusively local concerns, it enhances station status and prestige. It also provides a consistent "product image" for sponsors, who prefer to allocate funds to centralized institutions. However, local identity remains equally important to public radio stations. A station's mission often is based on local service: serving local needs, addressing local issues, and reflecting local culture. Stations depend on local business and listener support, and local programming enhances organizational morale by giving staffers a sense of participation. Local programming also provides more direct control over the station's product and decreases the complexity of decision making. Yet "localism" has never been well defined. As Lewis Friedland notes, "many local stations define it simply as autonomy from the [national] system."[1]

Given the disparate licensing arrangements and missions of public radio stations, federal funds provide the glue that binds the system.

The CPB's Community Service Grant (CSG) program is the only funding source that affects the entire public broadcasting system. In addition to the CSG program (essentially an entitlement arrangement, over which station managers exercise broad discretion), the federal Public Telecommunications Facilities Program (PTFP) supports station construction and maintenance. Beginning with fiscal year 1987, the CPB also provided to stations National Program Production and Acquisition Grants (NPPAG) to produce and acquire national programming. Federal funds also come from the National Endowment for the Arts, the National Endowment for the Humanities, the National Science Foundation, the National Institute for Health, and other government agencies. These funds tend to be program specific.[2] Federal funding also lends legitimacy to other funding proposals and so has an effect far out of proportion to its size. The director of marketing for New York City's WNYC has stated that "every one dollar in federal funding for public radio leverages five dollars in other funding from corporations and helps draw legitimate sponsors."[3] One in ten public radio stations relied on CPB funding for 20 percent or more of its budget in 1995, and a CPB-sponsored report by the National Economic Research Associates described the probability that revenues from other sources could match losses in federal aid as "highly unlikely," concluding that "the nature of public broadcasting will inevitably change" if public funding is lost.[4]

Public organizations usually are funded at increases of 3 to 10 percent over the previous year's appropriation.[5] Funding for the Corporation for Public Broadcasting has risen from five million dollars for 1969 to $300 million for 2000. However, fluctuations in funding have significantly eroded these gains (see Table 3.1). Unlike most public-service organizations, public broadcasting has high fixed costs in the form of equipment and multiyear commitments for interconnection and programming; also, public broadcasters seek to remain technologically and culturally competitive with their commercial counterparts. William Siemering testified before Congress in 1987 that the BBC's radio service "operates on a per capita annual rate of $5.98 while the United States public radio receives only 19 cents a year in federal support."[6] Federal support for public broadcasting continues to lag far behind that of other industrialized countries. In 1993 the U.S. government spent $1.09 per capita on public broadcasting, while Japan spent $32.02, Canada $31.05, and the United Kingdom $38.99.[7] By contrast, the U.S. government's licensing of the spectrum to commercial broadcasters has created an indirect subsidy amounting to millions of dollars a year, a figure that dwarfs by orders of magnitude public broadcasting's meager federal subsidies.

Federal funding is instrumental in maintaining the public radio system, but this funding has been highly vulnerable to political manipulation. Refusals to guarantee funding for more than two or three years

Table 3.1
CPB Appropriations, Fiscal Years 1969–2000

Fiscal Year	Administration Request (millions of dollars)	Final Appropriation (millions of dollars)	Percent Change (adjusted for inflation)
1969	9.0	5.0	—
1970	15.0	15.0	183.0
1971	22.0	23.0	46.9
1972	35.0	35.0	47.4
1973	45.0	35.0	- 5.9
1974	45.0	50.0	28.0
1975	60.0	62.0	13.6
1976	70.0	78.5	19.7
1977	70.0	103.0	23.2
1978	80.0	119.2	7.6
1979	90.0	120.2	- 9.4
1980	120.0	152.0	11.4
1981	162.0	162.0	- 3.4
1982	172.0	172.0	0
1983	172.0	137.0	- 22.8
1984	110.0	137.5	- 3.8
1985	85.0	150.5	5.7
1986	75.0	159.5	4.0
1987	186.0	200.0	21.0
1988	214.0	214.0	2.8
1989	214.0	228.0	1.6
1990	214.0	229.4	- 4.5
1991	214.0	298.9	25.0
1992	242.1	327.3	6.3
1993	306.5	318.6	- 5.5
1994	260.0	275.0	-15.8
1995	275.0	285.6	.99
1996	292.6	275.0	- 6.5
1997	292.6	260.0	- 7.1
1998	296.4	250.0	- 4.5
1999	275.0	250.0	—
2000	325.0	300.0	—

Source: CPB[8]

have hindered attempts at long-term planning. The increasing use of nonfederal financial support (NFFS) to determine how federal money is distributed between individual stations has concentrated the system's overall resources, punished broadcasters who serve small or "uneconomical" audiences, and forced stations to devote more time and energy to the scramble for private money. Federal funding patterns also have limited the potential for public participation and accountability. The bulk of these funds are allocated with minimal oversight to station managers, and linking federal funds to nonfederal financial support has led public broadcasters to focus on affluent sections of the population. These patterns have severely undermined the public radio system's ability to serve as a public forum.

Public broadcasters regard the lack of long-term, insulated funding as their chief external pressure. The conflict between the need for system-wide subsidies to ensure overall growth and stability and the system's avowed goals of decentralization and pluralism has led to what G. Gail Crotts and Willard Rowland, Jr., term a continuing "federalist" debate: "How much local, state and regional control must the stations retain as against the efficiency perceived to exist in national-level centralization?"[9] This debate, however, exists entirely between NPR and its member stations. While public funds are intended to help insulate public broadcasters from marketplace pressures, the "public" has had virtually no voice in determining their dispersal and use throughout the system's history. Initial federal funding criteria were defined almost exclusively by educational broadcasting insiders, particularly those affiliated with large university stations that already enjoyed substantial subsidies. Since then, federal funding patterns have allowed the largest stations in the system to control the lion's share of resources, while the CPB makes periodic, token efforts to divert funds to minorities and smaller operations. This chapter describes the history of federal funding for public radio and how large, well-entrenched stations have exploited antifederalist sentiments within the system and coalesced into pressure groups that increasingly dominate public radio's policy agenda, thereby working against the goals of pluralism and local service they espouse.

TRIAGE AND TUMULT

Section 396 (g) (2) of the 1967 Public Broadcasting Act authorized the newly chartered CPB to make payments to noncommercial educational broadcast stations for programming and operational purposes. After consulting the NER board and CPB's Radio Advisory Council, the CPB Board of Directors approved the *Policy for Public Radio Station Assistance* on September 26, 1969. To receive an initial grant of $7,500, stations had to broadcast at least eight hours per day, six days per week, for forty-eight weeks per year, and at least half of the station's broadcast schedule was to be specifically noninstructional. Stations also had to broadcast at a minimum of 250 watts and "have a staff of sufficient size and professional ability to provide a competent service," which in the eyes of the CPB required one full-time and four half-time staffers. Finally, to encourage local programming, stations had to have "an adequately equipped control room and studio . . . for program production and origination."[10] The only stipulation on the grant's use was that no more than a thousand dollars could be spent on equipment.

The adoption of the CPB criteria marked a watershed in public radio's development. Money would be distributed selectively rather than across the board, and therefore larger educational stations would continue to dominate the system. Four-fifths of the nonreligious noncommercial radio stations in the United States were excluded from funding.[11] While the broadcast-hour requirements were intended to help stations maintain a more consistent product image, former NPR president Lee Frischknecht acknowledged that "the programming criteria [were] certainly aimed at precluding support for stations whose efforts were targeted to narrowly defined groups or which were dominated by a particular kind of programming."[12] Given the dearth of ten-watt stations in many urban areas, the CPB decided to push for a few broad-appeal stations that would transcend the perceived parochialism of minority or "neighborhood" interests. Conversely, many stations operated in frequency-saturated markets or adjacent to VHF-TV Channel 6 stations, which meant that their low power ratings excluded them from CPB eligibility. The FCC had provided in 1962 a nationwide table of allocations for commercial FM stations; its failure to do so for the twenty channels reserved for noncommercial stations, on grounds that it could not determine where educational stations should be placed in order to provide universal service, ensured that many metropolitan areas initially would lack public stations.

The CPB's funding criteria has always been determined by size (budget, staff, and power), never by station performance or service to listeners. Although the CPB called for "quality" programming, the empirical measure of station staffing, or "professionalism," was chosen for convenience, since "quality" is highly subjective. Al Hulsen, who as head of the CPB's Radio Advisory Council was instrumental in determining funding criteria, rationalized the CPB's intent that stations use federal money to add full-time staff: "You have to be on the air if you're going to serve anybody, and you have to have people involved who are dedicated to that service if you're going to provide any service that was meaningful."[13] This conflation of a salary with "dedication" is unsurprising, given the fact that the RAC was populated by managers of large stations that operated under traditional organizational hierarchies. How-

Table 3.2
CPB Radio Funding Criteria, 1971–1976

	1971	1972	1973	1974	1975	1976
Staff						
Full-time	1	2	3	3	4	5
Part-time	4	2	—	—	—	—
Broadcast Schedule						
Weeks per year	48	52	52	52	52	52
Days per week	6	6	7	7	7	7
Hours per day	8	12	12	14	16	18
Minimum Budget	—	—	—	—	$75,000	$75,000

Source: CPB

ever, many stations believed they had functioned effectively without full-time staff, arguing that "their volunteers and students were every bit as 'equivalent' as full-time or part-time paid persons."[14] The emphasis on professional staffing rather than public participation also ensured that station overhead costs would increase and lead to greater dependence on private funding.

Of the CPB's five-million-dollar appropriation for fiscal year 1969, 10 percent, or $500,000, went to public radio. Each of the 438 noncommercial stations on the air could have received more than a thousand dollars, which would have been a godsend for the half whose annual budgets added up to less than $10,000. However, as a result of the CPB's triage, only seventy-three stations received the base grant of $7,500.[15] In contrast, no funding criteria were established for public television stations, and all received grants ranging from $12,500 to $32,500. In 1971, the CPB adopted a six-year plan based on a carrot-and-stick approach to station growth, in which stations could double their base grant to $15,000 if they met the minimum criteria for fiscal year 1976 (see Table 3.2).

The CPB defined "service" exclusively in quantitative terms, a tendency that continues to the present and minimizes the difference between commercial and public broadcasting. In addition, the haste and lack of public deliberation surrounding the adoption of federal funding standards rivaled (or exceeded) that surrounding the 1967 Public Broadcasting Act itself. Documentation of the early CPB criteria indicates that nobody outside of the educational radio system was consulted. CPB funding criteria would make no mention of public participation in "public" radio for another nine years, when nonfederal financial support became a criterion for supplemental CPB grants. Even this criterion was tied to fundraising and voluntarism in nonbroadcast roles; actual public participation in decision making and programming was left to the discretion of the individual stations. Rather than creating a "public" radio system based on public discourse and participation, the CPB criteria unilaterally determined that public radio would be a professionalized medium, enhancing the status of the larger, more established public broadcasters.

In the early 1970s the CPB was embroiled in controversy, as President Richard Nixon attacked what he deemed to be aggressively anti-administration public affairs programming on public television. In 1970, Nixon formed the Office of Telecommunications Policy, to provide direct executive oversight of the Public Telecommunications Facilities Program (PTFP) and national telecommunications policy. His ironically named "New Federalism" exploited the tensions seething within public broadcasting, by attempting to shift the balance of power from national organizations like CPB and PBS to station managers.[16] Public television stations increasingly resisted PBS's control over programming and distribution, feeling that much programming (especially controversial programming) was "unsuited" to their audiences. A White House memo drafted by OTP head Clay Whitehead in 1971 stated:

We stand to gain substantially from an increase in the relative power of the local stations. They are generally less liberal, and more concerned with education than with controversial national affairs. Further, a decentralized system would have far less influence and would be less attractive to social activists. Therefore, we should immediately seek legislation to (a) remove CPB from the business of networking; (b) make a drastic cut in CPB's budget; and (c) initiate direct federal operating support for local stations on a matching basis. . . . [L]ocal stations' support for our proposals could be bought for about $30 million.[17]

On June 30, 1972, Nixon vetoed a bill that would have authorized a two-year CPB appropriation of $65 million the first year and $90 million the second. Although the bill had passed the Senate by a vote of eighty-two to one, Congress failed to override the veto. Federal funds eventually were appropriated, but a cowed CPB directed these funds to the production of "neutral," high-culture programs and met with administration officials to review programs.[18] Nonetheless, Nixon dragged the "independent" Corporation for Public Broadcasting deeper into a political morass by packing the CPB board with administration loyalists. The public failed to rally to the defense of public broadcasting. One observer noted that "there was no widespread public indignation, no ground swell of support, no clear public demand that public broadcasting be permitted to play its obvious role in the consideration of national public issues."[19] Although public radio featured a highly centralized production process, virtually all attention was focused on public television, since radio received only a fraction of public broadcasting's federal revenues, and many major markets, like Chicago, lacked NPR affiliates. While PBS bore the brunt of Nixon's attacks, public radio also suffered from financial uncertainty, which would ultimately lead to the debacle of Operation Independence a decade later.

In the waning days of his presidency, Nixon proferred an olive branch to public broadcasters by recommending a five-year CPB appropriation. As with previous and future federal funding measures, what would become the Public Broadcasting Act of 1975 represented a compromise between insulation and accountability, in which long-term repercussions were overlooked or ignored altogether for political expedience. The 1975 act included funding authorizations that ensured that the CPB would remain in operation for at least five years. However, House and Senate amendments resulted in a process by which funding would be provided for only *two* years in advance rather than the full five-year period. Short-term funding offered ample opportunities for congressional interference.[20] Although they now had to lobby for funds only biannually, rather than annually, public broadcasters were still accountable to whatever political ideology held sway at the moment. To encourage public broadcasters to reach out to their constituencies, the 1975 act included a formula in which $2.50 raised from private sources would be matched by one dollar in federal funds. Although intended to encourage multiple funding sources and reduce the systems dependence on federal money, this formula encouraged stations to focus on economically lucrative audience segments; it penalized stations serving poor or rural audiences.

Critics have charged that the matching formula was chosen over a dedicated tax because the latter was politically untenable.[21] Although it lowered the ratio to one federal dollar for every two private dollars, the Public Telecommunications Financing Act of 1978 made CPB, PBS, and NPR even more susceptible to political pressures. The 1978 act whittled the overall five-year authorization to three years, and the congressional practice of operating under continuing resolutions rather than actual federal budgets meant that the CPB never received the full amount of funding it was promised. The CPB was finally forced to heed concerns about public involvement. In response to demands by minorities, women, and independent producers, the 1978 act also called for the CPB to pay stricter attention to equal employment standards and to set guidelines for financial management and public accountability, including open meetings and system access by independent producers. However, the upshot of the Act was that the already heavily politicized CPB was effectively "to serve in nothing less than an official, 'federal' regulatory capacity."[22]

By 1978 the number of CPB-qualified radio stations had grown to 198; the public radio audience had nearly doubled in five years, to 4.2 million listeners. By the early 1980s, state and federal funding for public broadcasting were evenly matched; however, only 26 percent of CPB-qualified radio stations received direct state funding—unlike public television, radio was not seen as primarily "educational."[23] Consequently, federal money was crucial to public radio's survival. A 1980 CPB study found that 63 percent of Community Service Grants (CSGs) went to salaries and personnel, 8 percent for programming, 7 percent for equipment, and the remaining 22 percent for support services.[24] Small stations with scant local resources relied on NPR programming to fill their broadcast schedules to maintain CPB funding, which caused these stations to kick more and more of their already limited funds back to NPR as the network hiked its fees. NPR also provided a conduit for CSGs to local stations, and allocation of these grants became a focal point for controversy. Small stations sought these grants to acquire programs from NPR, while large stations wanted CSGs to be specifically targeted for improving local service (including the use of translators, or "ghost" stations, which extended station coverage areas and occasionally led to direct competition with struggling local stations). The situation was further complicated by the fact that CSG money would have to be divided into smaller and smaller percentages as more stations became eligible for federal money. To counter growing criticism that CPB policies favored large, university-licensed stations, the CPB in 1978 inaugurated a series of expansion grants intended to increase the number of nonprofit, community licensees (particularly those controlled by minorities). As with legislation in 1975 and 1978, "community support" was defined exclusively by fundraising. However, the number of CPB-funded stations had remained relatively flat in the final years of the decade (two hundred stations received CSGs in 1980). To allow more stations to receive CSGs and encourage local fundraising via "incentive" grants, by 1983 the basic CSG also would be reduced from $30,000 to $25,000.[25]

As private support of public broadcasting increased, federal support diminished. In 1980, the Carter administration cut CPB funding for fiscal year 1983 to $172 million, $48 million less than the amount authorized by Congress.[26] This cut set the precedent for the Reagan administration's fiscal attacks on public broadcasting. After initial attempts to completely defund the CPB failed, the Omnibus Reconciliation Act of 1981 rescinded the CPB's appropriation for fiscal year 1983 from $172 million to $137 million; the average CPB-qualified radio station lost an average of $13,000 in CSG money.[27] As a result, stations placed increasing emphasis on corporate underwriting and audience financial support. The Reagan administration argued that the private sector would pick up the funding slack, but the inverse proved to be true: both foundation and business support fell, in response to diminished public funding. The result was that "stations, caught in the dual squeeze of rising inflation and lowered appropriations, were forced to trim or eliminate local programming."[28]

The 1981 Omnibus Act created the Temporary Commission on Alternative Financing for Public Telecommunications (TCAF), which convened in October under the aegis of the FCC. Chaired by FCC commissioner James Quello, the TCAF supervised an eighteen-month experiment beginning in March 1982 in which seven public television stations aired clusters of advertisements, while two stations broadcast "enhanced underwriting" announcements, which included business slogans but no comparative claims. National Public Radio declined to participate and was officially neutral on the experiment. With characteristic hubris, NPR president Frank Mankiewicz claimed, "We already know what the public is going to tell us."[29] Advertising, while it could help counterbalance uncertain local, state, and federal support, remained highly problematic for public broadcasting. Stations might lose CPB and institutional support, and small and medium-market stations could not hope to recover basic costs for sales and traffic personnel. Viewer donations would cease to be tax deductible, and community and college licensees would lose their tax-exempt status. Production costs would increase as unions and copyright holders demanded rates equal to those paid by commercial broadcasters. Finally, there was no agreement on whether profits should go to individual stations directly or be grouped and distributed system-wide, like community service grants. According to Ralph Engelman, the TCAF experiment "ended in a stalemate that satisfied none of the contending parties."[30] On the grounds that advertising would primarily benefit VHF stations in major markets, the TCAF ultimately rejected commercial support for public broadcasting. After considering a national lottery, subsidiary services, and tax incentives, the TCAF advocated continued federal appropriations and loosened underwriting restrictions, a position later adopted by the FCC.

SPLINTERING AND SECTARIANISM

The Public Telecommunications Act of 1981 further tinkered with the federal funding mechanism, restricting the CPB's administrative costs to 11 percent of the total federal appropriation for public broadcasting. Of the remainder, public television received 75 percent and public radio 25 percent. The increase from the previous 10 percent testified to public radio's higher profile (due in part to its increasing emphasis on Washington politics) and Frank Mankiewicz's lobbying skills.[31] Since CPB budget cuts meant that base grants would have consumed all CSG money by 1983 and left little for the "incentive" grants that favored large stations, 15 percent of the CSG pool was set aside for base grants and was split equally among stations. The remaining 85 percent was apportioned according to each station's nonfederal financial support, an arrangement that benefited the largest stations in the system. Despite the federal cutbacks, by 1984 the average CPB-qualified public radio station had a cash income of $483,000: 26 percent from listeners, 14 percent from CPB, 5.5 percent from business, plus $129,000 in indirect and in-kind support.[32] However, the system was reeling from NPR's near bankruptcy in the early 1980s. As the U.S. economy underwent a recession in the mid to late 1980s, major portions of the public sector faced bankruptcy. Debt-laden states were forced to slash spending on social services, and public radio and television were often viewed as nonessential. University administrators faced with shrinking enrollments and spiraling tuition costs were unwilling to allocate additional money to their licensees. Because of plunging oil and agricultural prices, stations in the West and South were particularly hard hit. Public radio operations in Alaska, Wyoming, Idaho, Montana, New Mexico, Nebraska, Kansas, Iowa, Oklahoma, Texas, and Louisiana lost 5 to 15 percent in state funding during the mid-1980s. Many of these stations were forced to lay off staff, cut programming, and reduce operating hours. Minority stations were particularly hurt by taxpayer revolts, like California's Proposition 13; as a result of state budget cuts, six California stations targeting minorities lost CPB eligibility in 1984. On the other hand, large stations on the East Coast and in southern California flourished from listener and business support.[33]

The growing polarization between public radio's haves and have-nots was underscored when fifteen large-market stations formed the Station Resource Group (SRG) in the summer of 1984.[34] The SRG's chief spokesperson was Tom Thomas, who ironically was the founder of the National Federation of Community Broadcasters (NFCB), which is composed of public radio stations who failed to meet CPB funding criteria. As a mouthpiece for large stations, the Station Resource Group resembled the old APRS; like the APRS, it wasted little time in challenging NPR's domination of public radio policy. At its first meeting, in August 1984, the SRG urged CPB to set a $10.7 million annual ceiling on NPR funding; any additional money would go into a CSG pool for stations to use to purchase greater amounts of programming, much of which was produced by SRG members. Douglas Bennet immediately criticized the action as a "challenge to the concept of a membership organization"; Thomas countered that "to the extent that NPR does not represent the entire system, these 15 stations want a voice."[35] The most pressing concerns for the ambitious station managers who populated the SRG were the same as those of commercial broadcasters, including "hard-nosed scrutiny of current operations and programming, a realignment of investments and services and the creation of new, more ambitious development goals." SRG membership swelled to forty stations by early 1985, and the organization was often cited as an authority on station interests, legitimizing its self-appointed status as "public radio's most important think tank."[36]

Also in the mid to late 1980s, regional groups emerged in Alaska, California, the Rocky Mountain region, the Midwest, the South, and the East Coast. While ostensibly reflecting greater regional diversity, these groups were run by public radio professionals representing their singular interests; this growing factionalization did nothing to advance actual public participation and accountability.

The most serious challenge to NPR's leadership of public radio has been posed by Public Radio International (PRI), founded in January 1982 as American Public Radio Associates (later American Public Radio, or APR) by Minnesota Public Radio, New York's WNYC, Cincinnati's WGUC, San Francisco's KQED, and KUSC in Los Angeles. Minnesota Public Radio president William Kling chaired the organization. A founding member of the NPR board and the former president of the Association of Public Radio Stations, Kling remains a major power in public radio, unmatched in his ability to work the system to his advantage. APR's formation was triggered by station complaints that NPR was more interested in perpetuating its role as the sole producer and distributor of public radio programming than in serving the interests of its member stations. Specifically, several producing stations saw NPR's ability to distribute its own programs and those of member stations as a clear conflict of interest. Rather than following NPR's membership model of government by an elected board of station managers, APR operated under an independent board of directors. Whereas NPR produced the majority of its programs in house, using staff and facilities subsidized by member stations, APR distributed shows from stations and independent producers. NPR offered an entire programming service for a single price to member stations, but APR provided individual programs to stations on an exclusive basis, depending on their coverage areas. In 1983, APR dropped "Associates" from its name and incorporated itself as a fully independent organization. Shortly thereafter, it achieved the dubious distinction of introducing marketplace economics in public radio.

APR's initial offering was *A Prairie Home Companion*, which had been syndicated since 1980 by Minnesota Public Radio after Frank Mankiewicz had rejected the program as "too parochial."[37] Beginning in 1981, APR assessed stations a weekly carriage fee of ten to twenty dollars, depending on market size. *A Prairie Home Companion* skyrocketed in popularity, ranking second to *All Things Considered* as an audience (and fundraising) draw. The following year, APR established an annual affiliation fee of a thousand dollars for stations in the top thirty markets and $850 for those in other markets, and the weekly fee for *A Prairie Home Companion* doubled, ranging from twenty to thirty dollars. Although stations were not charged for additional APR programming (primarily classical music programs produced by member stations), this material was restricted to one station in a given market. These measures were strongly resisted by smaller stations, who noted that affiliation and weekly fees amounted to a fourfold increase for carriage of *A Prairie Home Companion*, but Kling claimed that the program was one of public radio's "golden geese . . . and we're pampering it." He imperiously added, "We are willing to exist in a market. The stations can choose to join us or not."[38] Ron Kramer of KSOR Ashland, Oregon, noted that APR's five producing stations had received more than $2.6 million in public funding from the CPB to establish production facilities, and he questioned the legality of these stations producing programming to which access was restricted. Referring to APR as a "dictatorship," Kramer prophetically concluded: "If APR is successful, NPR will be left carrying responsibility for the less popular 'conscience' items in the national programming mix and APR will control the cream of the crop."[39]

By 1985, APR hiked affiliate fees to a range of $1,100 to $1,500, depending on market size, and the price of *A Prairie Home Companion* jumped to ninety-five dollars per week. For 1986, APR raised its fees between $1,600 to $2,800 for affiliation and $100 to $120 for each episode of *A Prairie Home Companion*. APR cited rising production costs to justify the increases, yet *A Prairie Home Companion* aired original episodes only six months out of the year. APR also demanded that the program air no later than 6 P.M. local time on the day of broadcast, since simultaneous transmission afforded better promotional opportunities, and insisted that stations carry a toll-free number announcement encouraging listeners to order *A Prairie Home Companion*–related merchandise.[40] On March 26, 1986, APR announced that stations would pick up all, rather than the previous 49 percent, of APR's administrative budget costs, and station fees would range from $2,500 to $18,000 annually for fiscal year 1987, to take advantage of new CSG funding arrangements to stations. Kling stated that the average station would pay $7,500, which he termed "probably the best bargain in public broadcasting."[41] Nevertheless, the new fees represented a 750 percent increase in only five years. Referring to APR's status as a challenger to NPR, Kling told a House subcommittee in 1987 that "competition . . . maximizes quality in programming, it maximizes customer service, meaning the stations. It stimulates a more careful review of ideas for new programming."[42] In fact, it is hard to imagine a better refutation than APR of the canard that competition reduces prices.

APR began to distribute *Monitorradio*, a news and public affairs program produced by the *Christian Science Monitor*, in January 1984. Because of an aggressive marketing campaign subsidized by the *Christian Science Monitor*, *Monitorradio* began cutting into the carriage of Sunday *All Things Considered*, particularly among Southern stations, which objected to *All*

Things Considered's perceived "liberal" bias.[43] In 1985, APR surpassed NPR as the largest supplier of cultural programming in public radio. Drawn by higher carriage fees, programs such as *Fresh Air, Mountain Stage,* and *Whad'ya Know* began to jump from NPR to APR, and NPR responded by further paring back its cultural programming in favor of news and public affairs. Reflecting its global designs on public broadcasting, American Public Radio changed its name to Public Radio International in July 1994. Two years later, PRI made its first venture into program production with *The World,* an ambitious news and public affairs program produced in conjunction with the BBC and Boston's WGBH. Although the program was offered free for a year to build carriage, many key stations failed to pick it up, since it competed with NPR's flagship *All Things Considered.* Although budgeted at five million dollars annually, the *Boston Globe* claimed, *The World* had "burned through" $16 million in one year. Citing the "inexcusable waste of precious system resources that have gone into *The World,*" PRI news director Ken Mills resigned in September 1997. In early 1998, production of the program was consolidated in Boston. *Monitorradio* ceased production in June 1997; the program had been losing money for the *Christian Science Monitor* for several years.[44] However, PRI found another "golden goose" with *Marketplace,* underwritten by General Electric and the A. G. Edwards brokerage firm. Host Stephen Brancaccio has stated that *Marketplace* is designed to "reflect ideas that aren't commercially driven," a strange claim for a show devoted exclusively to business news. Reflecting the demographic tilt in public radio, *Marketplace* draws 4 percent of all corporate underwriting money for public radio and rakes in the highest underwriting income of any public radio program.[45]

In 1997, PRI had 591 affiliates, while NPR had 635 members. While APR/PRI is a remarkable success in financial terms, its contribution to "public" radio is debatable. According to Engelman:

NPR took some steps to reach out to diverse audiences through its cultural programming despite the increased emphasis on demographics in public radio. The thrust of APR's programming was more unapologetically upscale. APR's emphasis on classical music contrasted with NPR's greater effort to present jazz, blues, gospel, and Latin music. APR's most important initiative in news and public affairs, *Marketplace,* targeted professional strata interested in business and economic programming.[46]

More than any other organization, APR/PRI's activities have highlighted the growth of marketplace ideology in the public radio system. Although PRI has benefited from extensive public subsidies throughout its history, its efforts have been geared toward increasing profits first and foremost. Its usurious pricing policies (as evidenced by *A Prairie Home Companion*) and dubious funding practices (described further in Chapter 4) have seriously challenged public radio's ethical standards. Most important, PRI has played a primary role in defining the "public" as a market. While it has profited handsomely by emulating its commercial counterparts, it has done so at great cost to the credibility of the public radio system.

THE STATIONS GAIN CONTROL

In 1981, representatives of more than thirty public radio and television stations drafted legislation that would have eliminated the CPB and passed all federal funds directly to stations. The bill was based on arguments that the CPB's dithering reduced its effectiveness while its administrative costs devoured 10 percent of the federal appropriation for public broadcasting; James Day notes that the Ford Foundation "had managed to dole out far more money to public broadcasting with a staff of only six."[47] The bill also would have removed the requirement for community advisory boards and eliminated "restrictions on use of federally funded equipment to generate revenues for support and maintenance."[48] In effect, the bill would have made the commercialization of public broadcasting a fait accompli. Although quickly defeated, it set in motion events that significantly redefined public radio. On February 6, 1985, the NPR board unveiled a five-year business plan in which CPB would send its radio funds directly to stations, and NPR members would then pay between 8 and 10 percent of their total income to access NPR programming and representation services. By directing federal funds to stations, the plan would buffer NPR from unstable federal funding and CPB's meddling and give local stations more control over programming. The plan was also triggered by thinly veiled threats from large producing stations. The Station Resource Group advised that 10 percent of NPR's stations might drop their membership if the network could not meet their "diversity of programming needs."[49]

By a vote of 159 to five, NPR's member stations overwhelmingly approved the five-year business plan at the Public Radio Conference in Denver on May 22, 1985. Beginning with fiscal year 1987, all federal dollars would go directly to stations (with the exception of three million dollars, or 7 percent, for what would become the CPB Radio Fund, devoted to experimental and minority programming). Membership and programming fees would be assessed separately; all NPR member stations would be required to pay the membership fee, but they would not be required to purchase programming. This policy would increase station leverage over NPR, since stations could vote on organizational matters even if they had no stake in programming. Lastly, all programming would be bundled under a single purchase price (an amendment for separate programming streams failed by a vote of seventy-seven to 124).[50] The stations also adopted the SRG's proposal for an annual NPR budget subject to station approval, which was to lead to intense wrangling over NPR's finances in the future. As the *Los Angeles Times* reported, "The Denver conference ended with the stations that NPR has served since 1970 in firm control of the network—not vice versa."[51]

The NPR business plan was adopted by the CPB on November 22, 1985, and the increased federal payments to stations had tremendous repercussions for the public radio system. Federal funding would now constitute up to 20 percent of large stations' operating budgets, and up to 35 percent at smaller stations. The increased CSGs to stations would give stations much greater discretionary income (the average station CSG would increase by 15 percent, to $84,441).[52] Before the plan, stations had paid nothing for programming; all costs had been included in NPR dues. Since station managers used their increased power to favor its competitors, NPR would have to expend more energy on promotion. As money flowed to stations rather than NPR, the network raised its station fees. This led some large-market stations that used a partial schedule of NPR programming to threaten to drop their membership (KUSC in Los Angeles terminated its NPR affiliation in 1985 and used the money to establish a news department). As more stations fled NPR, overall programming prices would rise for others. Many of NPR's member stations, faced with revenue shortfalls, claimed that NPR marketing practices forced stations to buy programming they did not want. Ten million dollars in CPB funding would go to a newly created National Program Production and Acquisition Grants (NPPAG) program, which was restricted to funding "more than local" programming (the remaining eight million dollars would be allocated to a radio fund for experimental and minority programming). The NPPAG arrangement allowed the CPB to maintain a direct role in station programming; it was based on congressional mandates to fund "balanced and objective" programming from diverse sources. The NPPAG funding was opposed by some stations and independent producers, but as the CPB's Rick Madden told the sixteenth annual Public Radio Conference, "The purpose of the fund is not to provide a living for producers trying to eke out a living. The purpose is to provide major national productions."[53]

The 1985 business plan allowed the stations unprecedented leverage over NPR, and an old idea now enjoyed a new resurgence: unbundling, or offering discrete programs rather than a comprehensive service. A program-by-program buy-back proposal had been floated in the 1977 APRS-NPR merger talks but had been dropped when NPR agreed to assume representation functions as well as program production. In March 1985, a month after the NPR board proposed the plan that would channel federal money directly to stations, the Station Resource Group issued a report, *Financing NPR*, proposing that stations have an option to purchase "programming streams" instead of the entire NPR schedule. However, the NPR board initially resisted pressures to unbundle its programming. Chairman Donald Mullally claimed, "This really isn't a market system. Congress puts money into the system because it has programming that the market won't support."[54] Although it gained substantially from the influx of funds to stations, APR resorted to more overt intimidation in efforts to thwart NPR's continued domination of programming. In a March 12, 1986, letter to Douglas Bennet, William Kling attached a legal brief charging that NPR's "practice of bundling magazine news services . . . with other services is an illegal tie-in under the antitrust laws."[55] This statement conveniently overlooked the fact that APR also bundled programs by requiring stations to pay an affiliation fee in order to obtain the rights to air *A Prairie Home Companion*.

NPR estimated that twenty-four stations would leave the system if programs were not unbundled, resulting in a loss of $1.4 million. Succumbing to what appeared to be the inevitable, in the spring of 1987 NPR proposed three membership tiers. Tier One would be based on representation and administration, Tier Two on programming overhead costs, and Tier Three on the programs themselves. To receive programming, stations would have to purchase Tier One or Two; stations could then decide to buy any or all of seven distinct programming services, including morning news, evening news, events, arts and performance programs, *Performance Today*, and "other services, produced or acquired."[56] While this arrangement would help large stations, it would hurt small stations that aired large amounts of NPR programming. Although fees would be based on market size, the plan would raise overall rates about 8.5 percent and increase the price for all news programming by 10 percent. A majority would buy only some programs (particularly high-profile news offerings like *Morning Edition* or *All Things Considered*), leaving the rest of the stations to subsidize "marginal" programming. As *Current* stated, "The more pieces the network divides the programming into, the more each piece will cost to compensate for the smaller number of stations which NPR expects to pay for individual programs."[57]

Proponents of unbundling claimed it would allow stations that did not air the entire NPR programming package to purchase one or two programs at a lower price. Other programming vendors, such as independent producers, the major producing stations, and American Public Radio, could compete more effectively, and stations would have more control over program production. The proposal pleased large producing stations, since programming prices would be disengaged from station financial support. On the other hand, opponents of unbundling, noting that programming previously had been included in general dues, argued that programming costs would rise dramatically. Larger stations would benefit as both programming producers and consumers; some stations forecast that unbundling would reduce costs for less than thirty of the three-hundred stations airing NPR programming.[58]

NPR member stations narrowly approved the plan on December 8, 1987, by a vote of ninety-three in favor, eighty-five opposed, and seventy-seven abstentions. Beginning with fiscal year 1989, NPR's programming would be divided into morning news, evening news, and cultural packages. The costs of unbundling would be phased in over two years, but all stations would pay more to compensate for those who dropped out of NPR as a result of price increases. Trying to put the best spin on events, NPR president Bennet claimed that unbundling would allow NPR to develop more diverse programming, in that a new program idea would no longer have to pass muster with the entire NPR membership before it could be produced.[59] In response to station pressures and the growing defection of programs attracted by APR's higher carriage fees, the NPR board of directors voted in early 1990 to offer all arts and performance, or cultural, programs individually or as part of a bundled "stream." Bennet again rationalized the move: "I'm not sure we should have the ability to maintain a program that does not have carriage. I think that what you do . . . is move on."[60]

Unbundling nudged public radio farther in the direction of the marketplace and reduced diversity on the national and local levels. National programming decisions were now driven by stations, who increasingly relied on commercially derived audience research methodologies to determine their schedules. Stations sought shows that would retain audiences in midday and during evenings (after the "tent poles" of *Morning Edition* and *All Things Considered*), as well as shows that could be "stripped," or programmed at the same time every day in a consistent schedule. Unbundling was intended to unfetter competition and reduce programming prices, but it had the opposite effect. NPR relayed the costs of production back to the stations through fees for individual programs, and the price of successful shows shot up dramatically; if purchased individually, *Car Talk* by 1992 cost nearly as much as NPR's entire cultural programming package.[61] These costs, in turn, forced stations to narrow their program offerings. The previous all-or-nothing approach to program bundling had enabled NPR to protect new shows and allow programs to run higher budgets than station carriage dictated. Now, programs had to pay their way and faced immediate pressures to be "salable."

Unbundling also produced little incentive for NPR to increase or retain the number of its member stations, since revenues were now based on the aggregate costs of programming. The network received the same amount of money whether it gained or lost members, as remaining stations picked up the expenses when others left; the annual debates over NPR's budget became increasingly contentious as it poured more and more money into its high-profile news operations. NPR asked for a $17.2 million dues assessment for fiscal year 1987, which meant individual station fees would rise an average of $13,500 to $15,500. After heated station opposition the assessment was reduced to $15.8 million, and NPR eliminated all funding for national promotion and fundraising. Spiraling dues rates led to continued haggling between NPR and its member stations.[62] NPR requested a budget of $43.6 million from its members in 1993, which would have required a 9.7 percent increase in dues. By this point, many stations were in open rebellion at the consistent dues hikes, and NPR was forced to set programming fees at a fixed percentage of station revenues. The 1993 budget eventually was settled at $40 million, and dues were locked for five years at a little more than 10 percent of station revenues. In 1997, consultant David Giovannoni proposed that dues be based on station listenership; the larger the audience for a given show, the more the station would pay for the program. This strategy would be accompanied by a complete unbundling of programming and push NPR farther toward an exclusive focus on high-profile news programming.[63] Another proposal would change NPR to a system of shareholder governance, rather than the current system of one station, one vote. Stations would get one share for every thousand dollars they paid NPR in dues, program fees, and distribution fees.[64] If adopted, these proposals would allow a cabal of larger stations to determine public radio policy—a goal of these stations since the system was founded in 1970.

FEDERAL FUNDING IN THE 1990s

While large stations in major markets benefited greatly from direct CSG payments and "incentive" grants, many others suffered—particularly minority broadcasters. By mid-1990, less than 3 percent of all the stations in the system received over 10 percent of all CPB station funds, while the top 10 percent (thirty-seven stations) received 30 percent. In contrast, only seven noncommercial stations licensed to African-Americans received CPB funding.[65] In response, an alliance of minority and community broadcasters bypassed the CPB and appealed directly to Congress to revise the CSG formula. Their testimony before a House subcommittee in June 1991 starkly illustrated the growing divisions within the public radio system. Citing a CPB study that found sixty-four public radio stations and eleven public TV stations had no full-time minority employees, Rep. Bill Richardson (D.–New Mexico) charged that funding had "fallen far short of CPB's goals and has frustrated minority groups." Richardson's statement was seconded by Hugo Morales, general manager of Radio Bilingue in Fresno, who claimed, "We are punished for serving our people. Those serving affluent audiences get rewarded. . . . [T]he rich get richer and the poor get poorer."[66]

An ensuing congressional mandate to improve service to minorities and rural areas begot the formation of three CPB-sponsored review panels in late 1991: one for radio, one for television, and one for both systems. The radio review panel proposed $2.2 million in targeted grants to stations aimed at minority, rural, or unserved audiences. It also readjusted the grant formula to place more money in the "base grants" that all stations share equally, and less in "incentive grants" that are proportional to station fundraising. Stations that met two of three minority criteria (50 percent staff, 50 percent board, and 35 percent listenership) would receive a 25 percent bonus grant. If a station met all three criteria, this amount would jump to 50 percent. According to one observer, "[the CSG reviews] were the first inclusive processes ever. . . . They turned have-nots into haves, and empowered a much larger universe of stations."[67]

What Congress giveth, Congress also taketh away. As the CPB's funding stalled in the 1990s, Congress began pressuring the public radio system to eliminate "redundant" programming between stations. In May 1995, a CPB Task Force recommended that radio community service grants be geared to "audience service" criteria, based on a station's average-quarter-hour listenership or its status as the sole public radio provider to at least half of its coverage area (minority-operated stations would be exempted from either criteria). After station complaints, an optional criterion based on fundraising was added. In September, the CPB formally proposed that beginning with fiscal year 1988, stations would receive funding according to average-quarter-hour listenership figures (based on CPB's "Areapop" listening index) or nonfederal financial support.[68] The CPB board unanimously approved the proposal on January 22, 1996. By gearing funding to audience ratings and income, CPB would place at risk many of the stations that offer small-niche programming in major markets. A staffer at Portland's KBOO told Current,

No, it doesn't make any sense to program in Vietnamese, that's true. However, that's an underserved audience we've attempted in some marginal way to service. Spanish-language programming in our broadcast area—no, that's not a smart programming move. Is it part of our mission statement? Is it part of what we say we're all about? That's why we do it.[69]

Paradoxically, Lynn Chadwick of the National Federation of Community Broadcasters (and who served on the CPB Task Force) welcomed the emphasis on ratings, stating that "taking the criteria off cash and into service has been what we're after for years."[70] Tom Thomas of the Station

Resource Group estimated that one in six stations would have to improve "audience service" in order to meet the new federal funding criteria.[71] Ultimately, six stations lost the matching portion of their CPB funding. These stations included KBOO; KCSN in Northridge, California; KDHX in St. Louis; KVCR in San Bernadino; WNYE in Brooklyn; and WYPL in Memphis, a radio reading service whose visually impaired listeners have difficulty filling out Arbitron diaries. According to the CPB, nearly twenty other stations failed to meet the standards but "have demonstrated 'aggressive efforts' to do so" by working with professional consultants.[72]

The CPB also created a three-year "Future Fund" in 1995 to boost listener and corporate support for public radio through competitive proposals by stations and other groups. A third of the Future Fund's $11 million was diverted from CSGs that had previously gone to stations; NPR affiliates opposed the fund's creation by a vote of eighty-nine to sixty-two. Some managers argued that the fund would divert monies from an already-shrinking CSG pool, while one station manager cited the precedent of allowing the CPB to spend funds as it saw fit: "What's to prevent them from spending $20 million or $40 million on a discretionary basis, unless someone calls them on it?" The Future Fund also diverted money from small stations to large, well-funded stations like Minnesota Public Radio. One manager claimed, "The basic problem is one of fairness. . . . If you take money from the CSG pool, how can you use it so that all 'contributors' to the fund derive some benefit?"[73] The Future Fund, in conjunction with the new CSG standards, indicated the CPB's tacit approval of public radio's commercialization. The first Future Fund grants, awarded in May 1996, included station fundraising collaborations, the consolidation of Alaska Public Radio stations, the dissemination of audience research data, and a mail-order book service devised by Minnesota Public Radio.[74]

Nevertheless, the Future Fund's patchwork attempts at reducing funding uncertainty are stopgap measures. The great dream of public broadcasters remains a long-term funding source insulated from political pressure. In May 1995, public broadcasters proposed that a trust fund of five billion dollars be established for the CPB, estimating that an annual return of 5 or 6 percent (the norm for foundation and university endowments) would match the mid-1990s subsidy of $250 million. Two proposals were crafted. The CPB's version was purposely vague on how the trust fund would be financed, whereas a rival proposal drawn up by NPR, PRI, PBS, and the Association of Public Television Stations advocated a combination of proceeds from the auction of unused spectrum, a 2 percent transfer fee on sales of commercial stations, contributions from commercial stations in exchange for release from public interest obligations, and tax benefits for private donors. Rep. Mike Oxley (R.-

Ohio) quickly scotched the plan, claiming, "We couldn't get 100 votes on the floor of the House. We'll be very lucky to sell $1 billion."[75] In February 1996, Rep. Jack Fields (R.-Texas), the head of the House telecommunications subcommittee, countered with the "Public Broadcasting Self-Sufficiency Act," a bill that would establish a trust fund of a billion dollars received from auctioning 343 vacant noncommercial TV channels. The bill would freeze CPB appropriations at $250 million for fiscal years 1998, 1999, and 2000, and it would cut off all federal appropriations to public broadcasting as of September 30, 2000.[76]

Despite their disappointment with the trust's funding level, public broadcasters found other sections of Field's proposal more palatable. One provision would allow an overlapped TV station in a market to be operated as a commercial station or sold for commercial use. Another would enable public stations to accept payment for airing programs produced by other networks. For example, The Discovery Channel could buy time on PBS stations and sell thirty second announcements. Underwriting guidelines would include a "call for action" and "strictly quantifiable comparative descriptions." Finally, the proposal would authorize the CPB to create programming for the first time, and the CPB board would have appointees nominated by the majority and minority leaders in the House and Senate, with approval by the president. The Fields bill failed, due to mixed support from public broadcasters and congressional concern about lack of oversight.[77]

However, Fields's successor, Rep. W. J. (Billy) Tauzin (R.-Louisiana), also favors a trust fund. Unlike Fields, Tauzin is adamantly opposed to commercialization of public broadcasting; instead, he has proposed to deregulate commercial broadcasters if they agree to pay spectrum fees, which would be given to public broadcasting.[78] Given the bellicosity of commercial broadcasters at the slightest mention of spectrum fees, such a proposal is highly unlikely to be realized, but the trust fund issue promises to remain a political hot potato for years to come. Public broadcasters surely will continue to push for a trust fund, as they have since the system received its first federal funding in the late 1960s. Yet it is unlikely that they will gain a fund that matches their desired funding figures or that will be totally insulated from political concerns. The potential for congressional hotdogging during reauthorization hearings is irresistible for politicians seeking personal publicity on an issue with little financial consequence for the federal budget.

FUTURE TRENDS IN PUBLIC RADIO

Public broadcasters are constrained by a number of external factors besides federal funding. First, substantial barriers to entry exist. Spectrum space is finite, and regulation has limited the number of channels devoted to noncommercial broadcasting. While public broadcasters struggle for funds, commercial broadcasters have significantly reduced public-interest obligations in the wake of the deregulatory zeal of the late 1970s and 1980s. While this deregulation was designed to encourage new technologies and services by shifting concern from ownership and content regulations to market controls and economic efficiency, the relaxation of ownership rules led to increased programming syndication and format duplication.[79] The further slackening of these rules in the 1990s transformed the FM band into a speculative commodity, which further raised the costs of entry; the few noncommercial radio channels that remain are increasingly absorbed by religious broadcasters. Although reserved frequencies cannot be sold for commercial purposes, a religious broadcaster can transfer its operation to the noncommercial license and sell its commercial station. In addition, the FCC no longer requires applicants to establish their eligibility for noncommercial licenses; misrepresentation claims are examined only if they are already under litigation in state courts.[80] In 1997, the University of the District of Columbia attempted to sell WDCU-FM to an associate firm of Salem Communications, the country's largest Christian station group, for $13 million. Attempts by the SRG and a proposed coalition of NPR and Washington's WETA to buy WDCU both failed. NPR nevertheless threatened a license challenge, and Salem withdrew its offer. WDCU, a jazz station with the nation's fourth-largest African-American audience, was eventually purchased by C-SPAN.[81]

Second, like their commercial counterparts, public broadcasters face significant competition for audiences. Media delivery channels have grown at a nearly exponential rate in the last two decades (although programming diversity has scarcely kept pace), and a number of these channels have challenged radio's particular strengths. Radio's benefits as a mobile medium have been undermined by portable cassette and CD players, and new technologies like downloadable MP3 sound files and digital satellite broadcasting promise to further erode its standing. Additionally, financial pressures on public radio have mounted as the system has matured. Public radio now faces declining surpluses as it switches from public to private money to sustain its operations. Soliciting money from private sources is much more time and labor–intensive than tapping government funds, which requires little more than filling out forms. As WXPN station manager Mark Fuerst predicted,

In a general sense, these pressures will make public radio more "business-like." Productivity will become more important at a national and local level. Managers will be forced to weight the actual dollar return of their spending. By the end of the [1990s], efficiency criteria (such as listeners served per dollar, or money raised per hour) will be key measures of station performance.[82]

The contemporary structure of National Public Radio differs radically from that envisioned by its founders. Rather than reflecting localism and diversity, stations increasingly have adopted a business mode in which "listener support and business underwriting correlate with the size of a station's audience in general and the audience for specific programs in particular."[83] "Audience awareness" is driven by the threat of declining subsidies and the desire for institutional growth and organizational prestige. As a result, the future structure of public radio will be characterized by regional consolidation, national "superstations," greater use of syndicated programming and formats, and commercial ventures. Each of these will be considered in turn.

System Consolidation

Public radio had a negligible presence in most major markets when CPB began funding the system in 1971, largely because of educational radio's base in midwestern land grant colleges. In 1975, the CPB devoted a million dollars through the Coverage Expansion Grant Project to help establish public radio stations in major major markets. The following year, Thomas Warnock (then director of radio activities for CPB) proposed that stations be established in thirty-six major cities and four states then lacking public radio service. Wamock specifically called for multiple public radio stations in major population centers, some of them to be created through direct purchases of existing commercial stations for noncommercial use.[84] To meet the needs of rural operations, the NPR board established "auxiliary" memberships in early 1985. These stations, which would pay lower fees in exchange for not being given exclusive rights to NPR programming in their areas, had coverage areas of less than 150,000 people and minimum gross revenues of $50,000. A third category, associate members, consisted of stations that extended the coverage of full-member stations.

By 1986, public radio was inaccessible to only thirteen markets and 14 percent of the population. Expansion into these areas was inhibited by startup and maintenance costs, terrain problems, and a lack of available frequencies. A 1989 study by the National Telecommunications and Information Administration (NTIA) found that no new "stand-alone," full-service public radio and television stations were needed to reach the public; full service could be accomplished by translator and repeater stations. Nevertheless, NPR convened a Public Radio Expansion Task Force in March 1989 to explore expansion possibilities. Its report estimated that extending public radio's reach via eighty new stations would cost $62 million over five years. Because further penetration into rural areas was not cost-effective, service extension increasingly focused on establishing multiple stations in large markets. An NPR audience researcher claimed that "clearly . . . if we are to serve more listeners better, we've got to fish where the fish are."[85]

By the mid-1990s, most medium and large markets had two to five public radio stations. Yet the federal funding pool shrank as appropriations dropped and more stations tapped into what money remained. In addition, nearly 90 percent of public radio and TV stations lost some state and local funding in the early '90s, and one-third lost more than 20 percent of their budgets. The emphasis on private fundraising continued to polarize large and small stations; in 1996, nearly half of all public radio stations had less than $500,000 in nonfederal financial support, while 8 percent had more than two million dollars. Stations also were battered by inflation and spiraling program fees. Halfway through the decade, a significant shakeout within the public radio system was in progress. Alaska public broadcasting lost 40 percent of its state funding between 1986 and 1995, and consolidation reduced sixteen public radio stations to five "master" stations with repeaters throughout the state.[86] More stations began merging aspects of their operations, including fundraising. WSKG in Binghamton, New York, transformed itself into a "virtual" station by contracting its scheduling and financial operations and automating its signal. According to *Current*, "Deejays record a four-hour shift in about an hour and a computer merges their remarks with music from an automated 'jukebox' that holds some 130 compact discs." WSKG's remaining employees are given incentives to attract outside funding, thereby maximizing fundraising efficiency by turning everyone into a salesperson.[87]

Such "virtual" stations, ludicrous as they may be, may become more common as public radio increasingly emulates the practices of its commercial counterparts. Equally troubling are the blatant land-grabs by large stations within statewide areas. In Grand Junction, Colorado, KPRN carried a substantial amount of programming from Denver's KCFR when it signed on in 1984. Two years later, KPRN station manager Marsha Thomas (who was a leader in the station expansion movement) advocated that the station develop self-sufficient programming, telling officials at the Public Telecommunications Facilities program, "Denver is 250 miles away and the programming of the major metropolitan station does not meet the needs of the local audience."[88] The station developed blocks of eclectic, volunteer-produced programming that aired in the evenings, but insufficient fundraising forced KPRN to drop its independent programming and lay off its expanded staff; KPRN and KCFR merged in October 1991. The merger was designed to take advantage of economies of scale and build KPRN's audience through "consistent" classical music programming; KPRN station manager Thomas claimed, with great precision, that classical listeners gave an average of eighty dollars a year, and jazz listeners fifty-eight dollars a year.[89] The merger was strongly opposed by KPRN's Community Advisory Board, which learned of it only through the press. The board petitioned the FCC to deny transfer of the station's license to KCFR, but the transfer was approved. Tom Thomas of the Station Resource Group, which earlier had spearheaded the station expansion movement calling for more public radio stations, cited the event as a watershed. He noted approvingly that the only code of ethics in public broadcasting is that "if you can provide a service and people use it, do it. If it hurts another station, that's their problem, and it probably means you're doing a better job."[90]

His remarks clearly evince the laissez-faire ideology that increasingly motivates the actions of public broadcasters. KCFR manager Max Wycisk drew national attention when in 1997 he sent fundraising letters to areas of the state outside KCFR's signal and drew donations from listeners who confused Wycisk's operation with their local stations. KCFR is the hub of Colorado Public Radio, which by 1998 had blanketed 80 percent of the state through four stations and twelve translators. Its aggressive expansion directly threatens KDNK in Carbondale and KAJX in Aspen, stations that "offer several programs that serve as the main source of news for the 22 percent of the local population that is primarily Spanish speaking."[91]

The Growth of National "Superstations"

Cincinnati's WVXU has expanded into northern Michigan, Oregon's KSOR reaches into Northern California, and Philadelphia's WRTI can be heard in Delaware and New Jersey. The leader, however, is Minneapolis-based Minnesota Public Radio (MPR), which had extended into six states and Canada by 1996. MPR originated with KSJR-FM, which went on the air in Collegeville, Minnesota, on January 22, 1967. The station's licensee, St. John's University, hired William Kling as program director. Kling left the station for a job as Associate Director of Projects for Radio at CPB in 1969, returning two years later when St. John's turned control of the station over to a nonprofit, Minnesota Educational Radio. The group changed its name to Minnesota Public Radio in 1974, completing a six-station network in 1975.[92] To capitalize on the success of *A Prairie Home Companion*, MPR launched the Rivertown Trading Company in 1981 for program merchandising. MPR established a statewide network of twelve stations by 1985; two years later the Rivertown operation was reorganized as the Greenspring Company, a for-profit subsidiary of MPR. Kling's entrepreneurial skills are reflected in the fact that MPR received nearly five million dollars in listener support, more than three million dollars in government funding, and close to eight million dollars in revenues from broadcasting and other activities, including *Minnesota Monthly* magazine and catalog sales, in 1988.[93]

By 1989 MPR was operating seventeen stations, with another under construction and applications for four more on file with the FCC. These expansionist policies unsurprisingly led to direct conflicts with local stations. In late 1989, residents of Sun Valley, Idaho, applied to the FCC for a permit to install a thirty-watt translator and a hundred-watt Class A station with MPR's assistance. The Sun Valley group had approached the nearest public station, KBSU in Boise, for assistance, but the issue had stalled at the Idaho State Board of Education eighteen months later. The group had then turned to MPR, which "presented a much more attractive package and could provide their expertise getting us on the air via translator." By the early 1990s, MPR's signal was bouncing off the mountains of Idaho.[94] MPR also established a transmitter near Grand Forks, North Dakota, in 1990, although the area already was served by AM and FM public stations licensed to the University of North Dakota. Much of MPR's programming was the same as that of the local stations, who could not hope to match MPR's marketing resources. These stations were forced to turn to "marginal" audiences and programming, while MPR skimmed off the cream of their subscriber base.

MPR president Kling claims that MPR moves into an area only after community requests; and he insists that new communities finance station construction and the first year of operation. In fact, these stations are frequently financed by state grants, while MPR reaps the benefits of programming fees and promotions—yet another example of the ways in which public subsidies serve private profits. MPR also has often been a free rider on NPR's programming. Using translator and repeater stations, MPR requires only one NPR affiliate in order to receive NPR programming. This loophole allows MPR to save thousands of dollars in affiliation fees, at NPR's expense, and increases the burden on other NPR affiliates.[95]

Increased Use of Syndicated Programming and Formats

Several producing stations also are extending their reach through syndicated programming. A 1993 study of public television by the 20th Century Fund had called for the CPB to discontinue the CSG program and earmark all television funds to PBS, while suggesting a shift away from "ephemeral" broadcasting to programs with a longer "shelf-life."[96] Although the report neglected to address public radio, consultant David Giovannoni has adapted its arguments to the medium:

A service that maintained the library, chose the cuts and paid the talent could be far less expensive than the aggregate cost of repeating these activities across dozens of licensees. The cost per station per program hour could be reduced significantly. And if this programming is better than the local production it displaces, audience service may very well increase.[97]

Chicago's WFMT directly supplies classical music programming to 371 cities, and it also syndicates the Fine Arts Network and Beethoven Satellite Network. The station began also offering twelve hours of jazz in 1995; in 1996 more than a hundred stations relied on MPR's *Music through the Night* satellite service.[98] Several proposals have been made for "sharenets," or decentralized networks of stations sharing programming based on appeal to specific demographic groups—for example, jazz for national news listeners, jazz for older "white guys," or jazz for African-American listeners. Although proponents claim this approach increases audience "service" by freeing personnel for education and outreach, the realities are more prosaic. Dave Carwile, the program director at WOSU, has stated, "you don't have to have somebody doing the programming, and you don't have to have the programming staff."[99]

Commercial Ventures

Several "superstations" like Minnesota Public Radio have publishing ventures (WFMT also publishes *Chicago* magazine), and marketing spin-offs are an attractive source of revenue for public radio organizations. MPR's entrepreneurial activities rewarded director William Kling handsomely: while earning slightly less than $75,000 as head of MPR in 1996, he also received over $382,000 from Greenspring.[100] MPR's profits from Greenspring (which Kling termed an "experiment in 'social purpose' capitalism") also began to attract considerable attention from outside the organization. The director of a nonprofit group in Minnesota has noted, "One of the biggest issues was that this non-profit had a very large and successful for-profit and very few people knew about it." Another observer stated, "Unlike the nonprofit organizations with which they are associated, for-profit offshoots can dance around how much they spend on salaries, whom they employ or who receives consulting contracts."[101] Although MPR is ostensibly a separate entity, its employees worked at Greenspring during the 1995 Christmas sales rush, which led to an inquiry by the Minnesota attorney general's office as a potential conflict of interest. MPR ultimately was cleared of wrongdoing, yet its activities clearly ventured into ethical gray areas. In March 1998, MPR sold its catalog business to Minneapolis retailer Dayton Hudson for $120 million. The sale raised MPR's endowment by $90 million, and Kling personally received $2.6 million from the deal.[102] MPR's activities were seeded indirectly with public funds; two years earlier, the CPB awarded $2.43 million in grants to MPR.

Music also provides a means for public radio to milk audiences for money. NPR's *Performance Today* released a "Christmas around the Country" CD on the newly formed NPR Classics label in 1995. PRI's *Mountain Stage* also has released several CDs of performances culled from the show. But the most brazen commercial venture in public radio's history is the Public Radio Music Source (PRMS), which Minnesota Public Radio began operating in January 1993 in conjunction with sixty-six stations. Participating stations plug a toll-free number for listeners to purchase the CDs on their station's playlist. In return, the station earns up to 10 percent of the gross from sales. The PRMS also provides local stations with the names, addresses, and phone numbers of users, who then get a membership pitch from the station. KUSC in Los Angeles estimated it received $30,000 from PRMS in 1993 and hoped that annual profits eventually would reach $60,000 to $70,000. By 1997, more than three hundred stations subscribed to the service.[103] PRMS provides a dependable revenue stream to stations and a convenient means for record companies to promote certain releases aggressively. According to James Ledbetter, "Public radio stations are therefore twice subject to the whims of the marketplace: first by industry hype and solicitation, second by knowing that if they play something palatable to a wide audience, the station's share of royalties will grow."[104] In addition to alienating local record stores that sponsor programs, PRMS also encourages stations to narrow their programming. Although participating stations surely would claim that their song rotations are not affected; the fact that they could directly benefit by playing certain recordings places them in a blatant conflict of interest.

Another craven attempt at wringing money from listeners surfaced in 1996, when a scheme with the remarkable title of the Listener Alliance for Public Radio was cooked up by a group of station representatives to capitalize on the purported groundswell of support for public broadcasting in the 1995 funding debate. The group administering the Listener Alliance called itself the Alliance for Public Broadcasting (APB). The Listener Alliance would generate revenues for stations by making deals with companies offering products and services. These companies would give listeners discounts of 10 percent on merchandise, and the station would receive a 2 to 5 percent return on each transaction. According to Mary Bokuniewicz, development director of KUNM-FM in Albuquerque and the vice president of APB,

We know a lot about what our listeners spend their money on. So we target the vendors of those goods and services, and secure discounts for them (on stuff they're going to buy anyway!). Delighted to have our loyal listeners become their loyal customers, vendors rebate a small percentage of every [Listener Alliance] transaction to [the Alliance for Public for Public Broadcasting]. APB distributes the proceeds to participating stations. APB will develop and administer the program. Stations need only promote it.[105]

Table 3.3
Sources of Public Radio Station Programming, 1972–1992 (in percentages)

	1972	1982	1992
Local stations	67	56	48
NPR	8	25	27
Other syndicators	25	19	25

Source: NPR

After paying the APB an annual fee according to the size of their re-spective listening audiences, participating stations would air six an-nouncements throughout the broadcast day. In addition to cluttering broadcasts with more overt commercialism, the Listener Alliance would further implicate public radio with businesses involved in potentially controversial activities, from telephone services to oil companies. One station manager recalled:

Once upon a time, we felt most of our underwriters were of a certain . . . caliber. At least it was clear they all were ardent backers of public radio. These days we do check the color of their money. . . . But, honestly, I sure would worry if our listeners considered that all of our underwriters have our endorsement.[106]

FROM FEDERALISM TO FEUDALISM

The percentage of local programming aired by CPB-qualified stations has declined markedly since the early 1970s (see Table 3.3). This decrease is partly due to a vastly expanded number of program suppliers. In addition to NPR, public radio stations may air programs from other pro-ducing stations, commercial stations and news networks, independent producers, outside organizations, and such foreign productions as the *BBC World Service*. This programming often is heavily subsidized and available at little or no cost. Moreover, the programming "marketplace" is highly concentrated; the number of programming *distributors*, as op-posed to producers, is quite small. In 1985, Tom Thomas and Theresa Clifford found that 91 percent of nonlocal station programming was mo-nopolized by a handful of distributors, including NPR and APR/PRI (half of whose programming is produced by five stations). Of the re-maining 9 percent, half went to popular series produced by independents or individual stations, and the rest was "completely disaggregated and the subject of intense competition among smaller syndicators and dis-tributors such as the NFCB Program Service, Pacifica and the Southern Educational Communications Association, scores of independent and station-based producers, and a few state networks."[107] In short, hundreds of programs compete for only six and a half hours of airplay per week (based on a station average of 6,698 broadcast hours per year).

Thomas McCain and G. Ferrell Lowe define a broadcasting locality as "a discrete but nonstandardized geographic area corresponding to a relatively unique and commonly shared collection of situationally and/or culturally determined values and interests represented by the people who live there."[108] Indeed, "localism" has been a central tenet throughout the history of American broadcast regulation. Robert Horwitz argues that the FCC's emphasis on localism fundamentally misconstrues the nature of the American broadcasting system:

The Commission's image of the broadcaster in the mythic haze of the small-town Jeffersonian public sphere served only to veil the actual practices and consequences of a commercially organized, national system of network broadcasting. In doing so, the FCC may have robbed itself of the available means to make broadcasting better and more diverse.[109]

Yet Horwitz is not denouncing localism per se; instead, he is referring to patterns of ownership and control. The structural deficiencies of the FCC have made localism a moot point. Commercial broadcasting was built on a legal basis of localism, yet programming ultimately was determined by networks. The cultural shortfalls of the commercial radio and television networks were used to rationalize federal support for public broadcasting; paradoxically, the national system of public radio and television was built to redress the failures of the decentralized educational broadcasting system.

Despite the homage paid to "localism" in regulatory policy and decentralized operations, the bulk of public programming originates with networks and syndicators. Public radio managers are primarily concerned with the local image rather than local programming: Thomas and Clifford find that "over 86 percent of 'local' programming consists of announcers-plus-recordings, with the recordings themselves constituting a 'nonlocal' program source. Local content/local production programming (i.e., locally originated programming that is *not* announcer-plus-recording) constitutes less than eight percent of the average station's schedule."[110] Due in part to the gradual reduction in federal money, public radio stations are concerned primarily with attracting consistent, faithful audiences as a stable funding base. The result, according to Thomas Looker, is that "they will therefore pressure NPR for programs which their audiences *are used* to, with which they are *familiar*, and which fulfill clearly perceived needs—such as hard news, weather and traffic."[111] Network programming reduces diversity, yet stations devote an ever-increasing part of their broadcast time to programs offered by NPR and other syndicators. Because this programming attracts the upscale demographics beloved by station managers, syndicated programming increasingly squeezes out local production.

The efficiencies of network programming and regional collaboration in operations pose a fundamental challenge to public radio's mission. The stations located in large markets, who also are the major programming producers, command the most resources and enjoy the most power in the system. Consequently, these stations seek to expand their operations, while local broadcasters become increasingly marginalized. Localism may have served as a subterfuge to mask corporate consolidation and control of both commercial and public broadcasting, yet it remains central to configurations of an open and participatory public sphere. As Michael Hunstberger, the manager of Olympia, Washington's KAOS, has stated:

From a pure management perspective, consolidation makes sense. It's the MBA's answer: merge management, consolidate operations, close outlets, eliminate staff, make big profits. It's ruthlessly efficient—and inhuman. . . . As the private sector has shown over the past 15 years, consolidation serves the interests of those who already have the power and influence.[112]

To reduce costs, many public broadcasters believe, the system must follow in the footsteps of its increasingly automated commercial counterparts. While enhancing operational efficiency, these actions also signal the abandonment of any "mission" other than the straightforward pursuit of profit.

The federalist model in public radio lasted only fifteen years, from 1970 to 1985. The agreement to channel CSGs to stations put the stations in control of the system. While ostensibly meant to lead to greater pluralism, this arrangement has in fact resulted in regional operations maximizing economies of scale. The federalist conundrum has been resolved: public radio is now headed toward a feudal system of interlocking ties between regional entities, in which "kings" are acclaimed by followers on the basis of their ability to wage war against lesser dominions. NPR's sovereignty has diminished; it now shares authority with a number of regional powers. Like the Catholic Church in the Middle Ages, the CPB remains an overarching, if often ineffectual, authority. Rather than on holy writ, its mandate is based on the heated subjectivity of politics and the cold objectivity of dollars and demographics.

While listenership figures increasingly define the value of public broadcasting, this drift toward numbers dates to the beginning of the public radio system. The stage was set when the CPB used strictly quantitative terms to established funding criteria, and it was reinforced by such reforms as the 1978 Public Telecommunications Act, which did little to redress the marginalization of the public in public radio. Instead, reform was targeted to meet the demands of pressure groups within the public radio system, and federal allocations were quantitatively based on nonfederal financial support. Since this support was crucial to gaining federal subsidies, stations became more preoccupied with building consistent audiences rather than with serving diverse publics. Organizations like the Station Resource Group and American Public Radio divided station against station and increased conflicts within the public radio system. Their ceaseless efforts to increase their stature within the system eventually forced NPR to unbundle its programming and sanction the marketplace model in public radio. The result has been a bias against innovation, local involvement, and service to minorities—all of which are central tenets of public broadcasting's mission.

NOTES

1. L. Friedland, "Public Television as Public Sphere: The Case of the Wisconsin Collaborative Project," *Journal of Broadcasting and Electronic Media* 39 (2), Spring 1995, p. 156.

2. See W. Powell and R. Friedkin, "Political and Organizational Influences on Public Television Programming," in *Mass Communication Review Yearbook 1983*, E. Wartella and D. Whitney, eds. (Beverly Hills, CA: Sage, 1983).

3. D. Petrozello, "Public Radio's Worst Fear, 'Zero Funding Means Death,'" *Broadcasting and Cable*, March 6, 1995, p. 50.

4. S. Behrens, "Consultant Field Is Worth Millions to the Public," *Current*, March 20, 1995, p. 3. This claim was underscored by a 1989 Texas A&M study of sixty-six public radio stations. The study found that contributions from individuals dropped an average of 14 percent when federal funding was increased, but it concluded that these levels were unlikely to rise if federal aid dropped (ibid.).

5. M. Lashley, *Public Television: Panacea, Pork Barrel or Public Trust?* (Westport, CT: Greenwood Press, 1992), p. 69.

6. "What They Said on Capitol Hill," *Current*, December 8, 1987, p. 13.

7. J. Ledbetter, *Made Possible by . . . The Death of Public Broadcasting in the United States* (New York: Verso, 1997), p. 4.

8. Percentage changes calculated from Consumer Price Index.

9. G. Crotts, and W. Rowland, Jr., "The Prospects for Public Broadcasting," in *Telecommunications in the U.S.: Trends and Policies*, L. Lewin, ed. (Dedham, MA: Artech House, 1981), p. 208.

10. L. Frischknecht, *The Policy for Public Radio Station Assistance of the Corporation for Public Broadcasting: 1969–1978* (Washington, DC: CPB, 1978, pp. 15, 17.

11. P. Fornatele and J. Mills, *Radio in the Television Age* (Woodstock, NY: Overlook Press, 1980), p. 178.

12. Frischknecht, *The Policy for Public Radio Station Assistance*, p. 14.

13. J. Haney, *A History of the Merger of National Public Radio and the Association of Public Radio Stations*, unpublished dissertation, Iowa City, University of Iowa, 1981, pp. 56–57.

14. Frischknecht, *The Policy for Public Radio Station Assistance*, p. 21.

15. L. Josephson, "Why Radio?" *Public Telecommunications Review*, March/April 1979, p. 10.

16. See G. Gibson, *Public Broadcasting: The Role of the Federal Government, 1912–1976* (New York: Praeger, 1977).

17. Cited in J. Witherspoon and J. Kovitz, *The History of Public Broadcasting* (Washington, DC: Current 1987), pp. 43–44.

18. S. Harrison, "Prime Time Pablum: How Politics and Corporate Influence Keep Public TV Harmless," *The Washington Monthly*, January 1986, pp. 34, 37.

19. R. McKay, "Financing Public Broadcasting: Problem or Symptom?" *Public Telecommunications Review*, March/April 1976, p. 31.

20. Aside from battles over funding authorizations on the national level, Congress has occasionally interceded at the local level. In July 1988, Cleveland's WCPN-FM dumped its Sunday schedule of ethnic programming in favor of extending the station's weekday format of jazz and public affairs programming. Shooshan and Arnheim state that "before making her decision [the general manager] met with the station board and concluded that the ethnic programming was not helping WCPN to 'build' its audience. According to the station, their audience of 50,000 listeners on weekdays dropped to 5800 on Sundays" (H. Shooshan and L. Arnheim, *Public Broadcasting* [Washington, DC: The Benton Foundation, 1989], p. 22). The ethnic producers filed suit against the station, and the matter became a political football in a Senate race between incumbent Howard Metzenbaum and his Republican challenger, Cleveland mayor George Voinovich. Metzenbaum held up passage of the 1988 bill reauthorizing funding for public broadcasting after WCPN's board refused to reinstate the ethnic broadcasters, withdrawing his resistance only after requiring the CPB to allocate more funds for production of non–English language programs, as part of the Public Telecommunications Act of 1988. In June 1989, the station agreed to recarry nine of twelve hours of foreign-language programming, while retaining *Weekend All Things Considered*. In exchange, WCPN was assured that it would receive a total of $185,000 in foundation or corporate support drummed up by the Greater Cleveland Roundtable, a group of area business leaders (J. Robertiello, "WCPN Settles Ethnic Program Dispute," *Current*, June 21, 1989, p. 19).

21. McKay, "Financing Public Broadcasting: Problem or Symptom?" p. 32.

22. W. Rowland, Jr., "The Struggle for Self-Determination: Public Broadcasting, Policy Problems and Reform," in *Telecommunications Policy Handbook*, J. Schement, F. Gutierrez, and M. Sirbu, Jr. eds. (New York: Praeger, 1982), p. 79; W. Rowland, Jr., "The Federal Regulatory and Policymaking Process," *Journal of Communication* 30 (3), Summer 1980, p. 146.

23. S. Behrens, "In Form and Amount of Aid, States Vary All over the Map," *Current*, March 18, 1981, p. 1.

24. Lashley, *Public Television*, p. 37; also see Corporation for Public Broadcasting, *An Overview of Community Service Grants for Public Broadcasting* (Washington, D.C: CPB, 1980).

25. J. Walker, "Radio CSGs to Change," *Current*, July 14, 1980, pp. 1, 4.

26. "Carter Clips CPB '83 Request," *Current*, April 14, 1980, p. 1.

27. S. Behrens, "What Gives in '83," *Current*, June 25, 1982, p. 1.

28. Lashley, *Public Television*, p. 81; J. Day, *The Vanishing Vision: The Inside Story of Public Television* (Berkeley: University of California Press, 1995), p. 287.

29. "Final Clearance for Ad Project," *Public Broadcasting Report*, March 26, 1982, p. 3.

30. R. Engelman, *Public Radio and Television in America: A Political History* (Thousand Oaks, CA: Sage, 1996), p. 191; W. Park, "What Would It Cost PTV to Go Commercial?" *Current*, October 26, 1981, p. 5.

31. K. Bedford, "Congress Adds New RTL Line to '96 Funding," *Current*, October 18, 1993, p. 9.

32. "NPR Endorses New Formula for '83 CSG's," *Current*, March 30, 1982, p. 8; Witherspoon and Kovitz, *The History of Public Broadcasting*, p. 47.

33. R. Barbieri, "Some Public Broadcasters in a 'Whale of Hurt,' " *Current*, June 10, 1986, pp. 1, 4–6; J. Mastroberardino, "California Cuts Hit Some Stations Harder," *Current*, May 30, 1984, p. 1.

34. The founding members of the Station Resource Group included KUSC (Los Angeles), WGUC (Cincinnati), WGBH (Boston), KLON (Long Beach), WEBR (Buffalo), KERA (Dallas), WAMU (Washington), KNPR (Las Vegas), WBEZ (Chicago), WBGO (Newark), KUOW (Seattle), KUER (Salt Lake City), KCFR (Denver), WUWM (Milwaukee), and KSJN (Minneapolis/St. Paul).

35. C. Cowan, "CPB to Allocate Supplemental," *Current*, September 11, 1984, p. 1.

36. A. Kossof, "Public Radio—Americans Want More," in *Radio: The Forgotten Medium*, E. Pease and E. Dennis, eds. (New Brunswick, N.J: Transaction Press, 1995), p. 176.

37. M. Collins, *National Public Radio: The Cast of Characters* (Washington, DC: Seven Locks Press, 1993), p. 55.

38. B. Gladstone, "APRA: Willing to Exist in a Market," *Current*, April 30, 1982, p. 5.

39. R. Kramer, "Kramer Takes Issue with NPRA," *Current*, August 20, 1982, p. 6. Without the knowledge of NPR's board of directors, NPR chairman Maurice Mitchell sent copies of the Kramer letter to each board member of the five APR founding stations, bypassing their station managers. Mitchell resigned in the ensuing controversy, although some NPR board members called for Mankiewicz's removal. After resigning, Mitchell told *Current*, "Parts of NPR are held hostage by power plays. The time has come when the big stations resent the Washington operation because money is being diverted from them. They will tell you that NPR has no business being so big in Washington. The problem is—for the ordinary guy in Sioux City, NPR is priceless" (B. Gladstone, "Aftermath: We Shot the Wrong Man," *Current*, August 20, 1982, p. 6).

40. F. Werden, "Public Radio Bows to Market Imperatives in PGC Contacts," *Current*, June 11, 1985, p. 6. APR could dictate station scheduling and promotion, since it did not represent member stations.

41. J. Yore, "Public Radio Upbeat for Annual Meetings," *Current*, April 8, 1986, p. 3.

42. "What They Said on Capitol Hill," p. 13.

43. C. Cowan, "International Newspaper Finds Its Voice," *Current*, October 9, 1984, p. 4.

44. J. Conciatore, "PRI Exec Cites 'Inexcusable Waste' in 'World,' " *Current*,

September 22, 1997, p. 1; J. Conciatore, "Church Puts Monitor Radio Up for Sale," *Current*, April 28, 1997, p. 1; I. Peterson, "Christian Science Radio Service Is Signing Off," *New York Times*, June 28, 1997, p. 6.

45. A. Adelson, "Talking Stage," *New York Times*, November 24, 1997, p. C11.

46. Engelman, *Public Radio and Television in America*, pp. 126–127.

47. Day, *The Vanishing Vision*, p. 259.

48. B. Gladstone, "Wirth Bill Keeps CPB As Is; Station Bill Would Dump It," *Current*, April 13, 1981, p. 4.

49. "NPR Funding Is Annual Meeting's Bottom Line," *Broadcasting*, May 20, 1985, p. 97.

50. F. Werden, "Business Plan Is Approved by NPR Members," *Current*, May 28, 1985, p. 6.

51. D. McDougal, "Public Radio Mainstays Survive Latest Crisis," *Los Angeles Times*, May 25, 1985, pp. 1, 7.

52. J. Yore, "A New Era for Public Radio," *Current*, December 3, 1985, p. 1.

53. J. Yore, "Public Radio Looks to the Future." *Current*, April 22, 1986, p. 1.

54. F. Werden, "Station Resource Group Recommends Revisions of NPR Business Plan," *Current*, April 30, 1985, p. 1; "Federal $$$ to Stations—Tithe to NPR," *Current*, February 13, 1985, p. 3.

55. J. Yore, "NPR May Violate Trust Laws," *Current*, April 22, 1986, p. 1.

56. A. Glick, "To Bundle Or Not to Bundle," *Current*, April 21, 1987, p. 16.

57. J. Yore, "NPR Program Pricing Proposal Receives Mild Response," *Current*, September 8, 1987, p. 1.

58. "Funding, Unbundling Top Public Radio Conference," *Broadcasting*, May 4, 1987, p. 38.

59. A. Glick, "NPR and Unbundling: A Network Grapples with New Market Realities," *Current*, December 22, 1987, p. 11.

60. "Public Radio Celebrates, Questions Growth," *Broadcasting*, April 16, 1990, p. 66.

61. J. Wilner, "Radio Restive over Dues on Eve of PRC," *Current*, April 27, 1992, p. 24.

62. See "NPR Passes the Buck," *Broadcasting*, February 8, 1988, p. 54; "Public Radio: New Audience, Old Problems," *Broadcasting*, May 13, 1991, p. 53.

63. J. Conciatore, "NPR Eyes Changes in Dues Formula, Memberships," *Current*, March 3, 1997, p. 8.

64. J. Conciatore, "Dollar-Based Voting Plan Eyed for NPR," *Current*, February 17, 1997, pp. 1, 11.

65. See Corporation for Public Broadcasting, *From Wasteland to Oasis: A Quarter Century of Sterling Programming* (Washington, DC: CPB, 1992); Engelman, *Public Radio and Television in America*, p. 121.

66. J. Robertiello, "Congress Indicates Upper Limit for CPB Spending," *Current*, July 22, 1991, p. 13.

67. J. Wilner, "Radio Factions Seek Common Hill Strategy," *Current*, November 16, 1992, p. 13.

68. The Areapop index is derived by multiplying a station's average-quarter-hour rating by one hundred and dividing the answer by the coverage area's population. To receive CPB funding, the listening index would have to be greater than 12 percent for large market stations, and 15 percent for stations serving

population areas of less than three million. Both index levels would rise 3 percent in fiscal years 1999 and 2000. To meet the fundraising criteria, station revenues from listeners, businesses and foundations would have to equal 18 cents per capita for larger markets and 20 cents per capita for those markets with less than three million residents (K. Bedford, "Proposed Radio Grant Criteria Previewed for CPB Board," *Current*, December 18, 1995, p. 3; J. Conciatore, "The Amazing Shrinking Dis List," *Current*, March 16, 1998, p. 25; K. Bedford, "CPB Grant Policy Review to Consider Rural Stations' Plight," *Current*, May 25, 1998, p. A-5).

69. R. Freed, "KBOO Made the Difference? 'It *Is* the Difference,' " *Current*, March 16, 1998, p. 12.

70. J. Conciatore, "A Few at NFCB Must Scramble to Meet New Grant Criteria," *Current*, February 26, 1996, p. 3.

71. "CPB Board Sets Audience Criteria for Radio Grants," *Current*, January 29, 1996, p. 4.

72. J. Conciatore, "The Amazing Shrinking Dis List," pp. 1, 13.

73. J. Conciatore, "Who Will Get CPB's Shrinking Radio Dollars?" *Current*, July 3, 1995, p. 1; "Howe Contends That Future Fund Plan Violates the Law," *Current*, October 23, 1995, p. 1; "How the CPB Future Fund Could Help Radio Sell Underwriting," *Current*, November 6, 1995, p. 30.

74. "CPB Future Fund Backs Its First Joint Projects in Radio," *Current*, May 13, 1996, p. 12.

75. E. Rathbun, "Public Broadcasters Seek Trust Fund," *Broadcasting and Cable*, May 8, 1995, pp. 78–79; "Conferees Okay Smaller Cuts for '96–97," *Current*, May 15, 1995, p. 8; S. Behrens, "Vacant Spectrum: A Divorce Settlement with 'If's,' " *Current*, March 11, 1996, p. 8.

76. D. Mullally, "There Are Other Ways to Capitalize a Trust Fund," *Current*, April 8, 1996, p. 12; S. Behrens, "Fields Seeks Support for His Bill—Or He'll Give Away Vacant Channels," *Current*, April 8, 1996, p. 14.

77. S. Behrens, "Fields Proposes $1 Billion Trust Fund," *Current*, March 11, 1996, p. 8; "Pressler Bill Also Favors Panel to Plan Trust Fund," *Current*, May 13, 1996, p. 1; S. Behrens, "Trust Fund Bill Motionless in Last Rush of Congress," *Current*, September 2, 1996, p. 11.

78. S. Behrens, "Key Chairman Eyes Spectrum Fee to Aid Pubcasting," *Current*, December 16, 1996, p. 1; S. Behrens, "Spectrum Fees Central to Tauzin's Purist Vision," *Current*, June 2, 1997, p. 1.

79. R. Horwitz, *The Irony of Regulatory Reform: The Deregulation of American Telecommunications* (New York: Oxford University Press, 1989), p. 280.

80. R. Kramer, "Lucky to Get Reserved Spectrum, We May Now Have to Work to Keep It," *Current*, October 16, 1997, pp. 25, 26.

81. J. Conciatore, "$10 million + Station Sale Raises Fears," *Current*, June 23, 1997, pp. 1, 19; J. Conciatore, "Lewis Tries to Save WDCU, But College Is Selling It," *Current*, July 7, 1997, p. 3; J. Conciatore, "WDCU Broker Is Trying Again 'to Pry Something Loose,' " *Current*, August 4, 1997, p. 7; J. Conciatore, "C-SPAN Steps In as Buyer of WDCU in Washington," *Current*, August 25, 1997, p. 1.

82. M. Fuerst, "What Could Make Public Radio Alter Its Course?" *Current*, February 14, 1994, p. 17.

83. T. Thomas and T. Clifford, *The Public Radio Program Marketplace* (Washington, DC: CPB, 1985), p. 21.

84. T. Warnock, "Public Radio: Taking Off at Last?" *Public Telecommunications Review*, January/February 1976, p. 30.

85. J. Robertiello, "Full Service Stations Not Needed, Study Finds," *Current*, August 2, 1989, pp. 1, 22; J. Robertiello, "Task Force See $62 Million Cost," *Current*, November 6, 1989, p. 3; D. Giovannoni, "Fishing Where the Fish Are," *Current*, November 27, 1989, pp. 4, 6.

86. K. Bedford, "We Paddled against Increasingly Troubled Waters," *Current*, December 14, 1992, p. 8; M. Fuerst and S. Behrens, "On Scale of Fundraising Effectiveness, Most Pub Radio Stations Way Too Small," *Current*, May 25, 1998, pp. B-11, B-12; J. Conciatore, "Regionalizing Underway As Alaska Cuts Aid to Stations," *Current*, May 29, 1995, p. 7.

87. R. Schatz, "Public Radio Being Pressed to Turn Its Success into Independence," *New York Times*, March 25, 1996, p. C8; S. Behrens, "Shifting to 'Virtual Station,' WSKG Flees the Death Spiral," *Current*, June 2, 1997, pp. 19, 20.

88. S. Behrens, "Great Divide," *Current*, May 27, 1991, p. 10.

89. Ibid.

90. A. Platt, "Empire of the Airwaves," *Twin Cities Reader*, May 24, 1989, p. 9.

91. B. Ortega, "A Public-Radio Maverick Generates Lots of Static," *Wall Street Journal*, March 30, 1998, pp. B-1, B-10.

92. P. Francisco, "The Life and Times of MPR," *Minnesota Monthly*, January 1987, p. 50.

93. Platt, "Empire of the Airwaves," p. 8.

94. S. Singer, "MPR Move into Idaho Draws Fire," *Current*, October 16, 1989, p. 17.

95. J. Wilner, "Minnesota Public Radio Emerges as a Regional News Superpower," *Current*, May 3, 1993, p. 18.

96. Twentieth Century Fund Task Force on Public Television, *Quality Time? The Report of the Twentieth Century Fund Task Force on Public Television* (New York: Twentieth Century Fund Press), 1993, p. 129.

97. D. Giovannoni, "What Will Help the Stations That Are Put at Risk?" *Current*, September 11, 1985, p. 38.

98. J. Robertiello, "Chicago Licensee Sued by 'Friends,' " *Current*, July 5, 1989, p. 3; J. Conciatore, "Syndicated Music Services Multiply in Public Radio," *Current*, September 25, 1995, p. 18.

99. D. Giovannoni, "Coming Soon: Do-It-Yourself 'Sharenets' Based on Appeal," *Current*, November 15, 1993, p. 21; J. Conciatore, "WETA and Minnesota to Offer Classical 24 Hour Feeds," *Current*, July 3, 1995, p. 12.

100. S. Behrens, "Uproars over Exec Salaries Blow Up, Then Blow Over," *Current*, April 22, 1996, p. 8; S. Behrens, "State Inquiry Finds No Wrongdoing in MPR's Business," *Current*, February 2, 1998, p. 3; R. Abelson, "Charities Use For-Profit Units to Avoid Disclosing Finances," *New York Times*, February 9, 1998, p. A12.

101. S. Behrens, "Operating Woes, State Inquiry Beset Kling," *Current*, May 27, 1996, p. 12; R. Abelson "Charities Use For-Profit Units to Avoid Disclosing Finances," pp. A1, A12.

102. J. Miller, "Public Radio Outlet in Minnesota Reaps $120 Million in Sale of Direct Marketer," *Wall Street Journal*, March 24, 1998, p. B-9.

103. S. Coolidge, "Public Radio Stations Take Cut of CD Sales," *Christian Science Monitor*, November 30, 1993, p. 8; S. Behrens, "MusicSource Established as a Public Service That Pays, Too," *Current*, March 28, 1994, p. 11; Ledbetter, *Made Possible By . . .* , p. 137; J. Conciatore, "Booksellers Resent Pub Radio Ventures in Their Market," *Current*, July 22, 1996, p. 6.

104. Ledbetter, *Made Possible by . . .* , p. 138.

105. M. Fuerst, "New Ventures? Let's Invest to Improve What We Do Well," *Current*, December 4, 1995, p. 17.

106. Ibid.

107. Thomas and Clifford, *The Public Radio Program Marketplace*, pp. 45, 47.

108. T. McCain and G. Lowe, "Localism in Western European Broadcasting: Untangling the Wireless," *Journal of Communication* 40 (1), Winter 1990, p. 90.

109. Horwitz, *The Irony of Regulatory Reform*, p. 194.

110. Thomas and Clifford, *The Public Radio Program Marketplace*, p. 37.

111. T. Looker, *The Sound and the Story: NPR and the Art of Radio* (New York: Houghton Mifflin, 1995), p. 137.

112. "What 'Consolidation' Should Mean, and How the Future Fund Could Help," *Current*, November 20, 1995, p. 16.

4

The Surrogate Public: Boards, Funders, and Producers

The total service should be trustworthy, enhance intellectual development, expand knowledge, deepen aural esthetic enjoyment, increase the
pleasure of living in a pluralistic society and result in a service to listeners
which makes them more responsive, informed human beings and intelli-
gent responsible citizens of their communities and the world.
—William Siemering, "National Public Radio Purposes," p. 2

Characterizing a broadcasting system as "public" implies public ownership and control, yet the Corporation for Public Broadcasting, Public
Broadcasting Service, and National Public Radio are private nonprofit
organizations. Many CPB-funded radio stations also are licensed to private groups and institutions. The fact that private nonprofit organizations control substantial parts of the system represents a very important
contradiction. A public medium should be collectively owned and freely
accessible, and it should provide services to all members of the public.
Private individuals and groups—even if they measure success in terms
of cultural, rather than economic, capital—simply cannot own a "public"
medium. One way in which public broadcasting has attempted to defuse
the issue of private ownership (and differentiate itself from its commercial counterparts) is through the use of volunteers at the local level. In
this regard, public broadcasting invokes the traditions of voluntarism,
self-sufficiency, and individualism in American political and cultural life
that Alexis de Tocqueville found in the early 19th century.

Voluntarism has been a primary means of achieving social welfare throughout American history, and private nonprofit organizations serve to mediate between the state and the individual. The legitimacy of these organizations is based on their altruistic origins and ostensible freedom from state coercion. In a late 1980s study, 72 percent of respondents believed that "private charities are generally more effective than government programs."[1] However, the fact that these organizations serve as state surrogates in many areas raises a host of complications. First, the boundaries of the state are blurred, as private organizations provide public goods and services. Second, private organizations often lack stringent accountability mechanisms for maintaining the standards of these goods and services. Third, the need to maintain funding and respond to government demands for oversight has led these organizations to become increasingly professionalized. As these organizations become more businesslike, their professionalization distances them from their communities. The public is relegated to the status of consumers, whose defining characteristic is that "they are not invited directly into decision-making processes concerning production."[2]

Nonprofit cultural organizations present a special case. These firms, which serve cultural rather than physical needs, are funded under the classic model of arts patronage, which involves private support from individuals or groups. According to Nicholas Garnham, "such funding leads to direct ideological control, legitimated as the cultural extension of private property, namely personal taste."[3] Private elites, or narrow cliques whose cultural standing is based on wealth, kinship, and carefully monitored membership, historically have controlled cultural organizations in the United States. This control has given them a voice far out of proportion to their numbers in setting the cultural agenda on the local and national levels. The organizational structure of public radio ensures that the public must continue to adhere to standards of taste instituted by elites and articulated by nonprofit concerns. Public broadcasters may bewail their unstable funding, but these fluctuations give them a convenient excuse to avoid issues of public access and accountability. While the system has begun to shift its emphasis from upholding the traditional standards of "high" culture to serving cultural "authenticity," as a result of demands from internal and external pressure groups (as well as a need to target differentiated audiences for donations and marketing purposes), it remains tied to paternalistic notions of cultural uplift according to which the audience must be "reformed, educated, informed as well as entertained."[4]

This chapter examines how National Public Radio and its affiliate stations have incorporated the roles of public representatives (or rather, private surrogates for the public) into their operations, and how the institutionalization of these surrogates (including boards, managers, funders, and producers) have influenced their activities. I argue that these surrogates have been ineffective in articulating public concerns; instead, they have manipulated the system, or vice versa, to suit private agendas. The chapter concludes with a discussion of how public broadcasting's mission is internalized by managers and production personnel, and how trends toward professionalization have affected public participation and accountability in the public radio system. As these trends grow steadily, the professionals themselves increasingly serve the funders, not the users, of the system. Public participation in public broadcasting is limited by the need to maintain institutional stability, occupational continuity, and demographic certainty in the face of an uncertain environment. In the process, the public continues to be eclipsed.

THE NONPROFIT TRADITION IN AMERICAN LIFE

Nonprofit cultural organizations in the United States emerged in the 18th century under the leadership of social elites. The patrons of these organizations hired professional curators to define the artistic canon and frame standards for consumer behavior. These patrons also set norms that defined "authentic" aesthetic experience in ways that would limit it to elites.[5] While appealing to classical liberalism's admiration for individual initiative and wariness of government, the privately endowed foundations built by industrialists like Andrew Carnegie and John D. Rockefeller in the 19th century also were intended to contain potential disruptions from the new "mass" society, particularly conflicts between the working class and industrial capitalism. Noblesse oblige combined with faith in social science in the early 20th century to foster technocratic solutions to social problems, resulting in the entrenchment of rule by "experts." Hence, the role of nonprofit organizations as service and cultural providers primarily is based in political circumstances rather than the market's failure.[6]

The size, number, and diversity of foundations and nonprofit organizations grew dramatically following World War II. The Ford Foundation, established in 1936, towered over all others, with assets "about four times as great as those of Rockefeller and twelve times those of Carnegie."[7] The Ford Foundation, in conjunction with the federal government, worked with other private sources and businesses in the areas of education, agriculture, the arts, and population research in the 1950s and '60s. The overall pattern was one in which the seemingly altruistic introduction of large-scale technology to solve educational and social problems had the actual effect of promulgating capitalist ideology, neutralizing economic and political opposition, and expanding foreign markets.[8] The Ford Foundation's domestic agenda sought to rationalize the existing social system and elite leadership via mechanisms "through which grievances could be aired, brought into the mainstream, and eventually rectified—within the framework of existing society."[9]

Local nonprofit organizations received little federal money until spending on social welfare programs rose significantly in the late 1960s. The Ford Foundation's successful efforts at social engineering, combined with the Johnson administration's activism, were major catalysts for the funneling of federal dollars into private organizations. Federal expenditures in social and cultural areas nearly tripled between 1965 and 1970, from $812 million to $2.2 billion, and much of this money went to private nonprofits.[10] The formal, hierarchical nonprofit model was federally sanctioned with the creation of the National Endowment for the Arts in 1965, and it added an aura of legitimacy to new agencies and services. Consequently, organizations that deviated from the form tended to be small and peripheral. Although the Pacifica stations' policies on public access programming shaped the activities of community stations for years to come, these policies were defined by a private, centralized board that held the station licenses. William Barlow asserts that Pacifica founder Lew Hill "believed in community service, support and involvement through volunteer associations, but not community control—which he felt was unworkable because there would be too many factions in competition with each other."[11]

Board members, as trustees of the public, are collectively the ultimate authority for nonprofit organizations in the United States. They affirm the organization's nonprofit status, provide funding oversight, and monitor community needs.[12] These individuals legitimate the organization, and the organization in turn legitimates their social status. In addition to redeeming their wealth, nonprofit cultural organizations create prestige for their benefactors and participants by defining and legitimating specific cultural artifacts and activities. Similarly, radio and television broadcasting of "high culture" provides a higher public profile and prestige for licensing institutions. Philanthropic boards provide a site for interaction and networking. Exclusive fundraising events provide ritualistic occasions for emphasizing elite solidarity, and personal donations affirm success and social status. Although Robert Bellah and others argue that America lacks the Old World's aristocratic traditions and sharply defined class distinctions, philanthropy has served an important function for staking out the cultural and organizational world of elites, who use philanthropy to justify their wealth and legitimate their position in society. As Max Weber observed, "Good fortune thus wants to be 'legitimate' fortune."[13]

Conversely, board members may meddle overtly in organizational services and missions, although their sole qualification for participation consists of their privileged social status. In addition, the highly status-laden nature of philanthropy may result in superficial and frivolous commitment, in which the most important aspect of philanthropy becomes being seen at fundraisers. According to Francie Ostrower,

Somewhat cynically, one might say that their philanthropy is conducted in such a way that elites can enjoy the sense that they are making a contribution to society without actually having to interact with members of that society outside their class. . . . Philanthropy, in short, allows elites to enjoy the sense that they are making a contribution to society, while defining social benefit on their own terms.[14]

Public broadcasting has relatively low prestige compared to other arts endeavors, since it is easily accessed. Although private philanthropy has therefore been a secondary means of financial support throughout public radio's history, NPR's organization is based on the nonprofit model. It initially established a fourteen-member board of directors whose structure paralleled that of the Public Broadcasting Service: nine from stations, one each from CPB and NPR, two from the general public, and the chief executive officer. Shortly thereafter, the board was changed to accommodate nine managers, six public members, and the CEO. Following the 1977 merger of APRS and NPR, the board consisted of twenty-five members—twelve members of the public, twelve station managers, and NPR's president. When this size proved unwieldy, the board was reduced to seventeen: eight public members, eight station managers, and the CEO. In January 1983, an NPR task force recommended that the board be expanded to twenty-one members and the number of station managers on it to twelve.[15] This proposal was rejected, but the board was reshuffled yet again in 1989, to six public members, ten station representatives, and the CEO. In a move to make the board more democratic, NPR member stations voted in 1992 for the right to remove national board members by a two-thirds vote.[16] The shifting structure of NPR's governing board reflects chronic conflicts between station managers, who wanted funds to improve existing service, and public members, who pressed for greater extension of service. However, managers have had the upper hand since NPR's inception. They have a direct, professional interest in the system and generally attend meetings more frequently. Yet the shift of weight toward managers has lessened, rather than increased, democracy in NPR's governance. Station managers serve their own interests as well as those of the national organization; in 1981, James Haney claimed that

the users of the system, the managers, are trying to guide the system. Objectivity is difficult to achieve when the decisions you are making will have an impact on your own station. . . . Given the desire of the system to be a member station organization, public radio is forced to live with a system of governance which inherently promotes greed and self-serving actions.[17]

BOARDS AND AUDIENCES

In interviews with public broadcasting station managers, William Hoynes has found that the issue of direct public involvement in operations and programming is rarely, if ever, discussed.[18] Instead, public advisory boards serve as surrogates for local audiences in station decision making. All CPB-funded radio and television stations are required to maintain community advisory boards, whose members are drawn from the ranks of the local service area. These boards serve as a "public check in return for public monies"; they evaluate the station's activities and serve as outreach tools for governing boards and management. Federally funded agencies began using public advisory boards after passage of the Economic Opportunity Act of 1964, which mandated that antipoverty programs seek input from boards drawn from local populations. *The Hidden Medium* called for the establishment of citizens' councils on the national and local levels "to help formulate educational radio station policies, in the true spirit of 'public radio,'" but the role of advisory boards in public broadcasting was formalized only eleven years later.[19] The 1978 Public Telecommunications Act, whose provisions were in part a response to criticism from activist groups within and outside the system, required CPB-funded institutions to make a "good faith" effort to establish community advisory boards. Section 396 (k) (9) of the Act specified two functions for these boards: they were to review station programming goals, services, and policy decisions to determine if they were meeting the "specialized educational and cultural needs of the communities served by the station," and they were to make suggestions "as [they considered] appropriate."[20]

The 1978 act also mandated that stations open their board meetings to the public and allow greater public access to station records. However, critics argued that advisory boards and open meetings "are the very solutions both least necessary if local station management cares about local community service and least effective if it does not."[21] The Act stated that no individuals, organizations, or groups had automatic rights to representation on community advisory boards and suggested that stations had broad discretion in member selection (for instance, a statewide system was not obligated to select a board reflecting statewide needs and interests). Although members could be elected by the local population, Stevan Holmberg and H. Kent Baker have suggested that "the most prudent course would [involve] station management working with the respective governing board in the selection and with final formal appointment made by the governing board."[22] This process would prevent the public from having any say in the selection of its representatives. The 1978 act also stated that "in no case shall the board have any authority to exercise any control over the daily management or operations of the station." This proviso legitimated station control by governing boards and managers and rendered the community boards ineffectual. As with so many other attempts at system reform, the Act's qualifications meant that its purpose would never be realized.

Community advisory boards theoretically provide numerous benefits to organizations. They may contribute to decision making, link governing boards and managers to the local community, and provide a training ground for potential members of the governing board. Nevertheless, their use as public surrogates is highly problematic. First, their constituencies often are vaguely defined. Do boards represent the public to the organization, or do they represent the organization to the public? Station managers frequently appoint advisory board members: as a result, they rarely represent the composition of their communities. Instead, advisory board members tend to be powerful or affluent people selected for public relations and fundraising purposes, or for their ability to defuse external hostility. The closed nature of "old boy" networks usually results in a narrowly focused consensus on organizational issues and in unwillingness to change. Second, advisory boards have ambiguous roles and responsibilities. Do these boards initiate policies, or do they act as a sounding board for management proposals?[23] Because of other commitments, board members have limited time to devote to organizational matters. Since they depend on managers for much of their information, they cannot make independent decisions. Rather than playing a normative role in station policy, they may do little more than rubber-stamp management proposals. Advisory board recommendations are used more often if they promote the aims of managers; otherwise, managers may view them as little more than a "bureaucratic nuisance, an infringement on station management and governing board decisionmaking, and an unnecessary duplication of community input currently obtained through such groups as governing boards and community program advisory committees."[24] While creating a channel for public input into policy making, the very existence of community advisory boards circumscribes public participation by relegating the public to an ancillary, advisory role. Although pressures for public accountability led the CPB to require community advisory for tax-funded radio stations, these boards have been manipulated to serve the purposes of the organization rather than the public.

Advisory boards also may become increasingly insular and work against the very purposes that led to their creation. The first Carnegie Commission called for the formation of a national citizen's advisory council to suggest policies for public broadcasting, and the CPB created the Advisory Committee of National Organizations (ACNO) in June 1969 ostensibly to solicit public input on programming. In reality, ACNO was designed as a CPB-awareness project, a "lobby device for whipping up popular and legislative support at [CPB's] behest."[25] ACNO served as an umbrella for eighteen national organizations, including the American Bar Association, U.S. Jaycees, the NAACP, and the AFL-CIO. Although the CPB attempted to control ACNO to serve its own purposes, the group increasingly saw itself as a public advisory group for CPB. According to Steve Millard,

It was not a role CPB felt inclined to deny them, for two reasons: first, because it might have won more enemies than friends had it not created some "partnership" with the groups; and second, because ... CPB wanted a vocal advisory group—speaking on its behalf [during 1972 negotiations over congressional funding].[26]

In 1973, the AFL-CIO, the National Organization of Women, and NAACP abandoned ACNO over public broadcasting's reliance on imported programs, its poor salaries, and its lack of opportunities for minorities. Nevertheless, the group had grown to include forty-nine member organizations and had changed its name to the Advisory *Council* of National Organizations. ACNO adopted an increasingly hierarchical structure of committees and subcommittees and sought more members, many of whom were focused on their own priorities. Public broadcasters considered ACNO a source of "expert" advice, thus transforming the group into insiders whose power was tied directly to their participation in ACNO rather than their status as public representatives. The emphasis on "expertise" also meant that ACNO retained the same members year after year, which heightened its insularity and loosened its members' ties to their respective organizations as well as to the public. Rather than promoting diversity in employment and programming, the organization increasingly benefited narrow interests within CPB. The growing stridency of factions within ACNO, however, coupled with the CPB's awareness that it was failing to represent public needs and interests, led the CPB to disband the organization, in September 1977.

In addition to mobilizing public support for purposes of fighting external influences and gaining subsidies, appointments to advisory and governing boards are an effective way to recognize and maintain long-term ties with major donors. Board membership provides prestige in exchange for money; a marketing consultant once suggested that "an excellent board development exercise is to require that every member *personally* solicit a major gift from another board member each year. If some board members balk at this, put them on notice."[27]

National Public Radio inaugurated a major fundraising operation, targeting "big money," when it created the NPR Foundation in November 1992. The Foundation was chaired by former NPR board chairman Edward Elson, and its thirty charter members have included executives from W. R. Grace, the Shaklee Corporation, Northwest Airlines, Nike, Random House, Valvoline, and many banking interests. Each foundation trustee contributed $10,000 and was expected to use his or her extensive contacts to pry donations of at least $100,000 from foundations, corporations, and individuals. The foundation's target is seventy-five trustees; by late 1997, the Foundation had created an endowment of six million dollars.[28] In the early 1990s NPR also established a bipartisan committee of "honorary trustees" comprising officials in Congress and the executive branch, and the Development Exchange (a professional membership group with annual dues of six hundred to $2,500 a year) to push for greater private funding.[29] A development parallel to PBS's Major Gifts Acquisition Program, the Development Exchange sought the fundraising efficiency afforded by large donors. A spokesperson for the Exchange stated, "it's so much more efficient to raise $100,000 with contributions of $1,000 and $5,000 than to raise it $40 at a time." The importance of big private money on the local level is reflected in an informal survey of radio stations, which indicated that such major giving programs bring in about 4 percent of station's annual budgets, while some larger stations rake in as much as 10 percent.[30]

However, attracting large donations requires a substantial commitment of time from management and staff. According to one estimate, "managers can expect to spend 30 percent of their time on relations with donors, thanking them, hosting them at the station and asking for funds."[31] Development professionals may be hired to cultivate donors over many years, and at least one staffer may be devoted full time to their care and feeding. In addition, station activities may be planned to meet the needs of donors rather than audiences. NPR's Development Exchange suggests that stations invite potential donors to functions that reflect their interests (or, by implication, that they create these functions). This emphasis on development creates a cycle in which more development personnel mean more overhead costs, more costs mean more donations, more donations mean more development personnel. One analyst noted that overhead and development costs can devour 40 percent of total revenues from listeners.[32] In addition to skewing the station's mission away from public service, the devotion to private fundraising (which the CPB condones by making federal support contingent on non-federal financial support) increases the disparity between large stations and those that lack resources and development personnel. This disparity further heightens tensions within an already fractious system.

Audience financial support has become essential to public broadcasting, and it also provides credibility with other funding agencies. As Table

Table 4.1
Listener Income for CPB-Qualified Radio Stations, 1971–1990

	1971	1975	1980	1985	1990
Number of contributors	40,000	190,000	487,000	979,000	1,275,000
Avg. contribution per person	$24.33	$18.55	$24.84	$41.06	$51.37
Overall listener income (in millions of dollars)	.97	3.5	12.1	40.2	65.5

Source: Adapted from *Current*, September 11, 1995, p. 8.

4.1 illustrates, listener donations have risen dramatically over the course of public radio's history. Voluntary audience subscriptions to public broadcasting originated with the Pacifica Foundation in the late 1940s, and on-air pledge drives traditionally have been the mainstay of audience fundraising for public radio and television stations. As part of a systemwide effort at increasing efficiency, coordinated pledge drives became increasingly common in the 1990s. The On-Air Fundraising Partnership, created in 1992 with the help of CPB money, offers fundraising editions of *Morning Edition* and a production service for scripts and on-air promotions. One of the principal stations in the Partnership, Boston's WBUR, offers a "how-to" guide, for $750 to $1,500 per package. The Partnership held its first national pledge drive in October 1993, with 140 participating stations; by 1996, three-quarters of NPR affiliates used the service extensively.[33]

On-air pledge drives are a proven method for drawing new listeners and viewers, since they often are organized around special programming (particularly in public television). These drives also create a sense of community for volunteers as well as viewers and listeners, since they are geared toward attracting new patrons of similar socioeconomic standing—"viewers [and listeners] like you." Indeed, they are *the* most common form of public participation in public broadcasting. However, their incessant handwringing and evocations of guilt may alienate audiences as well as disrupt viewing and listening patterns; also, they are costly in both time and labor. Income from public radio listeners, adjusted for inflation, peaked in 1988 and has declined since.[34] In the late 1980s, consultant David Giovannoni proposed replacing radio pledge drives with twenty or thirty-second pledge spots run throughout a station's broadcast day as a standard programming element.[35] Although Giovannoni claimed that this method would effectively reach noncontributing listeners, the scheduling of regular fundraising "spots" throughout the day would further blur the boundary between commercial and public radio. More significantly, radio stations may modify programming practices solely for fundraising effectiveness. For example, WETA in Washington, D.C., tightened its playlist during pledge drives in the early 1980s, playing only selections that were "bright and not too long," and announcers were restricted to selections that had been prerecorded onto tape cartridges, in order to minimize choice.[36]

The result of this obsession with money means that on-air fundraising and formulaic music programs are the major or sole local productions of many public broadcasting stations. This lack of local programming origination also increases public broadcasting's identity as an outlet for national programming. While minimizing local production, public radio paradoxically seeks more and more money from local listeners.

THE MARRIAGE OF FUNDING AND CONTENT

In 1983, the Temporary Commission on Alternative Financing upheld the notion of diversified funding sources, on grounds that it "encourage[s] the provision of programming that serves many different purposes and audiences."[37] Former PBS president Lawrence Grossman took a more realistic view:

Every source of money is tainted. With federal funds we worry about becoming a governmental broadcasting arm. Corporate money means you stay away from controversy. Membership money means you cater to upper middle class viewers. The saving grace is that we have diversified sources.[38]

Foundation support of public radio has remained relatively small throughout the system's history, ranging from 2 to 4 percent annually. Throughout the 1950s and '60s, the Ford Foundation's support of noncommercial programming fell into the category of what Erik Barnouw terms "the safely splendid," or noncontentious programming with implications of cultural uplift.[39] This programming was to be much beloved by the corporations that were increasingly to finance public broadcasting in the 1970s.

When programming and sponsorship intermingle, conflicts of interest are inevitable. By the end of the 1980s, 85 percent of corporate and foundation support for NPR news programming was in the form of grants restricted to coverage of specific areas or issues.[40] NPR board member (and former CBS News president) Richard Salant worried that nearly one-third of NPR's news budget came from targeted commercial and foundation grants. To Salant and others, this meant funders would set the agenda for news coverage, rather than allow NPR reporters to use their own journalistic standards. During the 1988 presidential campaign, NPR received a million-dollar grant from the John D. and Catherine T.

MacArthur Foundation to cover national security issues. Salant argued that "[we] were going to do stories on national defense as a campaign issue regardless of whether it was an issue or not. And maybe it should have been, but, as it turned out, it wasn't." He urged NPR's board of directors to support a motion that grantors be required to give their money less restrictively; the motion was opposed by NPR president Bennet, who claimed that NPR first determined topics to be covered and then sought interested foundations, not vice versa. Bennet convinced the NPR board to table the motion, and Salant resigned from the board in protest.[41]

In addition to being subject specific, foundation support is often contingent on particular presentational approaches. When *Soundprint* prepared a series of programs on breast cancer, producers were unable to obtain funding from two groups working against the disease. One producer stated, "We weren't using their preferred spokespeople. We weren't being positive enough. You have to present things from their perspective. You have to compromise your journalistic integrity."[42] Even the most seemingly benign funders may attempt to interfere with coverage. In 1988, aided by a grant from UNICEF, *Weekend Edition Saturday* host Scott Simon and a crew filed several reports on relief efforts in Ethiopia. When Simon attempted to investigate rumors of a massacre in the country, UNICEF tried to dissuade him, on grounds that negative coverage would get relief workers evicted. Simon covered the story anyway, noting that "it was a very uncomfortable relationship with the funder—and those are some of the best people in the world."[43] In 1992, the Japan Foundation's Center for Global Partnership (which is funded by the Japanese government to further its business interests) awarded grants to NPR and American Public Radio for coverage of Japanese affairs. NPR received $55,000 for a series on economics, while APR requested $100,000 for *Marketplace* and another $100,000 for news and cultural programs about Japan. NPR returned the grant after it was informed that the CGP was a government-sponsored entity, but APR had no such ethical qualms.[44]

Unlike foundation support, corporate funding for public broadcasting tends to be reserved for continuing series and "showcase" vehicles rather than discretionary or development money.[45] Corporate support for public radio more than tripled between 1979 and 1991, growing at an even faster pace than audience funding (see Table 4.2). Although NPR has a long-standing policy of refusing to reveal the amount of money it receives from individual underwriters, the *New York Times* found that corporate underwriting for public radio grew about 69 percent from 1989 to 1994, to $76 million, while business support for public television rose only 15 percent.[46] Since its programming is skewed toward audiences from high socioeconomic levels, corporations view public broadcasting

Table 4.2
Public Radio Funding Sources, 1979 and 1995 (in percentages)

	1979	1995
Listeners	9	25
Businesses	5	17
Corporation for Public Broadcasting	24	16
Colleges and universities	31	13
State and local governments	14	6
Foundations	2	5
Other	15	18

Source: CPB

as a cost-effective way to reach upscale decision makers. In particular, corporations working in controversial areas seek to develop favorable publicity through acts of philanthropy.[47] David Rockefeller commented that support of public broadcasting "can provide a company with extensive publicity and advertising, a brighter public reputation, and an improved corporate image." Mobil's sponsorship of "high" art and nature programs on PBS has been frequently cited as an example of corporate support for public broadcasting as a means of public relations and damage control.[48]

The same holds true for NPR's relationship with corporations dealing in socially contentious products and services. A $100,000 grant from Waste Management, Inc., saved the weekend edition of *All Things Considered* in mid-1985, and the company's advertising director told the *New York Times* "that the company has been pleased by NPR's 'upscale' audience and that it has been congratulated for its support by chief executives and political figures."[49] One critic found that

NPR's on-air credit for Waste Management, Inc., which has given money specifically for environmental coverage, describes it as a company "providing comprehensive waste services world-wide." Greenpeace called it "one of the worst corporate criminals in the country." According to the environmental group, Waste Management, Inc., has been the most frequently fined corporation in EPA history.[50]

In 1996, NPR continued to accept underwriting support from Archer Daniels Midland (which also contributed six million dollars annually to PBS's *NewsHour*) despite its admission of price fixing in agricultural products. According to an NPR spokesperson, "We have an open access policy for accepting underwriting."[51] Underwriting policies were never clearly defined in the 1967 Public Broadcasting Act, and individual stations exhibited wide disparities in the procedures used to give on-air credit to program sponsors. Much of the growth in public radio's corporate support may be attributed to changes in enhanced underwriting policies since the early 1980s. These changes, triggered by reduced federal subsidies and trends toward deregulation, increasingly blurred the line between subsidies and advertising. In the early 1980s, some public radio stations followed NPR's example and experimented with selling "shares" to corporate underwriters, in which credits would rotate through the schedule rather than being assigned to specific shows. This policy was designed to distance underwriters from specific topics; however, normal rotation might place an underwriter credit after a story about that company's activities.

In 1983, the Temporary Commission on Alternative Financing suggested that "broadened guidelines for on-air credits . . . would provide additional revenue for public broadcasting."[52] Following the TCAF's recommendations, on April 4, 1984, the FCC unanimously approved enhanced underwriting for public broadcasting. The new policy allowed the broadcast of specific brand or trade names and product or service listings, locations, the use of logos or slogans that "identify but do not promote" sponsors, and "value-neutral" descriptions of product lines or services. No qualitative or comparative language was allowed. Prices could not be mentioned, and such inducements as "no payments 'til February" were banned. The FCC ruling also stated that public broadcasters were "generally prohibited" from engaging in fundraising activities that suspend or alter regular programming on behalf of any entity other than the station itself.[53]

The FCC guidelines allowed for considerable interpretation, since "promotion" is a nebulous concept and may include corporate "imaging" as well as hard sells. In 1989, the FCC sent a letter of caution to WGBH, whose credits for *Morning Pro Musica* cited a sponsor as "a leading provider" of credit and services. Yet the FCC cleared Cincinnati's WVXU the following year of charges that six of its funding credits were qualitative. Two of the credits referred to the longevity of businesses, while another described an advertising agency as "offering creative services." A health-food restaurant credit described its specialty as "fresh and original foods," while an art gallery billed itself as offering "timeless traditional truths in contemporary visual vocabulary." In 1986, the FCC allowed sponsors' telephone numbers to follow program acknowledgments, and in October 1991 NPR began running exclusive underwriting credits on its hourly newscasts. Stations that did not air complete newscasts were provided with advance schedules and credit copy for announcers to read on the air. While the credits were estimated to raise between $250,000 to $300,000, having the announcers read advertising copy blurred the distinction between news and credits.[54] In 1995, the NPR board rejected a $500,000 underwriting commitment from an unnamed liquor manufacturer out of concern for NPR's public image, yet it allowed Hennessy Cognac to underwrite a New Year's Eve jazz special. The board also relaxed NPR's traditional ban on slogans and calls to action in underwriting announcements, allowing stations to air slogans that have become company identifiers—such as "Fly the friendly skies" and "Just do it"—on grounds that these are not "calls to action."[55] Corporate jingles and toll-free numbers also are appearing with increasing regularity on NPR broadcasts. While NPR limits underwriting announcements to eight seconds, many of its member stations allow fifteen to thirty-second announcements. Susan Harmon, the vice president of KERA in Dallas, told the *New York Times* that "everyone knows we need to support our habit, and so we're experimenting. We want underwriters to feel good."[56]

At least in theory, a key difference between commercial and public broadcasters is that the latter are able to separate program content from marketing issues. Yet programs must be "sold" to underwriters or sponsoring groups *before* they are produced. Jay Madigan, the Vice President for Corporate Communications for the Chubb Group, has suggested that underwriters must be actively involved in program selections and price negotiations, adding that "in public TV underwriting, everything is negotiable."[57] Corporations tend to support only certain kinds of programs—those that support their ideologies, appeal to particular audiences, or help public relations—which leads to self-censorship on the part of producers. Although the producers interviewed by William Hoynes vehemently deny any overt meddling by corporate funders, such as the right to review the "final cut" of programs, they still are faced with a fundamental constraint: will their concept sell to the right underwriter? While producers and programmers are concerned primarily with program quality, station development personnel look for programs that make it easier to cultivate long-term subsidies from outside sources. Consequently, they stress long-running series rather than "one-off" programs, which may provide insufficient return on investment, and they dismiss locally produced programming, on the grounds that it draws small audiences.[58] This strategy dovetails neatly with the intentions of corporate underwriters, who seek nationwide audiences to maximize their reach. The Chubb Group's Madigan has recommended that underwriters avoid local productions in favor of systemwide programming, adding, "If you negotiate hard, you can find sole corporate underwriter opportunities for surprisingly little money."[59]

Their thirst for money and muddled sense of mission led public broadcasters to bend the rules for important (that is, large or consistent) underwriters, and the relatively small number of such underwriters gives these firms great leverage.[60] Corporate-sponsored programs may be offered to stations at relatively low prices, which gives stations a strong financial incentive to broadcast them, and at the same time it strengthens corporate control over programming content. Honoring corporate preferences for national over local programming also runs counter to public radio's avowed goals of localism and pluralism. Finally, underwriting clearly represents a public subsidization of private profits. An independent producer told the Senate in 1987, "Corporate underwriting is . . . really a form of subsidized advertising, because of course public funds pay for most of the costs."[61] The growth of "enhanced underwriting" has increased the system's reliance on transparently commercial appeals. Barring the creation of a trust fund that would ban such appeals, NPR appears to be headed away from the "virtual" advertising of enhanced underwriting to blatant commercialism.

THE PUSH FOR PROFESSIONALISM

Clashes between programming and development personnel are another major source of conflict in public broadcasting, and these conflicts are compounded by the differing missions and structures of public radio license holders. While a number of stations are controlled by nonprofit corporations, the majority are operated by colleges and universities. These stations present particular complexities. University licensure assured some stability for educational radio stations before the 1967 act, but these stations (particularly ten watt operations) stood relatively low in university hierarchies. Ties to the licensing institution were (and are) often vaguely delineated or highly bureaucratized; a 1984 CPB-sponsored study found one station with twelve levels of administration between the station manager and the board of regents.[62] The license may be held by a board of trustees or a board of regents, who may live outside the station's coverage area and provide little or no input to management. Responsibility often is delegated to the university president, who may directly interfere with station operations. A case in point involves WUSF, licensed to the University of South Florida in Tampa. In 1968 the station switched from educational to "free-form" rock programming, a type of programming unique in the Tampa area. By 1973, the station was airing more than seventy-five hours of free-form programming each week, with the balance of the schedule devoted to NPR feeds, classical music, and local news and public affairs programming. Perturbed by growing on-air student activism, the university president fired the station manager and established ground rules for future programming. News and public affairs programs were dropped in favor of a uniform schedule of classical music and jazz. Despite protests from students and other listeners, the president claimed that although the First

Amendment protected the student paper from interference, "the station employed university staff members, and they were bound to obey administrative directives. . . . He argued that all rights to station operations resided in the president's hands."[63] The station continued its emphasis on high-culture programming.

More commonly, stations may be riddled with internal political maneuvering over issues of programming subsidies, and public control. KUNM, licensed to the University of New Mexico, has been hobbled by conflicts between management and volunteers over personnel responsibilities and programming. Following the advice of an outside consultant, the station changed its format in 1987 from volunteer-produced eclectic programming to jazz and greater amounts of NPR material. Program director Patrick Conley said:

If KUNM wanted an audience of sufficient size to support itself, it *had* to make changes in programming. Which we did. And the audience is growing, underwriting is growing, and the administration is growing tired of the quacking and honking of a small gaggle of volunteers who want to turn the clock back and return to free-form, an "institution" at KUNM for 20 years.[64]

Disgruntled listeners organized a Friends of Freeform Committee and asked that their donations be returned. A staff member was convicted of assault for choking an announcer denouncing the changes on-air, and volunteers brought a six-million-dollar lawsuit against the station, charging management with pursuing fraudulent trade practices, limiting public access, and breaching the First Amendment.[65] The suit was dropped when three hours of afternoon free-form programming were reinstated, suspended volunteers were allowed to return to the station, and the university interceded to create a fifteen-member advisory board comprising community representatives, faculty members, students, and university staff. The board required a thirty-day notice for all programming decisions, followed by a thirty-day review and public comment period; it would then make recommendations to the university vice president in charge of KUNM.

Nonetheless, battles continued between volunteers and successive general managers, leading the provost to announce in early 1992 that he would reduce the board from fifteen to nine members, all of whom would be picked by him and serve limited terms. After yet another general manager had been replaced (this time by a volunteer), a compromise reduced the board from fifteen to twelve members, of whom three (rather than all) were appointed by the provost.[66] Friction continued at the station. In 1993 elections to the board, community representatives were thrown out following charges of voting irregularities. In an election the following year, two candidates (who nevertheless won seats on the board) charged that the University of New Mexico had attempted to rig the election. Isolated wrestling and shoving incidents continued between volunteers and staff members, but one volunteer observed that "it's certainly not as bad as when there were police in the hallways."[67] In spite of the furor, the station won several state Associated Press awards for its news coverage and public service. The conflict between professionals and volunteers at KUNM, compounded by years of university indifference, underscores claims that "the principal purposes of the university and of the station may be only generally synchronous. In fact, the more broadly the station interprets its educational role—i.e., the more public its broadcasting becomes—the less clear and obvious the relationship."[68]

Alexis de Tocqueville claimed that voluntary action was the building block of democracy, yet public broadcasting policy has regarded volunteers mainly as servants of professional managers. A 1978 CPB report is particularly instructive in this regard. The report betrays its intrinsic paternalism when it calls for stations to open their records and meetings in order to "educate and inform the public on the goals, priorities and limitations of public broadcasting." The report also confuses promotion with participation, in that it suggests that stations should "continue and expand their present activities . . . [in] the use of volunteers in fundraising activities, with emphasis on helping volunteers understand their important role in such activities." The CPB report also recommends that stations "aggressively recruit volunteers to assist in or perform those activities which will enable professional staff to maximize their effectiveness or cost efficiency."[69] In short, the most appropriate activity for members of the public at a public broadcasting station is licking stamps. (The authors of the CPB report were not completely oblivious to its shortcomings, however; in an appendix, one of the participants complained that "our Task Force Report suffers from the maladies that infest so many committee efforts: platitudes, hedging and reduction to the least common denominator.")[70]

Other CPB reports define an equally limited role for the public. In a 1977 report on ascertainment (consulting community leaders to define local issues), one proposal called for the process to be integrated into day-to-day operations through the use of volunteers, recruited by stations to "man telephones or perform other tasks at various fundraising activities."[71] The CPB's *Public Radio Handbook* includes a brief section about public participation on the station level, but actual public involvement in programming is mentioned only in passing; instead, managers are urged to use the public for coordinating membership, assisting in the office, helping with pledge drives and program guide production, public speaking, coordinating special events, and conducting station tours.[72] Donald Mullally states that the development of a long-range plan on the station level "offers a unique opportunity for public participation" but later qualifies, "Does this invite a takeover of the management function by incompetents? Certainly not; public comments are advisory only, and one may find them constructive and useful."[73]

Professionalism is an effective means of control within organizations. It can be defined as the skills necessary to meet an organization's goals; like the goals themselves, it can shift across time. These shifts are exemplified by NPR's increasing emphasis on reportorial competence over skills like tape editing, as described by Thomas Looker.[74] Professionalism also serves to rein-in volunteers, who may have a strong ideological commitment to the institution, rather than to the manager. A 1986 study commissioned by NPR, the *Audience-Building Task Force Report*, advised stations to "professionalize" their operations by eliminating programs in cases where "each person selects program material on the basis of personal taste."[75] Citing the need to oversee their stations' on-air sound, managers are replacing what little volunteer programming they air with productions from paid staff and national sources. NPR-distributed research from commercial firms also is used to back claims that local "talent" is relatively unimportant. As managers consolidate their control over station operations, processes of professionalism and employment patterns within the industry ensure that the ranks of these managers will become increasingly homogenous. Since managers allocate resources according to their knowledge, experience, beliefs, and values, programming diversity likely will decrease.

As with "service," public radio's semanticists have worked their magic on "outreach." Rather than bringing the public into station operations or serving marginal or overlooked groups, one public radio producer defined "outreach" as "a constellation of activities bridging the areas of marketing, promotion, public relations and development."[76] Community involvement ultimately is driven by the need for public subsidies rather than public discourse; the station manager of KBSU in Boise, Idaho, once admitted that his station's outreach efforts were primarily "a way to build revenue streams."[77] The public radio audience lacks self-recognition as a "public" due to its circumscribed role in public broadcasting, and its lack of identification with the radio and television public broadcasting systems is plainly evidenced in the growing inability of public broadcasters to muster the public in their defense. Public testimonies before Congress during reauthorization hearings dropped from a high of 134 in 1969 to only twelve in 1986, and specialized interest groups with direct ties to the public broadcasting industry were the most vociferous supporters.[78]

Processes of professionalization also are evident at the national level, particularly in the development of NPR's news and public affairs programming. *All Things Considered* initially was designed to carry reports originating from stations around the country. During the program's first six months, however, nearly half of the stories submitted by stations were rejected on grounds of technical inadequacy or limited interest—despite the fact that *All Things Considered* employed only four reporters and relied heavily on phone interviews.[79] Although stations became increasingly upset at the lack of local feeds on *All Things Considered*, the program provided the backbone for many station schedules and was a major fundraising draw. The rising price of NPR affiliation, stemming in part from the costs of *All Things Considered*, forced many stations to cut back on their local news and public affairs operations. The network began hiring professional field reporters, or "stringers," to cover breaking stories, and it opened news bureaus around the world, which enabled NPR to strengthen its position as a player in the news business. By 1981, *All Things Considered* was budgeted at $800,000 a year and employed a staff of sixteen. Although the size of the program's staff had grown dramatically, the "experimental" pieces upon which much of NPR's early reputation rested became more infrequent. NPR's news programming became increasingly insular, relying on "experts," academicians, business leaders, and government officials for sources and commentary; these contacts provided NPR with increased access to inner circles of power and justified NPR's federal subsidies. When in 1990 *All Things Considered's* listenership exceeded the readership of the *New York Times*, Douglas Bennet crowed, "This may have begun as an experiment, but we're way beyond that now; we're in the big leagues, the very big leagues. People are now relying on us for the news, and this creates a whole new accountability we have to live up to."[80] However, as reporters became professionalized, they essentially became prisoners of their sources and hesitated to cover these sources aggressively. NPR's growing focus on government minutiae led it to ignore important breaking stories like the savings and loan crisis; the value of the service was defined primarily in terms of audience growth.

This audience was highly exclusive. In the late 1980s an analyst found that "in comparison to the general population public radio's audience is more male, higher income [41 percent over $35,000 annually], and higher in education level. In addition, fewer blacks, fewer Hispanics and fewer senior citizens listen to public radio in comparison to the general population."[81] As public radio's fixed costs climbed, stations focused on honing existing audiences, and analysts within and without the system began to refer to the "aging of public radio's core."[82] Mindful of the cultural transformations signaled by demographic changes in the United States, NPR attempted to resuscitate its moribund cultural programming with musical offerings like *Afropop Worldwide, Bluesstage, Club Del Sol*, and *The Thistle and Shamrock*. Cultural division head Peter Pennekamp claimed that NPR's separation of news and cultural programming had led to " 'culture' without a context and 'news' without depth."[83] Nev-

Table 4.3
NPR Funding Allocations for Programming, 1988–1993 (in millions of dollars)

	1988	1989	1990	1991	1992	1993
News programs	$10.5	$12.5	$14.3	$16.1	$17.3	$18.7
Cultural programs	$8.5	$8.4	$9.2	$9.3	$5.7	$7.3

Source: NPR

ertheless, NPR's subsidies for cultural programming continued to lag behind those for news and public affairs (see Table 4.3). The major new offering by NPR's cultural programming department, *Heat*, premiered in March 1990. The program was designed as a two-hour late-night program featuring talk and music. *Heat* was carried by more than forty stations (including ten major markets) and performed well in the Arbitron ratings. CPB-sponsored research by FMR Associates found that

Heat tests as positively as any spoken-word program we have ever evaluated with public radio listeners. What's more, the higher level of appeal indicated by "occasional NPR samplers" as well as the strong appeal among women and Hispanics . . . suggests considerable potential for this program if further developed and positioned in an appropriate daypart (either morning or afternoon drive).[84]

Yet many stations wanted NPR to sink more financial resources into news and information programming, particularly *Morning Edition* and *All Things Considered*. Although *Heat* was "over twice as expensive as the next largest project under development by NPR Cultural Programming," Pennekamp claimed that it "had the lowest cost-per-hour of any nationally produced news/cultural affairs program in public radio—about half the cost of *Fresh Air* and only a small percentage of the cost of NPR newsmagazines."[85]

Although it had been in development since 1986, *Heat* was canceled after only six months, due to its failure to attract underwriters. Pennekamp believed that part of the difficulties stemmed from bad timing; the National Endowment of the Arts had planned to give the program $100,000 but was itself fighting for its life in the wake of controversy surrounding a grant in support of an exhibition by photographer Robert Mapplethorpe. Producers estimated that *Heat*'s production costs for fiscal year 1991 would have exceeded $1.2 million.[86] New large-scale programs could no longer rely on NPR subsidies for support; the cancellation of *Heat* represented the difficulty in the "unbundled" era of developing ambitious programming without substantial corporate or philanthropic support. The cancellation also triggered resentment from NPR affiliates, since the organization had thus failed to follow through with its program commitment after stations had made holes in their schedules to accommodate it. Pennekamp left NPR in 1993, four years after his arrival. A 1995 reorganization resulted in the cancellation of several cultural programs, including the long-running *Horizons* series. By 1997, *Morning Edition* and *All Things Considered* alone consumed 40 percent of NPR's budget.[87]

INDEPENDENT PRODUCERS AS PUBLIC SURROGATES

As NPR channeled its money and energies into news and public affairs, independent producers became responsible for much of NPR's documentary and arts programming. In September 1983, the CPB defined an "independent" as a producer with "no affiliation with a public or commercial broadcasting licensee which could exercise content or fiscal control over the project.[88] Independent producers, as an aggregate, claim to represent the public's interest, in that they are separate from institutional interests. The budgets of some major independent production consortiums rival those of many stations, but most public radio producers are freelancers operating on a shoestring, and all compete to interest NPR and its member stations in their efforts. The resource discrepancies between large and small producers lead to the same conflicts that characterize relations between large and small stations. Major production centers and local stations receive substantial funds for production; in 1997, the CPB Radio Program Fund awarded $4.4 million to twenty-two programs, including $500,000 to NPR for developing Saturday programming. The following year, the Fund gave $4.5 million to twenty-two awardees; NPR received nearly $650,000. Consequently, "the small 'independent' producers [remained] the most disgruntled and strident lobbyists."[89] The "independent" market mode also leads producers to become a pressure group for expanding that market in attempts to stake out a niche for themselves. An organization called Audio Independents briefly represented independent producers after NPR's founding, but in 1982 the newly formed Association of Independents in Radio held the first meeting of independent radio producers in over a decade. Much like other special-interest organizations, AIR was formed as a pressure group for representation and funding. By 1994 it represented more than six hundred of the estimated 1,800 independent radio producers in the United States.[90]

The first major federal funding source for independent producers, the Satellite Program Development Fund (SPDF) stemmed from a provision in the 1978 act ordering the CPB to allot a "substantial" part of its programming dollars to independent productions. The SPDF was formally established in 1980 with $300,000 in funding from NPR, which also administered the fund. SPDF manager Dave Creagh claimed that the fund was intended to prime the pump for the upcoming satellite distribution system, but rather than explicitly fund independent producers, the SPDF allowed NPR to meet independent producers' demands for greater distribution and to keep control of SPDF funding.[91] Grants were based on a panel review of proposals, in which judges rated the first page of each applicant's proposal; one-third of the proposals were eliminated before tapes were auditioned—hence, marketing plans were crucial to a proposal's success. The remaining applications were narrowed from more than three hundred to twenty during marathon review sessions. While this procedure led to speedy results, it was criticized for relying on the whims and caprices of judges. One producer complained, "I know what to take to NEA, NEH, Markle—I can give you a two-paragraph precis of what each group is looking for. But I don't have the vaguest idea of what SPDF will fund. You can't hone things with SPDF—it's a total crapshoot. It drives producers crazy."[92]

The SPDF was designed to fund new and innovative work, but some grants were highly controversial. In 1982, the SPDF awarded $5,138 for production of "Tunnel Hum, USA"—in fact, recordings of people humming in various tunnels. "Tunnel Hum, USA" was aired by only a handful of stations and became a lightning rod for controversy, indicating the tension between experimentation and carriage that independent producers faced, as well as presaging growing right-wing demands for accountability in public funding of the arts. Some producers, contending that the SPDF concentrated on funding minor projects that would not compete with NPR's offerings, preferred a separate fund that would allow them to become major suppliers competitive with NPR. Dissatisfaction with NPR was heightened by the network's delayed payments to independent producers in the wake of the 1983 financial debacle. Calls grew for a discrete, insulated CPB program fund for independent productions.

Producers got what they wanted in 1986, when the CPB Radio Program Fund was created as part of the business plan that channeled CSGs to stations. Producers also lost what they had, since the SPDF was folded into the new fund and independent producers had to compete with stations, NPR, and other producing entities. Although the Radio Program Fund was initially opposed by NPR, which would surrender control over funding, it was supported by stations. Rather than emphasizing experimentation and diversity, the Fund's stated priority was to seed "national radio production [of] projects that . . . will yield at least one major new service or series."[93] Grants were determined by a small panel of station managers, producers, and audience researchers. Radio Fund director Richard Madden became a virtual czar for independent producers; he determined final funding based on recommendations of the review panel. In its first year, the fund received 172 proposals and awarded grants to eleven series. Half of these series already were airing at the time of their awards. The fund was quickly criticized for avoiding risky or innovative programming, but Madden told producers to assume the "context" of stations seeking to double their audience by the end of the decade.[94]

The CPB Radio Fund swelled to $4.2 million by 1990. When the CPB board reaffirmed its support for the radio fund the following year, it stated that the fund's goals were to "yield quality programming that is illuminating, inspiring, as well as appealing; take programmatic risk; and advance public radio's mission of serving an increasing number of Americans."[95] This statement represents the overall conceptual vagueness of public radio; one official complained, "it's hard to think of anything I've heard on the air that wouldn't qualify for support. I'd like to know what criteria, what choices I've made as a director by voting for these [guidelines], besides voting for motherhood and apple pie."[96] Producers wanted grants for a greater number of smaller projects, while stations desired more money for audience draws already in production. The CPB Radio Fund assumed greater importance as other subsidies began to dry up. In 1992, when the Fund handed out $4.48 million in grants, it was "the largest single source of money for public radio programming."[97] In addition to funding large projects that would show a return on investment, money increasingly was used to subsidize audience research (a Phoenix research project had received $81,000 in 1989).

In 1991, WXPN in Philadelphia received $1.1 million, or 27 percent of all the money in the Radio Fund, for *World Cafe*, a music program syndicated two hours daily. Designed to attract younger audiences to public radio, *World Cafe* was a heavily researched variation on the commercial Adult Album Alternative music format, which rotated recordings by established singer/songwriters like Paul Simon and Sting with some alternative and rhythm and blues artists, as well as reggae and other international music. The program was derided by Ruth Hirschman of Santa Monica's KCRW as "a jukebox program that has no credibility and barely discernible carriage.... *World Cafe* has eaten up a lion's share of [CPB Radio Program] funds and has proved to be a mouse."[98] Despite widespread criticism, the CPB Radio Fund awarded nearly a million dollars to *World Cafe* the following year but eliminated $300,000 to *Soundprint*, which was "public radio's only general-interest national documentary program and one of the most respected sources of radio journalism."[99]

The Radio Fund was intended to provide "start-up" funding only, to encourage producers to become self-supporting; programs were cut off from funding after five years. This marketplace strategy spelled the end for *Latin American News Service* in 1989. *Soundprint* was severed after five years and $1.6 million from CPB, because it had not attracted significant underwriter support.[100] The program did eventually attract enough funding from other sources to continue production, but the Fund's bottom-line reductionism hardly went unnoticed. Producer Larry Josephson summed up the situation:

The CPB Radio Fund claims to support innovation and to take risks, but it does neither. It is a temple of numbers, absolutely controlled by one person who is more into systems analysis than actual content. CPB gives grants to just enough independents and minorities to cover themselves politically, but the lion's share . . . has gone to six- and seven-figure projects that do produce numbers, but not much love from listeners. . . . [T]he $1.1 million *World Cafe* grant is a scandal, a thoroughly misbegotten attempt to buy young demographics with a service that is, in essence, a commercial radio music format.[101]

National Public Radio has a deep structural and ideological need for independent productions. They are less expensive than station-produced programs, whose administrative costs are passed along in budget requests to NPR and CPB. They enable NPR to cover events and topics that may not suit the discrete, demographically honed audiences sought by NPR's member stations. They also enable NPR to maintain its product image with listeners as a progressive institution outside the bounds of market forces. But the second-tier status of independent producers is reflected in the fact that these producers must buy their own equipment, cover their own expenses, and create a finished product in their own studios, independent of NPR and its affiliates. This marginal status is compounded by the miserly compensation NPR awards to independent producers. In 1988, NPR rates for independent productions averaged forty to fifty dollars per minute, which meant that producers earned an average of only seven dollars per hour for their labor. In 1993, NPR rates for completed and aired productions had risen by only five dollars per minute.[102]

While unbundling programming in the 1980s expanded the program marketplace and arguably produced more opportunities for independent producers, the supply of programming far outstripped available space on station schedules. The problem was compounded by the growing conservatism of public radio programmers. NPR had based much of its early reputation on creative freedom for producers, but by the late 1970s slots for discrete, freestanding programs had largely vanished from the schedules of major public radio stations. NPR's sole vehicle for one-shot documentaries, *NPR Journal*, disappeared, and late-night airtime was increasingly consumed by overnight services like *NPR Plus*. *All Things Considered* adopted a more "user-friendly" format in the late 1980s, with few pieces lasting longer than three minutes, while the program's spread to two hours ate up the only available half-hour on many station schedules. Stations also began to emphasize regularized "strip" programs, on the grounds that they drew regular audiences. The program director for KJZZ in Phoenix stated that for all new programs, "we always ask the question now, 'Will they raise enough money to pay for themselves?' " As a result, independent producers were often forced to *give* their programs away to ensure carriage. By 1989, nearly all independent productions acquired by NPR or APR were being obtained for token fees or no fees at all.[103]

Marketing became a central consideration for producers, and often it was incorporated directly into the production process. Leslie Peters, NPR's chief of marketing in the late 1980s, recommended that producers "get an advisory committee of stations [and] call them when you get the grant" before beginning production. Others suggested bombarding stations with press kits and demo tapes; one consultant claimed, "You need at least 30 markets to get good press coverage."[104] The marketing frenzy also extended to the qualification process for the CPB Radio Fund. Beginning in 1989, producers were requested to submit a business plan with each proposal.[105] Producers faced growing pressures to design their work so as to fit into the programming flow of formats and to assemble them into packages that were large enough to achieve a promotable "critical mass" on station schedules and attract underwriting support. Of course, this emphasis on packaging and collaboration was problematic for independent producers, who "work in isolation from and competition with each other, and are jealously protective of the style, approach and integrity of their productions."[106]

Perhaps the biggest change for independent producers has been the growth of "modula" pieces of thirty, sixty, or ninety seconds. NPR distributed at least seventeen modular programs in 1990, and independent producers complained that these programs "present the only entry to a public radio market increasingly dominated by heightened competition among the field's largest distributors."[107] Modules provided flexibility for programmers but allowed for only cursory coverage of issues and events while requiring the same amount of marketing as longer programs. The sheer volume of modules also complicated station scheduling and promotion. New delivery systems may afford new possibilities for independent distribution, but they threaten the status of independent producers in the short term. In late 1995, NPR defined all independent productions as "work for hire" and demanded the right to recycle the material via on-line services and CD-ROMs without compensating producers accordingly. An agreement reached in May 1996 would allow NPR to distribute independent production in new media for eighteen months without paying royalties in order to track potential revenues, which in turn would allow both parties to renegotiate.[108] The continued marginalization of independent producers leads to high rates of attrition within their ranks. Josephson finds, "There are very few middle-aged *producers* in the system. To survive, one must become a manager or administrator, struggle as an independent or leave."[109]

Independent producers provide a voice that is theoretically independent of public broadcasting institutions, but their viability as public surrogates is debatable. Independent producers traditionally view themselves as artists; early NPR producers asserted that audiences had to be "taught" to appreciate their efforts.[110] Yet works must fit public radio's distribution system to reach an audience, and producers who want their work distributed will not create products the system will not handle. Producers may have different standards of professionalism than programmers, but they nevertheless share the "professional" ideology of interpreting audience needs and tastes, judging value to output, and developing strategies for enhancing their status within the public radio system. Larry Daressa, one of the founders of the Independent Television Service, has written:

Producer's independence from commercial considerations is only a necessary but not a sufficient condition for community service. Production must in fact be closely dependent on (and strictly accountable to) the actual process of a community's development. . . . For example, community leaders consistently express the need for programs on education, jobs and health issues. Independents, in contrast, have been primarily interested in "cultural politics" or "personal documentary," not surprisingly the areas of their own immediate interest.[111]

Producers claim that their work is compromised by catering to commerce. Since they dress their intentions in the ideology of Romanticism, in which the artist consciously stands apart from society to pursue his or her singular vision, the efforts of independent producers, unsurprisingly, serve themselves rather than the public. The producers interviewed by Hoynes described public broadcasting exclusively in terms of individual goals (that is, creative freedom) rather than any collective mission or responsibility to the public.[112] Independent producers rationalize their efforts by claiming to appeal to underserved audiences. Yet instead of acknowledging the limited relevance of many of their productions to these audiences, independent producers claim that their productions would be enthusiastically received but for the timidity or reactionary tendencies of broadcaster programmers. Despite their "outsider" status, independent producers have become not surrogates for the public but merely another pressure group within the public radio system.

The public surrogates in the form of boards, finders, and producers described in this chapter are compromised by public radio's primary goal of organizational survival rather than public service. Although stations are licensed to both private and public groups, the nonprofit model is the primary structural model for public radio. This model lends itself to domination by elites who set the agenda for the system's mission, structure, and practices on the local and national level. The 1978 Public Telecommunications Act attempted to reform the system by mandating the creation of community advisory boards to provide public oversight of station operations, but this reform was halfhearted at best. Guidelines for the selection and roles of these boards were left to the discretion of station managers, who frequently manipulated them for purposes of financing rather than public input. Instead of encouraging public participation, managers increasingly have professionalized station operations. This process minimizes the need for decision making and ensures predictability. It also is reflected on the national level by NPR's diversion of resources to its news division, as a response to station demands and to the need to enhance NPR's institutional legitimacy.

Since the goals of nonprofit organizations are more heterogeneous and ambiguous than their proprietary counterparts, such organizations are particularly prone to the contradiction of "popularity" and "publicness," in which attempts at increasing audience size are counterbalanced by the necessity of maintaining production (and audience) "quality." Public radio's development in many ways harkens back to an earlier model. To Thomas Streeter,

it is perhaps no coincidence that public broadcasting today rather strikingly resembles the kind of broadcasting that Herbert Hoover seems to have had in mind in the 1920's: generally noncontroversial, patrician programming supported to a large degree by corporate donations in exchange for low-key, image-enhancing corporate "publicity."[113]

The separation of the public from any normative role in public radio has been a constant throughout the public radio system's history. Despite the rhetoric of public participation and social integration in NPR's mission statement, the fact remains that the public was shut out of the processes that led to the service's founding. Although pressures for public accountability led the CPB to require community advisory for tax-funded radio stations, indications are that these boards have been manipulated to serve the purposes of the organization rather than the public. The deceptive self-image of "service" conceals the fact that public radio essentially has disciplined its audience throughout its history, as elites, managers, and funders policed who might participate and what kinds of discourse were admissible. Certainly, public radio has aired programming that challenges the status quo, yet these programs remain part of a highly industrialized system. Corporate sponsorship has reinforced the shift from diversity of coverage to the packaging of product lines. Although underwriting practices help ensure stable flows of money to public broadcasters, they often lead to overt commercialism and further erase the distinctions between public and commercial broadcasting. The public is invoked by administrators, policy makers, and personnel, but nowhere does it actually act. Instead, actual democratization is shunned as undermining institutional legitimacy. How does one become a "member" of a public broadcasting station?—by making a financial contribution. All of these factors lend credence to charges of elitism in public broadcasting.

NOTES

1. F. Ostrower, *Why the Wealthy Give: The Culture of Elite Philanthropy* (Princeton, NJ: Princeton University Press, 1995), p. 128.

2. T. Streeter, *Selling the Air: A Critique of Commercial Broadcasting in the United States* (Chicago: University of Chicago Press, 1996), p. 302.

3. N. Garnham, *Structures of Television* (London: British Film Institute, 1978), p. 143.

4. I. Ang, *Desperately Seeking the Audience* (New York: Routledge, 1991), p. 29. For a detailed analysis of the behavioral consequences of for-profit, nonprofit and public organization, see P. DiMaggio, "Nonprofit Organizations in the Production and Distribution of Culture," in *The Nonprofit Sector: A Research Handbook*, W. Powell, ed. (New Haven, CT: Yale University Press, 1987).

5. See P. DiMaggio and M. Useem, "Cultural Democracy in a Period of Cultural Expansion: The Social Composition of Arts Audiences in the United States," in *Art and Society: Readings in the Sociology of the Arts*, A. Foster and J. Blau, eds. (Albany, NY: State University Press of New York, 1989).

6. S. Smith and M. Lipsky, *Nonprofits for Hire: The Welfare State in the Age of Contracting* (Cambridge, MA: Harvard University Press, 1993), p. 35.

7. W. Nielsen, *The Big Foundations* (New York: Columbia University Press, 1972), p. 78.

8. W. Rowland, Jr., "Continuing Crisis in Public Broadcasting: A History of Disenfranchisement," *Journal of Broadcasting and Electronic Media* 30 (3), Summer 1986, p. 258.

9. R. Engelman, *Public Radio and Television in America: A Political History* (Thousand Oaks, CA: Sage, 1996), p. 281.

10. Smith and Lipsky, *Nonprofits for Hire*, p. 54.

11. W. Barlow, "Community Radio in the US: The Struggle for a Democratic Medium," *Media, Culture and Society* 10 (1), January 1988, pp. 85–86.

12. C. Perrow, "The Analysis of Goals in Complex Organizations," *American Sociological Review* 26 (6), December 1962, pp. 857–858.

13. See R. Bellah, R. Madsen, W. Sullivan, S. Swidler, and S. Tipton, *Habits of the Heart: Individualism and Commitment in American Life* (New York: Harper and Row, 1985); M. Weber, "Class Status, Party" and "The Social Psychology of the World Religions," in *From Max Weber: Essays in Sociology*, H. Gerth and C. Mills, eds. (New York: Oxford University Press, 1946), cited in Ostrower, *Why the Wealthy Give*, p. 14.

14. Ostrower, *Why the Wealthy Give*, p. 129, 131.

15. B. Gladstone, "Panel Calls for More Managers on Board," *Current*, January 28, 1983, p. 6.

16. Engelman, *Public Radio and Television in America*, p. 123.

17. J. Haney, *A History of the Merger of National Public Radio and the Association of Public Radio Stations*, unpublished dissertation, Iowa City: University of Iowa, 1981, p. 217.

18. W. Hoynes, *Public Television for Sale* (Boulder, CO: Westview Press, 1994), p. 130.

19. J. Pearce and J. Rosener, "Advisory Board Performance: Managing Ambiguity and Limited Commitment in Public Television," *Journal of Voluntary Action Research* 14 (4), 1985, p. 36; Herman W. Land Associates, *The Hidden Medium: Educational Radio* (New York: National Educational Radio, National Association of Educational Broadcasters, 1967), p. iv.

20. S. Holmberg and H. Baker, "Community Advisory Boards: Managing the Challenge for Maximum Benefit," *Public Telecommunications Review*, May/June 1979, pp. 37–38.

21. T. Haight and S. Vedro, "Fighting the MGM Syndrome: Reform at the Station Level," in *Telecommunications Policy Handbook*, J. Schement, F. Gutierrez, and M. Sirbu, Jr., eds. (New York: Praeger, 1982), p. 99.

22. Holmberg and Baker, "Community Advisory Boards," p. 40.

23. See Pearce and Rosener, "Advisory Board Performance."

24. Holmberg and Baker, "Community Advisory Boards," p. 36.

25. M. Lashley, *Public Television: Panacea, Pork Barrel or Public Trust?* (Westport, CT: Greenwood Press, 1992), p. 24.

26. S. Millard, "ACNO: CPB and the Public," *Public Telecommunications Review*, March/April 1977, p. 8.

27. C. Dann, "Membership: Under the Grassroots Lies the Mother Lode," *Current*, September 16, 1996, p. 34.

28. J. Wilner, "NPR Rolls Out Very Red Carpet for Endowment Fundraisers," *Current*, March 1, 1993, p. 7; S. Behrens and J. Conciatore, "No 'Low-Hanging Fruit' in Sight to Solve NPR's Revenue Problem," *Current*, November 17, 1997, p. 18.

29. S. Behrens, "Development Exchange Regroups into Specialities," *Current*, March 2, 1998, p. 6.

30. J. Robertiello, " 'We've Gone at It Almost Backwards,' " *Current*, September 7, 1992, p. 12.

31. Ibid.

32. M. Fuerst, "What Could Make Public Radio Alter Its Course?" *Current*, February 14, 1994, p. 17.

33. K. Bedford, "Research-Informed Techniques Bring Sophistication to On-Air Pitches," *Current*, May 13, 1996, pp. 1, 29; S. Behrens, "Less-Pledging Experiments Satisfy Budget, Audience," *Current*, December 1, 1997, p. 9; S. Behrens, "Radio's October Pledging Benefits from Partnership," *Current*, November 15, 1993, p. 3.

34. S. Behrens, "Audience as Donor Pool: Pledge Trends Worrisome, Or at Best Unplanned," *Current*, December 16, 1996, p. 18.

35. D. Giovannoni, "On-Air Drive Is Yesterday's Technology," *Current*, March 29, 1989, p. 8.

36. S. Behrens, "About Eight Percent of Weekly Audience Now Subscribes on Honor System," *Current*, November 26, 1982, p. 1.

37. "Final Report: Temporary Commission on Alternative Financing for Public Telecommunications," *Current*, September 7, 1983, p. 6.

38. W. Powell and R. Friedkin, "Political and Organizational Influences on Public Television Programming," in *Mass Communication Review Yearbook 1983*, E. Wartella and D. Whitney, eds. (Beverly Hills: Sage, 1983), p. 420.

39. E. Barnouw, *The Sponsor: Notes on a Modern Potentate* (New York: Oxford University Press, 1978), p. 68.

40. "Public Radio Celebrates, Questions Growth," *Broadcasting*, April 16, 1990, p. 66.

41. B. Porter, "Has Success Spoiled NPR?" *Columbia Journalism Review*, September/October 1990, p. 32.

42. S. Behrens, "Victim of a New Darwinism?" *Current*, May 25, 1992, p. 13.

43. M. Fisher, "Underwriting the New," *Washington Post Magazine*, October 22, 1989, p. 38.

44. J. Wilner, "Japanese Grant Raises Conflict-of-Interest Questions," *Current*, June 22, 1992, pp. 3, 14.

45. See Powell and Friedkin, "Political and Organizational Influences on Public Television Programming."

46. R. Schatz, "Public Radio Being Pressed to Turn Its Success into Independence," *New York Times*, March 25, 1996, p. C1.

47. See M. Ermann, "The Operative Goals of Corporate Philanthropy: Contributions to the Public Broadcasting Service, 1972–1976," *Social Problems* 25, June 1978.

48. H. Schiller, *Culture Inc: The Corporate Takeover of Public Expression* (New York: Oxford University Press, 1989), pp. 92–93; M. Ermann, "The Operative Goals of Corporate Philanthropy," p. 504.

49. P. Pagano, "New Weekend Life for 'All Things Considered,' " *Los Angeles Times*, July 22, 1985, Part 6, p. 1. Also see J. Truscott, "NPR Gets Grant for News Show," *Washington Post*, July 26, 1985, p. D-7; E. Blau, "National Public Radio Gets By with Help from Its Friends," *New York Times*, February 27, 1989, p. D13.

50. S. Husseini, "The Broken Promise of Public Radio," *Humanist* 54 (5), September/October 1994, p. 26.

51. " 'ATC' to Continue Airing Donor Credits for ADM," *Current*, October 28, 1996, p. 6.

52. "Final Report: Temporary Commission on Alternative Financing for Public Telecommunications," *Current*, September 7, 1983, p. 5.

53. J. Mastroberardino, "Underwriting Policies in Flux," *Current*, April 24, 1984, p. 1.

54. R. Barbieri, " 'Leading' Out As Funder Credit," *Current*, February 15, 1989, p. 14; R. Barbieri, "FCC Clears WVXU in Credit Case," *Current*, April 9, 1990, p. 3; J. Wilner, "NPR Selling Newscast Credits on Cost-per-Thou Basis," *Current*, November 18, 1991, p. 7.

55. D. Uebe, "NPR Spurns $500K Underwriting from Liquor Industry," *Current*, December 1, 1995, p. 3.

56. D. Barboza, "The 'Enhanced Underwriting' of Public Broadcasting Is Taking a More Commercial Flair," *New York Times*, December 27, 1995, p. C2.

57. F. Werden, "Chubb Spreads Underwriting Gospel to National Advertisers," *Current*, April 19, 1985, p. 1.

58. See Powell and Friedkin, "Political and Organizational Influences on Public Television Programming."

59. Werden, "Chubb Spreads Underwriting Gospel to National Advertisers," p. 1.

60. See S. Emerson, "The System That Brought You *Days of Rage*," *Columbia Journalism Review*, November/December 1989.

61. "What They Said on Capitol Hill," *Current*, December 8, 1987, p. 17.

62. See Southern Educational Communications Association. *Editorial Integrity in Public Broadcasting: Proceedings of the Wingspread Conference* (Washington, DC: CPB, 1985).

63. M. Lucoff, "The University and Public Radio: Who's in Charge?" *Public Telecommunications Review*, September/October 1979, p. 23.

64. P. Conley, "Audience Building Can Ruin Your Whole Day," *Current*, October 26, 1988, p. 2.

65. D. Kirsh, "The Struggle for the Soul of Public Radio," *Extra!* April/May 1993.

66. J. Wilner, "University to Intervene in 'Radio War,' " *Current*, June 22, 1992, p. 1; J. Wilner, "Provost Backs Away from Plan for Overhaul in Albuquerque," *Current*, August 14, 1992, p. 1.

67. S. McCrummen, " 'It's Not As Bad As When There Were Police in the Hallways,' " *Current*, June 6, 1994, p. 3.

68. Corporation for Public Broadcasting, *The Public Radio Handbook: Starting and Operating a Public Radio Station* (Washington, DC: CPB, 1979), Sec. 3, p. 3.

69. Corporation for Public Broadcasting, *Public Participation in Public Broadcasting* (Washington, DC: CPB, 1978), pp. 25–26, 29, 31.

70. Ibid. p. 35.

71. A. Smith, P. Nester, and D. Pulford, "Volunteer Ascertainment Panels," in *Six Experiments in Ascertainment Methodology*, Office of Communication Research, ed. (Washington, DC: CPB, 1977), p. 19.

72. See Corporation for Public Broadcasting, *The Public Radio Handbook*.

73. D. Mullally, "Long-Range Planning and the Local Station," *Public Telecommunications Review*, March/April 1979, p. 40.

74. See Looker, *The Sound and the Story*.

75. Cited in R. Goodman, "Why Public Radio Isn't (and What You Can Do about It)," *Whole Earth Review*, Winter 1992.

76. D. Gediman, "Why Should I Worry about Outreach? What's in It for Me?" *Current*, June 20, 1994, p. 18.

77. D. Uebe, "PROVE's Point: Volunteers Are Part of the Solution," *Current*, March 25, 1996, p. 11.

78. Lashley, *Public Television*, p. 60.

79. S. Behrens, "ATC: Caught in the Act of Thinking," *Current*, April 27, 1981, p. 4.

80. Porter, "Has Success Spoiled NPR?" p. 27.

81. J. Carey, "Public Broadcasting and Federal Policy," in *New Directions in Telecommunications Policy*, Vol. 1, P. Newberg, ed. (Durham, NC: Duke University Press, 1989) p. 204.

82. J. Robertiello, "Has Public Radio Hit the Wall?" *Current*, May 13, 1991, p. 19.

83. " 'Heat'—Pennekamp's Elegy for a Late Program," *Current*, May 27, 1991, p. 17.

84. Ibid.

85. Ibid.

86. J. Robertiello, "NPR Cancels 'Heat,' " *Current*, September 3, 1990, p. 17.

87. J. Yorke, "NPR to Trim Staff in Reorganization," *Washington Post*, August 8, 1995, p. C-7.

88. "Hull Explains Broken Agreement," *Current*, March 27, 1984, p. 4.

89. "Weekend Radio Projects Win 40 Percent of Annual CPB Grants," *Current*, March 3, 1997, p. 1; J. Conciatore, "CPB Aids NPR Newsmags, Weekend and Native Programming," *Current*, February 16, 1998, p. 14; Lashley, *Public Television*, p. 75.

90. J. Yore, "Radio Independents Press for More Money," *Current*, September 28, 1988, p. 13; J. Conciatore, "Radio Indies Still Want Rights, Rates, Respect," *Current*, November 14, 1994, p. 1.

91. B. Gladstone, "Seed Money for Radio's 'Sparrows,' " *Current*, April 19, 1983, p. 5.

92. Ibid.

93. R. Barbieri, "Winners of $3 Million Radio Program Fund Competition Unveiled," *Current*, November 17, 1986, p. 1.

94. Ibid.

95. J. Robertiello, "Radio Fund Draws Fire for Vague Criteria, Specific Choices," *Current*, May 27, 1991, p. 3.

96. Ibid.

97. Ibid.

98. P. Viles, "Public Radio Flirts with Pop Format," *Broadcasting*, August 17, 1992, p. 22.

99. Engelman, *Public Radio and Television in America*, p. 119.

100. S. Behrens, "Victim of a New Darwinism?" *Current*, May 25, 1992, p. 1.

101. L. Josephson, "We're Drunk on Numbers, Boring to Our Listeners," *Current*, April 27, 1992, p. 31.

102. J. Yore, "Radio Independents Press for More Money," p. 13; S. Rathe, "Public Radio Needs an Independent Program Service," *Current*, March 15, 1989, p. 15; R. Mahler, "Cheap Air: Hard Times for Public Radio's Producers," *Columbia Journalism Review* 31 (6), March/April 1993, p. 17.

103. "Producers Drop Or Adapt Their Half-Hour Formats," *Current*, August 25, 1997, p. 6; J. Robertiello, "Money in the Driver's Seat," *Current*, August 20, 1990, p. 1; S. Rathe, "Public Radio Needs an Independent Program Service," p. 15.

104. J. Robertiello, "To Market, to Market," *Current*, September 28, 1988, p. 9.

105. "CPB Radio Funder on Criteria, Process," *Current*, March 1, 1989, p. 10.

106. T. Thomas and T. Clifford, *The Public Radio Program Marketplace* (Washington, DC: CPB, 1985), p. 57.

107. S. Singer, "The Long and Short of It," *Current*, May 7, 1990, p. 1.

108. J. Conciatore, "NPR Reaches Rights Agreement with Independent Producers," *Current*, May 27, 1996, p. 1.

109. "Wingspread Conference Papers," *Current*, February 28, 1984, p. 4.

110. T. Looker, *The Sound and the Story: NPR and the Art of Radio* (New York: Houghton Mifflin, 1995), p. 111.

111. L. Daressa, "Television for a Change: To Help Us Change Ourselves," *Current*, February 12, 1996, p. 20.

112. Hoynes, *Public Television for Sale*, p. 143.

113. Streeter, *Selling the Air*, p. 188.

5

The Reified Public: From Ascertainment to Ratings

National Public Radio will not regard its audience as a "market" or in terms of its disposable income, but as curious, complex individuals who are looking for some understanding, meaning and joy in the human experience.
—William Siemering, "National Public Radio Purposes," p. 5

Since "public" broadcasting theoretically serves the discursive needs of the public rather than the financial needs of the system, its effectiveness is virtually impossible to measure. At the prompting of government, public broadcasters initially attempted to determine public needs through ascertainment, or consulting community leaders to define pressing local issues. However, these ascertainment processes were marred by procedural difficulties, and station managers viewed them as little more than the result of government meddling. At the same time, dwindling federal and state subsidies led many public radio station managers to adopt audience research methodologies from the commercial broadcasting industry in order to aid their searches for new revenues. Empirical research into consumer behavior is a fundamental strategy for reducing producer uncertainty; unlike mission statements, which are based in subjective values, statistics appear to be precise, impersonal, and neutral. By emphasizing fact over value, empirical research carries an aura of expertise and objectivity. Results from audience research reinforce public broadcasters' claims of representing popular will, rationalize their decisions, and provide empirical proof of audience demographics for existing and potential funding sources. Public broadcasters adopted commercially derived audience research methodologies in order to justify continued tax-based support in the wake of increased competition from commercial programmers. This trend was accelerated by consultants with backgrounds in commercial broadcasting, consultants who were trained to seek numerically large, but demographically narrow, target markets.

However, such methodologies work against the formation of an inclusive and self-aware "public." Instead, they isolate the public's individual members and reconstruct them through demographic variables into a series of discrete markets that serve the interests of the system. Audience research is designed to mold audiences as well as reflect them; in the guise of reflecting popular demand, the institutionalization of empirical audience research makes paternalism a fait accompli. According to John Peters:

Public opinion research makes the public a demographic segment or data set rather than a realm of action. Citizens do not themselves produce public opinion today; it must be generated through the machinery of polling. The power to constitute the public space, then, falls into the hands of experts, not of the citizens.[1]

While supposedly improving fundraising effectiveness, empirical audience research has blurred the distinctions between public and commercial broadcasters. This blurring is compounded by fundamental changes in public radio programming strategies. Until the late 1980s, public radio was "programming centered," featuring "composite arrangements of discrete programs, each with identifiable starting and ending points, internal coherence, and, often, a linear or cumulative presentation of material."[2] Many public broadcasters now consider this strategy obsolete, given the large numbers of service providers in many markets, and have adopted the format strategies of commercial radio to draw stable audiences that will in turn attract underwriters. This programming practice has a long track record in the commercial broadcast industry, as validated by commercial research methodologies, and its ability to simplify decision making makes it irresistible to public radio managers. Consequently, stations seek audience-building "tent poles" and programming that is congruent with their narrowed formats, which further reduces uncertainty—and limits localism and diversity. This chapter examines how commercially derived research and programming strategies have seeped into public radio and discusses their implications for public radio's avowed mission of creating a pluralistic public sphere.

THE SHORT LIFE OF ASCERTAINMENT

The controversy surrounding federally mandated ascertainment exemplifies the public radio system's resistance to external influences on policy making. Ascertainment of community needs was implicit in the "public interest" standard of the 1927 Radio Act and the 1934 Communications Act, but the policy was made explicit in the FCC's 1960 *Programming Policy Statement*. The *Statement* required commercial broadcasters to report how they had measured the needs of residents within their station's coverage area, and how they proposed to meet them, when applying for new or renewed licenses. Considerations included use of local talent, news and public affairs programming, service to minority groups and children, and coverage of religion and politics.[3] Fearing a barrage of criticism that ascertainment policies infringed on broadcasters' First Amendment rights, the FCC granted broadcasters wide discretion to determine local needs and decide what "problems" to treat. Broadcasters consequently used broad topics rather than specific issues (for instance, "housing" rather than "housing for the low-income elderly") to meet the language of the *Statement*.[4] No official surveys were required until 1968, when the FCC's *Ascertainment of Community Needs by Broadcast Applicants* specifically described the methodologies broadcasters had to use to consult with community leaders and evaluate their suggestions.[5] Noncommercial broadcasters were exempted from ascertainment until 1976, and, *The Hidden Medium* reported, more than 50 percent of educational stations conducted no audience ascertainment or research. Interestingly, the oft-maligned ten-watt educational stations were planning or actively doing a significantly greater amount (46 percent) than other noncommercial stations (36 percent).[6] These patterns indicate the paternalistic tendencies of the more powerful noncommercial stations of the era. Despite reaching larger audiences, they were less interested in determining the needs and interests of their audiences than were their weaker counterparts.

The push for increased ascertainment standards continued throughout the 1960s, largely because of the growing number of license challenges from minority groups who felt that local broadcasters were neglecting their needs. The 1969 Supreme Court decision in *Red Lion Broadcasting Company, Inc. v. FCC* tacitly encouraged activist groups, by asserting that the rights of viewers and listeners to receive information from diverse sources superseded the rights of broadcasters to disseminate their views. *Red Lion* further emboldened citizen's groups to challenge license renewals on grounds that radio and television stations were not meeting the needs of minority groups (including the poor, the elderly, and children).

In 1971, the FCC responded by releasing the *Primer on Ascertainment of Community Problems by Broadcast Applicants*, which contained thirty-six detailed questions and was supplemented by a comprehensive *Report and*

Order. In addition to detailed community surveys, the report required station managers to interview a cross-section of community leaders to determine at least ten needs and problems of the community. Managers then would decide which of these needs and problems could be addressed; they could cite later programs that addressed them. Public broadcasters pleaded to be exempted from ascertainment requirements, on the grounds that any money for compliance would have to come from already-stretched programming funds. As to "community leaders," public broadcasters argued that program decisions were already influenced by state and local funding sources.[7] As a result, the FCC exempted noncommercial stations from specific and detailed ascertainment requirements, because "given the reservation of channels for specialized kinds of programming, educational stations manifestly must be treated differently than commercial stations."[8]

Yet the National Citizens Committee for Broadcasting, a broadcast reform group, argued that the audiences who stood to benefit the most from public radio and television programming were the least assessed for their needs, because they

could (1) seldom afford to become a member of a public broadcasting station . . . and thus did not receive the preference polls used by some stations, (2) that very few employees of minority groups were involved in the decisionmaking process on public stations, and (3) the composition of station boards and directors tended to exclude the least affluent and otherwise disenfranchised members of the community.[9]

While the demand for ascertainment was nearly universal in the broadcast reform movement, the reformers were not particularly impressed by its efficacy. The National Black Media Council acknowledged that "in giving our support to applying the ascertainment rule to public broadcasting, we know we are asking for more 'talking'—which is what ascertainment is—and not for more program performance."[10] Ascertainment guidelines were often complex and confusing. No clear rationale existed for determining "community leaders"; the FCC advised stations to interview the executives of social service agencies gleaned from local telephone directories. Consequently, "community leaders" who operated in unofficial or unrecognized capacities were ignored. McCain, Hofstetter, James, and Hawkins elaborated on the problems of relying on "community leaders" for input:

The "problems" community governments and organizations face may be quite different than the problems faced by individuals of the community on a daily basis. "Community" problems of drugs, alcohol, crime, etc., are people's *solutions* to problems, albeit socially unacceptable solutions.[11]

Meetings between station managers and community leaders often were cursory affairs, in which groups of station managers listened to a succession of prepared statements with little time for follow-up questions. Defining the community to be ascertained also presented difficulties, particularly in rural areas.

The FCC began chipping away at ascertainment procedures for commercial broadcasters in 1975, when markets of less than 10,000 people were exempted and detailed community surveys were discarded in favor of general demographic studies. Station personnel other than managers could conduct half of the interviews, which allowed ascertainment to be manipulated into a public relations vehicle for stations. A CPB guide to ascertainment recommended that using station personnel to conduct interviews "serves the dual purpose of reducing the manager's ascertainment burden and promoting the station's image by briefing community leaders on programs being produced in their own community or geographical region."[12] Noncommercial broadcasters were required to engage in formal ascertainment in 1976, but these requirements were nominal. Public radio stations had only to prepare a narrative report of how they determined community problems and to list the people they had contacted. Ten-watt stations and exclusively instructional stations continued to be exempted from all ascertainment requirements. Nevertheless, many public broadcasters were indignant. As Willard Rowland, Jr., states, "By definition, by their very existence, they felt they were serving many of those needs that ascertainment would presumably reveal."[13]

All ascertainment requirements for commercial broadcasters were dropped when the FCC deregulated commercial radio on January 14, 1981. Stations were no longer required to ascertain their communities' needs using a prescribed interview process; instead, they were free to devise their own, and the FCC would judge only the resulting programs. Public radio broadcasters immediately requested similar deregulation, and the FCC rewarded them with a unanimous decision on June 27, 1982. Requirements for ascertainment and program logs were voided; instead, public stations were to compile quarterly lists of community issues and programs for their public files. These lists were to include at least five to ten issues that the licensee had addressed in the previous three months.[14]

While community ascertainment procedures were highly problematic, these procedures did encourage public accountability. Rowland finds "ample evidence that the ascertainment procedures have improved the thinking of public broadcasters about their local communities and how better to produce and program for them."[15] In addition, ascertainment redressed the balance of power between management and board members. Regular ascertainment allowed station managers to bolster public affairs programming, against the desires of board members who preferred to see stations oriented exclusively toward education and cultural events. Nevertheless, many station managers complained about the time and labor costs required to conduct community surveys, which also threatened their hold on decision making and control. Others disdained community ascertainment, on grounds that the cold-eyed scientism of survey research would cripple the creative process. Their fears would soon be realized in an entirely different context, on a scale unprecedented in public radio.

THE RISE OF CONSULTANTS

Early educational radio grew out of engineering experiments at colleges and universities. Administrators, believing that engineers lacked pedagogical training, viewed audience research as a means to ensure that educational broadcasts were effective. Yet such research was infrequent and largely unsystematic, relying primarily on mail from listeners and limited largely to stations at land grant universities. In 1948, Ohio State University began using telephone surveys to report ratings and shares, rather than cumulative audiences, for its educational radio station.[16] National public broadcasting entities also were intrigued by the development of empirical audience research, and the NAEB considered hiring an audience research consultant as early as 1953. These plans were abandoned because of a lack of funds and due to concerns about commercialism, but they were revived in the late 1960s. Samuel Holt's 1969 public radio study found that audiences for educational radio stations were so small that the margin of error for audience measurement was often plus or minus 100 percent (he neglected to mention that the majority of these stations were ten-watt student operations lacking community-oriented programming). Holt recommended that the CPB's radio division establish ties to a research service that would provide regular data on noncommercial radio audiences, adding that "research, promotion, and the assistance of consultants where needed, should be considered integral parts of future thinking about noncommercial radio on all levels."[17]

The Corporation for Public Broadcasting commissioned an analysis of Nielsen ratings for public television in 1969 and purchased Arbitron ratings in 1973, making April/May audience estimates available to interested stations. Two years later the CPB began to buy radio audience data for additional "sweep" periods for markets with multiple NPR affiliates, and NPR retained Lawrence Lichty of Northwestern University as the research project's chief consultant. Lichty had studied under Harrison Summers, a former vice president for NBC who had been instrumental in WOSU's research activities. In 1976, after a three-year stint at Arbitron,

Tom Church joined CPB's Office of Communication Research and began buying Arbitron reports from the actual home markets of stations, rather than custom ratings based on a station's signal coverage area. Church's action marked a key demarcation point in the evolution of public radio research: Alan Stavitsky believes that "for the first time, public radio stations could compare their audiences to those of their commercial competitors."[18] In 1977, Church began sending cumulative audience reports to individual stations, urging them to use Arbitron data to extract demographic information. To Stavitsky, this "provided an opening for the research consultants who were to have a major impact on the rise of audience research in public radio."[19]

Given the fact that public broadcasting's grand obsession throughout its history has been getting more money, it follows that consultants with backgrounds in commercial radio would find a ready ear. The question remains: why would National Public Radio be so susceptible to commercial strategies that appear to be antithetical to its mission? First, the CPB, rather than NPR, PBS, or individual stations, provided the impetus for the use of empirical audience research: "The data were taken to Congress to demonstrate that people were indeed listening to public radio and that the CPB appropriation was justified."[20] Second, many stations operated at a remove from their communities. Station managers often were distracted by academic duties or had relatively little understanding of broadcast practices. Consultants expounded a rhetoric of expertise, claiming to know the client's needs better than the client did, and were given extensive exposure, through the public broadcasting trade press as well as in CPB-funded seminars. They attempted to convince public radio managers that commercial research and programming strategies were a matter of common sense, much as advertising agencies had convinced broadcasters of the "naturalness" of ads in the 1920s. As the system's overall resistance to ascertainment suggested, developing innovative methods of public accountability and participation would detract valuable time and resources from the pursuit of money. Commercial research methodologies fit into public radio's pursuit of the path of least resistance; the methodologies were *scientific*, they were *proven*, and with a bit of tinkering they were *ready to go*.

Yet commercially derived research was not universally embraced within the public radio system. Controversy over ratings erupted at the 1978 Public Radio Conference: "After a presentation by Church, E. B. Eiselein, an academic from Arizona and consultant to public radio stations, stood up and proclaimed, 'Arbitron is bullshit.' Many of the conferees cheered." Marvin Granger of WPBX-FM in Spokane stated that "the moment we ask research to answer metaphysical questions, and to help us find cultural integrity, that is the moment I believe we become commercial broadcasters."[21] Undaunted, consultants set out to convince programmers of the need for their services. In 1979, Church and George Bailey (a former student of Lichty's) held a series of CPB-funded workshops across the country. In a trade press article describing the seminars, Bailey and Church claim that

while certain critics assert that audience research leads inevitably to commercialism, ratings have no particular ethic of their own. . . . Audience research, like surgery, is best performed by professionals. . . . [Questions about listenership] can be answered with objectivity and reliability by a trained analyst of the Arbitron audience surveys.[22]

After enumerating their services for hire, Bailey and Church gravely concluded, "Our future depends on having objective, systematic and reliable information from authentic research. These data exist and are waiting to be used."[23]

In 1979 the CPB began using Arbitron's interactive computer system to enable stations to obtain estimates for time periods matching their own schedules. Before the arrangement, stations had to infer these estimates from commercial schedules, which varied greatly from their own.[24] By 1980, stations in sixty-five of the eighty-five public radio markets surveyed by Arbitron subscribed to this service. The previous year, NPR had hired Lawrence Lichty as director of audience research and evaluation. At the behest of NPR vice president Samuel Holt, Lichty, Leo Rosenbluth (the director of CPB's Office of Communication Research), and Lichty's former student David Giovannoni began developing the Public Radio Audience Profile (PRAP). Funded with $50,000 from the CPB and $20,000 in NPR money, the PRAP used Arbitron data to obtain information about listening habits at the program level. Audience research was still highly controversial, however. In 1980, a resolution by Public Radio in Mid-America lauding NPR for its interest in "meaningful audience research" passed by a vote of only sixteen to fourteen, with ten abstentions.[25] Nevertheless, the public radio system was now firmly locked into the chase for audience numbers.

The first significant use of audience research data to construct NPR programming took place in the late 1970s. *All Things Considered*, NPR's flagship program, was a ninety-minute show with three half-hour sections. Local stations could directly engage listeners only during brief pauses on the half-hour, which complicated local on-air fundraising appeals and abilities to "build empathy" with local listeners through weather and traffic reports. Responding to local station demands, as well as the uncertainty of future tax-based subsidies, NPR created *Morning Edition* in November 1979. It was designed on the "clock hour" formula used by commercial radio, with set time segments for stories and frequent cutaways to local stations. To Thomas Looker, *Morning Edition* represented a milestone in NPR's history: the transformation from a *program*, or series of contiguous programs, to a *service*, or "something that listeners would not listen to from beginning to finish."[26] Lawrence Lichty, described as the program's "conceptualizer," conducted extensive audience research to test news story preferences, scheduling, and even the program's name. Yet *Morning Edition* initially was resisted by large-market stations like Boston's WGBH and Cincinnati's WGUC, which featured their own morning shows, and fewer than half of NPR's affiliates carried *Morning Edition* at the time of its debut.[27] The program gradually increased in popularity, partially because the morning drive period (7:00 to 9:00 A.M.) is characterized by greater overall levels of listening than afternoon drive time, and *Morning Edition*'s cumulative ratings exceeded those for *All Things Considered* in 1989.

Cultural programming began to slide as NPR devoted more of its resources to news and public affairs programming, a trend that continues to the present. In 1977, NPR spent more than $671,000 on cultural programming and nearly $1.2 million on news and informational programming. By 1993, the budget for cultural programming was $7.3 million, or roughly eleven times the 1977 figure, while funding for the news division had ballooned to $18.7 million, or nearly sixteen times the amount allocated for news in the 1977 budget.

Cultural programming was a perpetual afterthought at NPR; one notable exception, the *Sunday Show* arts program, failed due to conflicting demands of stations. The *Sunday Show* stemmed from NPR's 1980 proposal for a Music and Arts Project that would supply two hours each night of music, drama, arts criticism, and documentaries. The proposal was defeated by the stations at the 1980 Music Personnel Conference, who did not want to surrender ten hours of evening airtime to NPR each week. After surveying a sample of stations, NPR proposed *Sunday Magazine* in 1981 as "an audio arts and leisure section," an arts counterpart to *All Things Considered*.[28] Funding was targeted by NPR at $1.4 million, but the program still was opposed by many stations, who preferred that NPR concentrate on news and public affairs programming. Large producing stations like Minnesota Public Radio and KUSC already supplied many NPR affiliates with music programs, and obtaining local funding for arts programs was relatively easy due to their noncontroversial nature. Nevertheless, the *Sunday Show* premiered April 4, 1982, as a combination of performances, features, and arts news hosted by David Ossman, a founding member of the Fireside Theater comedy troupe. Similar to *Morning Edition*, the program was designed as a compartmentalized service from which listeners could tune in and out.

Initial carriage figures were positive (130 stations carried at least two hours of the segmented service, and eighty-four carried the entire block of programming), but the show's eclecticism and innovative content alienated many station managers. The *Sunday Show* was intended to feature new music, rather than classical warhorses, but station programmers complained that the program was an example of NPR "trying to force the 'new music' down the audience's throat. . . . When [a piece by avant-garde composer John] Cage comes in you can hear radios click off for miles around. . . . In Mobile, Strauss is considered contemporary."[29] George Bailey complained that "it was too unpredictable, with bluegrass one week and a Samoan Church Choir the next." Station programmers claimed that ratings showed the program fared poorly with listeners, but the program had begun airing in the fourth week of a twelve-week ratings sweep, which allowed audiences insufficient time to become familiar with the program. Ossman was replaced as host in September 1982, and the program's focus switched to classical music, with less talk and more slots for station breakaways, but the program folded shortly thereafter. Ossman's parting words to the public broadcasting trade journal *Current* were, "The *Sunday Show* has been used as a political football by stations that are virtually at war with NPR—who needs that?"[30] *Sunday Show* producer Deborah Lamberton explained the program's demise: "[The producers] tried to appease the requests of particular key stations—major market stations—and sometimes those requests were quite disparate. The bottom line is that it creates a series of guidelines that were anathema to the program's integrity."[31]

In contrast, *Morning Edition*'s success further oriented NPR in the direction of hard news and led the network to devote more of its resources to audience research. It spent less than $50,000 on research in fiscal year 1978; by 1983, the network's Audience Research and Evaluation Department was budgeted at $225,000. Both Lichty and Church left NPR in 1981, the former to work on documentaries for PBS and the latter to form the Radio Research Consortium, a membership organization that provided public stations with research data and consulting services.[32] Church and George Bailey later formed Walrus Research and began consulting for CBS's FM stations as well as public stations. Also in 1981, the CPB abolished its Office of Communication Research. According to John Fuller, the director of research at PBS, "OCR studies had become 'very sociological' and were generating 'little actionable research."[33] David Giovannoni was named head of NPR research in 1981 and left five years later for full-time consulting to public radio stations. His "Radio Intelligence" columns were a fixture in *Current* throughout the late 1980s. The columns, tantamount to advertising for consultants, were subsidized by CPB, even though Giovannoni was raking in fees as a private consultant. After several interim managers, NPR hired John Sutton (described by Stavitsky as "a veteran of commercial radio programming and marketing") as its research director in 1990.[34]

The consultants described in this chapter repeatedly hyped their "sci-

entific" standards and methodological rigor, which allowed them to position their services as ideologically neutral and absolutely necessary to
the public radio system. They also touted empirical research for an ability to reduce uncertainty; in one trade press column, Giovannoni hailed
Arbitron data (which, of course, required "professional" interpretation)
as "inexpensive, offer[ing] a great return, and as such constitute[ing]
outstanding investment."[35] Yet the agendas of these consultants were
hardly "neutral" or "value free." Since commercial broadcasting was
saturated with consultants, public radio provided fresh territory for their
activities. Tom Church, George Bailey, David Giovannoni, and others all
established lucrative private consulting careers with the aid of public
funds. While presenting themselves as impartial "third parties" who
merely interpreted audience data, they ceaselessly shilled their services
in order to enrich themselves and entrench their positions in the public
radio system. Their efforts have been so successful that they now set the
agenda for public radio in the United States.

THE DRIVE TO DOUBLE AUDIENCE

In 1984, NPR's weekly listenership stood at eight and a quarter million.
Consultant Tom Church argued that eighteen to twenty million listeners
a week were required to make public radio self-supporting. That fall,
Church and NPR president Douglas Bennet hatched a plan to double
NPR's audience within five years, by concentrating on expanding the
network's average-quarter-hour audience, on the grounds that "core"
listeners would be likely to donate to NPR's member stations. An
Audience-Building Task Force chaired by Donald Mullally and comprising nine station managers and program directors was convened in May
1986. Its report, issued two months later, left little doubt about the future
direction of public radio. The report accused stations of failing to define
their "market position" and declared that stations should not "present
programs because they are worth presenting, whether or not they serve
audience needs." Instead, they should react to what were viewed as commercial news and "smooth jazz" competitors by adopting commercial
strategies; specifically, by defining a narrow niche or station "identity"
and replacing individual programs with "seamless" blocks of programming. The report also explicitly instructed public radio stations how to
increase the size of their audiences. Stations should develop average-
quarter-hour ratings goals for each section of the broadcast day, and
"each expenditure should be examined in terms of dollar per listener."
All training efforts should be geared toward building audience, and "un-
professional" on-air volunteers should be eliminated. In addition, "stations should avoid, and syndicators should not produce ... programs
which contain such a wide variety of music that they inhibit careful

dayparting [scheduling]." Furthermore, "no national production funds should be provided for programming which does not include a research component testing the appeal of the program and its concept." In a recommendation that undoubtedly thrilled consultants, the task force advocated using $22,000 in NPR funds for the immediate production of research "first-aid kits" that would include, among other things, a "list of safe/avoid classical music selections."[36]

The *Audience-Building Task Force Report* evoked a firestorm of criticism upon its release. Dave Kanzeg, the former program manager of WNYC, accused the authors of encouraging "anti-intellectual yahooism." William Siemering, then manager of WHYY in Philadelphia, offered a more measured critique. In response to the report's claim that "national promotion funds [should] be spent only in markets in which the local station is making a concerted effort to increase audience as part of a national goal," he asked, "What criteria and what effort will determine if a station is making a 'concerted' effort? Will funds be withheld if they play unsafe music?" Independent producer Everett Frost claimed that "audience development leads to an inordinate emphasis—sometimes an anxiety-ridden fixation—on packaging rather than substance and on formatting rather than programming." He also noted that in 1986 the CPB's Radio Program Fund had refused to fund proposals for serious radio drama (including works by Eugene O'Neill and Samuel Beckett) on grounds of "audience building."[37] Consultants had long dismissed radio drama as hopelessly antiquarian; during a presentation to program directors in the late 1970s, George Bailey quipped that the best time to schedule radio drama was "1938."[38]

Two years after the Audience-Building Task Force, consultants David Giovannoni, Tom Thomas, Terry Clifford, and Linda Liebold issued the CPB-funded *Audience '88* report, which further underscored the penetration of marketplace ideology into public radio. The authors measured "program efficiency" in terms of the cost of serving one listener for one hour. News and public affairs programming was considered the most efficient, followed by classical music. According to researchers, "Jazz programming is the least efficient of the three major formats: It consumes 17 percent of all program-hours, but generates only 10 percent of all listener-hours and only eight percent of all listener income."[39] The logical inference is that "public service" can be measured by listener contributions and underwriter support, which would make *Car Talk* the most significant program on public radio. *Audience '88* was problematic on other grounds. All ratings samples are biased in desirable directions, and *Audience '88*'s sample was weighted toward NPR members. The CPB cited one in ten listeners as a station member at the time of the test, yet 34 percent of survey respondents claimed to be members.[40]

Since the mid-1980s, at the urging of consultants, public radio broad-

Table 5.1
Audience Estimates for CPB-Qualified Radio Stations, 1971–1995

	1971	1975	1980	1985	1990	1995
Cumulative audience (millions)	1.3	3.3	5.3	9.8	13.9	19.7
Average-quarter-hour audience (thousands)	n/a	147	271	611	835	1281
Number of stations	103	165	199	270	343	421

Source: Adapted from *Current,* September 11, 1995, p. 8 and from various CPB reports.

casters have defined "audience service" in terms of "time spent listening," or the ability of stations to retain a core audience defined by average-quarter-hour (AQH) ratings (see Table 5.1). These ratings measure the number of people listening to a given station for at least five minutes within a given quarter hour, while cumulative ratings ("cumes") measure the number of people listening for at least five minutes a week. Cumulative ratings represent the total listenership for a particular time period, while AQH is an average. Despite consultants' emphasis on AQH ratings, their efforts yielded surprising results. While average-quarter-hour listening rose nearly 37 percent between 1985 and 1990 (down from a growth rate of 126 percent between 1980 and 1985), the cumulative audience grew nearly 42 percent from 1985 to 1990, down from 85 percent in the previous period (see Table 5.2). These figures indicate that overall listenership grew at a slower rate between 1985 and 1990 despite public radio's audience-building schemes, and that the growth in cumulative listenership actually *outpaced* average-quarter-hour listening. While these trends may be due in part to the greater number of CPB-qualified radio stations, they just as clearly undermine the conventional programming belief that listeners treat radio as an ambient medium, or "audio wallpaper."

Why, then, should public radio emphasize average-quarter-hour ratings rather than cumulative listenership? Simply put, the "core" audience defined by AQH ratings is seen as more willing to contribute financially to public radio stations, and the image of a fixed and stable audience is attractive to underwriters. Giovannoni stated that "[consultants] don't use cume because it counts every listener equally; the person who flows in from the previous program and listens for five minutes before tuning out counts as much as the person who makes a point to tune in the program and listen to every minute."[41] As government funding shrinks, listener income has become the fastest-growing sector of public radio support; hence the need to squeeze more money out of listeners, as well as increase the amount of money that can be easily controlled at the local level. The result is that listener contributions are

Table 5.2
Growth in Cumulative Versus Average-Quarter-Hour Audiences, 1975–1995 (in percentages)

	1975	1980	1985	1990	1995
Cumulative growth (over previous period)	153.8	60.6	84.9	41.8	41.7
Average-quarter-hour growth (over previous period)	n/a	84.4	126.3	36.7	73.0

used to index audience (or "public") service, and consultants define programming "value" as "the amount a listener will voluntarily pay to hear an hour of programming."[42] Financial value becomes a proxy for personal value: in his keynote speech to the 1997 Public Radio Program Director's Conference, Giovannoni announced that "the amount of money your listeners send you is a direct function of the public service your station is providing."[43]

Financial returns offer an unambiguous criteria for success, yet the fact remains that public service cannot be quantified. While "value" (as defined by consultants) has replaced "mission" at the core of public radio's ideology, "value" remains an equally subjective measure. Obviously, personal value has as much to do with the sharing of social and cultural values and engendering public discourse as it does with monetary "voting." Consultants may define value in terms of consumer sovereignty, yet this sovereignty is suspect when consumers have limited options because of broadcasting's barriers to entry.

The mandate to double NPR's audience by 1989 went unmet; in October 1988, the NPR board extended the deadline to 1992. But by the mid-1980s, Stavitsky finds, "discord over the use of audience research in public radio had largely faded. As station manager Marvin Granger noted, 'The issue was settled and the researchers won.' "[44] Average-quarter-hour ratings are now formally institutionalized as a means for determining federal funding eligibility. In July, 1996, KPCC in Pasadena, California, changed its programming emphasis from 1930s and '40s era jazz to a format of morning news/talk programs and Adult Album Alternative in the afternoons. The station was forced to increase its average-quarter-hour ratings by 20 percent to meet the new CSG criteria, despite the fact that its cumulative audience was the ninth largest in the United States. KPCC stood to lose $175,000 in CPB funds, or 16 percent of its budget. Reflecting the fatalism of many managers in the face of the consultant juggernaut, KPCC's general manager shrugged that the average-quarter-hour criteria "did force us into a more uniform format which looks more like commercial radio than noncommercial radio. It's not good public policy, but it's done."[45]

Ratings remain highly problematic for public radio. Arbitron ratings measure local audiences, not local needs, and the public radio system's image of its audience is shaped by the methodology it uses.[46] The listener diary system fails to account for listening in institutional settings like hospitals and dormitories, and it also skews data toward upper-income audiences, since they are more likely to return the diaries. In addition, the concept of a "fixed" audience is highly suspect. Ien Ang notes that the audience's composition is shifting and tentative; the need to "capture" this audience fuels producer speculation on audience behavior, which in turn creates a greater emphasis on more "accurate" and detailed scrutiny. Advanced research, which seeks to bring the audience under microscopic view, reveals that it is constantly dissolving and reforming. It is never fully captured; instead, it is pursued by accumulating more information, which further confirms that it is constantly shifting, which fuels the need for more data. Rather than facilitating control, audience measurement makes control more difficult, and the audience is ultimately defined in tautological terms.[47]

The use of national ratings also is highly politicized, because of the often fractious relationships between national organizations and local stations. David Leroy finds that ratings and research in public broadcasting are used as leverage over local stations, since individual stations are at a disadvantage in research expertise. He adds that "it is not in the immediate self-interest of the national organizations to change this situation."[48] Audience research also increases the disparity between large and small stations in the public radio system. Max Wycisk, general manager of KCFR, estimated that research duties consumed nearly 24 percent of his time and more than 50 percent of the program director's time.[49] Managers of small stations can scarcely afford such demands. Of course, others are more than willing to perform these services for an appropriate fee. A 1993 column in *Current* detailed a mind-numbing array of consultant services available to station managers: Tom Church's Radio Research Consortium could provide market and customer profiles for $3,600; Giovannoni's Audience Research Analysis firm would conduct custom surveys of listening areas for $650; George Bailey's Walrus Research "Program Economics" survey, which estimates how much revenue is produced by particular programs, was available for $15,000 to $20,000. Other services included Arbitron diary reviews for $600 dollars and up and focus groups for $15,000. An auditorium music test would cost approximately $45,000, with telephone surveys of listeners approximately $15,000.[50]

In September 1997, public radio consultants began to release the preliminary findings from *Audience '98*, the first comprehensive national survey of public radio listeners since *Audience '88*. Masterminded by David Giovannoni and funded by the Corporation for Public Broadcasting (CPB) at a cost of nearly half a million dollars, *Audience '98* represents the culmination of audience research in public radio. Listening and donation patterns will be interpreted from more than thirty thousand Arbitron diaries from fall 1996, as well as an Arbitron followup survey of 8,100 listeners. Reports are being solicited from public radio professionals as a part of the study; according to Giovannoni, using these reports "lets all of public radio buy into [*Audience '98*] by participating in it."[51] Of course, this strategy also is a shrewd tactical maneuver designed to lessen criticism within the public radio system. The report doubtlessly will deliver a dazzling array of constructed factoids, all clad in elaborate empirical finery. Among other things, *Audience '98* promises to determine the financial return, per listener hour, of specific public radio programs and formats. Audience research has been used for managerial, rather than civic, purposes since the advent of the public radio system. *Audience '98* represents the latest in a series of efforts by the public radio system to posit public radio stations as direct competitors to their commercial counterparts and define the "public" primarily in terms of its ability to sustain the system.

FROM DEMOGRAPHICS TO PSYCHOGRAPHICS

Public radio stations have long been interested in how many people are listening; increasingly, they are interested in what kinds of people are listening. A significant part of *Audience '98* is devoted to psychographic research, based on the Values and Lifestyles Program (VALS) typologies developed by SRI International of Menlo Park, California. In addition to providing demographic information about consumers, VALS delineates audience "clusters," based on attitudes, behaviors, and consumer tastes. Such techniques are commonly employed by the advertising industry. In 1981, WKSU in Kent, Ohio, became the first public radio station to employ psychographic research, using it to determine audience consumption patterns and listening preferences.[52] That same year, NPR began to purchase data from Simmons Market Research about public radio listeners. *The NPR Audience*, published by NPR in 1981 from Simmons findings, found three types of listeners. The first, constituting 34.6 percent of NPR's listeners, had a median age of twenty-nine, was health oriented (and likely to buy cigarette rolling papers), tended to attend concerts and films, and did not own their homes. "Type Two" listeners (30 percent) were female homemakers aged eighteen to fifty-five and likely to be college graduates, with an affinity for headache remedies and lipstick. The third group of listeners (35 percent) were "successful" males, who were more likely to own personal computers and fly their own airplanes than the general population.[53]

A detailed study of NPR's audience, conducted by NPR, Arbitron, and the Development Exchange, was published in 1985 as *Public Radio Lis-*

teners: Supporters and Non-supporters. In a telling reference, the study was commonly known within NPR as "Cheap 90," for the approximate percentage of public radio listeners who failed to donate to their local stations. When asked to describe their local public radio station, more than three-quarters of those surveyed used the words "high quality," "noncommercial," "entertaining," "informative," "educational," "a station I can trust and rely on." Yet the study also found that "fewer than half of all listeners consider[ed] public radio 'important' in their lives. . . . Only 34 percent of the cheap 90 consider[ed] public radio important, compared with 54 percent of supporters," and these were likely to be women over the age of fifty.[54] Three years later, *Audience '88* found that public radio listeners tended to be "inner-directed" professionals between the ages of thirty-four and forty-four, who "conduct their lives primarily in accord with inner values—the needs and desires private to the individual—rather than in accord with values oriented to externals." More than half of the public radio audience had attended college and boasted annual incomes above $30,000.[55] This information was crucial if public radio was to market itself to corporate underwriters. Alan Stavitsky notes that a spring 1991 survey found NPR news listeners "were 47 percent more likely than average to own an Acura automobile; public station underwriting salespeople could descend on their local Acura dealerships armed with such data."[56]

However, psychographics are used infrequently in radio. Simmons relies heavily on "ascription," a statistical method in which probability is applied to available data to supply unavailable information. This method leads critics to accuse Simmons of "making up numbers." The findings are not available on a routine basis, and "clustering" requires a substantial amount of subjective decision making. The typologies used in clustering, such as "old-fashioned" or "other directed," are arbitrary labels that may not accurately represent the data. Clustering also is most effective when the number of clusters is fewer than six, but that precludes effectiveness in areas with diverse populations, such as the largest radio markets.[57]

Focus groups are employed more frequently by commercial radio stations; they have been used by public radio since the mid-1980s. The first of these studies, funded by CPB, NPR, and participating stations KLCC in Eugene, KPLU in Seattle, and KJZZ in Mesa, Arizona, evaluated New Age, contemporary, acoustic, and "mainstream" music in 1986. Each station assembled two panels of college-educated people aged twenty-five to forty-nine. Staffers played a tape of song "hooks" to the groups, and participants indicated on a form how much they liked or disliked selections. Afterward, moderators asked participants which selections they felt were compatible when played together. The study found that "respondents in all three markets preferred contemporary and new age styles over traditional mainstream styles" and favored slower, more "lyrical" pieces over those that were "busy" or "aggressive," on grounds that they were better suited for "background music."[58] In addition to implying that "background music" was the appropriate use for public radio, consultants argued that New Age and acoustic music were incompatible with jazz, and that jazz programmers should either ignore them altogether or incorporate them while eliminating music that did not have "congruent" appeal.

The Denver Project, conducted at KCFR between 1988 and 1990, institutionalized the use of focus groups in public radio. The first year of the study was fully funded by a $125,000 grant from CPB, the second year by $90,000 from CPB and $45,000 from KCFR, and the final year by KCFR. Directed by George Bailey of Walrus Research, the Denver Project deployed the complete arsenal of consultant weapons. Individual Arbitron diaries were used to determine listener loyalty and financial support; music was tested in focus group settings of ten to twelve listeners, whose reactions were videotaped from behind a two-way mirror; auditorium tests using between seventy-five and a hundred respondents evaluated music via an electronic program that recorded listener responses; and telephone "perceptual" surveys of three hundred listeners checked the reliability of group data. After the study was completed, KCFR came to the startling realization that different musical genres appealed to different groups of listeners, and it used this hard-won knowledge to conclude that their music programming was "too broad and inconsistent." KCFR subsequently streamlined its playlist, eliminating selections that clashed with the "dominant" mode. WKSU followed a similar path in 1991 after focus groups objected to works by Stravinsky in favor of Beethoven.[59]

Focus groups also have been used to gauge the "effectiveness" of independent productions and to determine whether they would receive funding. In July 1989, Bailey tested listener responses to eight public radio series, including *Afropop Worldwide, Crossroads, Fresh Air, Good Evening, Marketplace, NPR's Latin File, New American Radio*, and *Soundprint*. The project was funded by the CPB Radio Fund at a total cost of $80,000. A sample of 440 people (340 listeners and one hundred nonlisteners) was chosen as representative of the public radio audience. The groups used keypads to register their responses while listening to five-to-seven-minute selections from programs; a computer linked responses to demographic variables like age, gender, and ethnicity. Participants also were asked "open-ended" questions about what they liked or did not like about particular programs. This methodology also was used to test strategies for a national public radio pledge drive in 1993, with $470,000 in CPB funding.[60]

The use of focus groups to drop "marginal" programming may reduce uncertainty, but such knowledge comes at a price. Researchers suggested that an "entry level" research package, including Arbitron data, two sets of focus groups with six groups per set, and a perceptual telephone survey, would cost approximately $50,000, while a single auditorium test for evaluating music can cost $60,000.[61] More importantly, the methodology used in these surveys is simplistic and reductive. Familiar music has a much better chance of eliciting favorable responses, while unfamiliar or stylistically innovative material inevitably fares poorly; the use of programming snippets rather than complete productions also favors modular programs at the expense of long-term documentaries. In addition, audience input is solicited only in carefully controlled, "scientific" surroundings that differ greatly from actual listening conditions. One critic argued that focus groups "can tell us only about how people talk about something when asked to, not whether and how they actually do so."

The use of qualitative audience research by public broadcasters poses particular challenges because of the varied goals and objectives of the system. Qualitative research "does nothing more than measure volume of applause," while disregarding the ability of programs to convey information, stimulate the search for additional information, and develop tastes and interests.[62]

By the mid-1990s, NPR's Audience Research Unit was engaged in a host of activities designed to help stations generate revenues. In addition to providing information about what programming styles and strategies most effectively wring dollars from listeners, the research unit provided stations and producers with Simmons data on demographics, zip-code analyses of where pockets of listeners live, and customized profiles of station contributors. The desire to reduce uncertainty was taken to cynical extremes. John Berky, the director of Connecticut Public Radio, once asked, "What good is a listener to public radio if they don't contribute[?] ... [To] get members you need the right kind of listeners." Anything not sanctified by research represented a squandering of time and money. George Bailey has referred to CPB program funds as "spillage. . . . Let's just consider that money lost, wasted." Bailey also ridicules station managers who reject research as either "classical missionar[ies]" who have "a holy obligation to program *the repertoire* on an annual cycle" or emblematic of "free-form, stoned-DJ, college-town radio." While consultants and managers steer public radio in the direction of its commercial counterparts, this orientation must be carefully concealed. David Giovannoni warns: *"Don't blow the public service image.* It's an accurate perception which public radio's increasing preoccupation with increasing audience could shatter. Discussions about 'audience doubling' should *never* reach the public's ears without careful characterization and presentation."[63]

Ralph Engelman finds that the direction taken by audience research "signaled two trends in public radio at odds with its original statement of mission: an emphasis on mass marketing and the cultivation of an elite membership base."[64] As they differentiate between audiences, research and ratings methodologies seek to divide and conquer the public for purposes of organizational control. The fragmentation of viewers and listeners diminishes their mutual self-recognition as a "public," and the system's conception of the public as an "audience" engenders passivity on the part of listeners. The public radio system's concentration on simplistic descriptive data, derived from commercially based polling and marketing research, continues to perpetuate audience stereotypes and marginalize actual public involvement. While ostensibly attempting to elicit audience responses, both qualitative and quantitative methodologies are instrumental in asserting organizational control in the guise of "value-free" science. By relying on research and ratings to determine "value" and "service," which are in fact undeterminable, public broadcasters have ignored their missions of participation, pluralism, and diversity. In that regard, we might well consider the money spent on consultants and audience research as "spillage . . . money lost, wasted."

FROM SERVICE TO SELLING

In addition to adopting commercial broadcasting's research methodologies, public radio increasingly emulates its programming practices. In the 1970s, classical music was the most common type of public radio programming, followed by news and informational programming, jazz, and radio drama.[65] Stations frequently divided their schedules into blocks, or segments of time that appeal to small audiences, in hopes of gradually building a large collective following. On weekdays, stations might air *Morning Edition* followed by locally originated programs based on classical music records. A morning opera program might be followed by a program featuring works by Romantic composers, which would segue into an hour of Baroque performances. A local arts program would lead into *All Things Considered*, and jazz programming would fill out the night. Weekends were devoted to bluegrass, folk, or jazz programs originating locally or from NPR. Block programming served several important purposes for public radio. Such programming attracted diverse groups of listeners and presented an image of pluralism to the public while reducing the station's dependence on one specific group of listeners. In addition, the "balanced portfolio" of block programming allowed the station to recover if a commercial station adapted one of its blocks.

As public broadcasters faced funding inconsistencies throughout the 1980s, station managers began coveting the consistent and marketable audiences associated with commercial radio. Public radio leaders complained that attempts to serve varied groups resulted in patchwork scheduling that fragmented listenership and placed public stations in a reactive posture with respect to other stations. One program manager claimed that the station's block programming strategy had balkanized the schedule: "We didn't want to isolate the communities and say, 'this is *your* half-hour, and this is *your* half-hour.'" Above all, they feared that the lack of a consistent "product image" drove away potential underwriters. Consultants claimed that block programming discouraged one group from listening most of the time and cut into the all-important average-quarter-hour ratings that could be used as bait for sponsors.[66]

Unlike block programming, formats provide consistent programming throughout the broadcast schedule and so deliver measured and defined groups of consumers to advertisers. Format radio was inaugurated in the early to mid-1950s in medium-sized Midwestern markets, and its convenience for programmers and advertisers soon established it as the dominant form of commercial radio programming. Although radio stations competed against each other for overall ratings, programming strategies were increasingly niche oriented; broadcasting began to evolve into "narrowcasting," in which station owners became preoccupied with staking audience boundaries. One of the keys to format consistency was a "clock hour" formula that specified every element of programming and explicitly stated when it was to occur. Format radio was designed to demand little concentration from listeners, since station managers found that 50 percent of their audience was mobile.[67] Station managers also used the standardization of the clock hour to centralize programming control, by winnowing out "incompatible" material and reining in announcers. The adoption of a single music and presentational style radically reduced the number of programming choices and simplified decision making. As one station manager noted, "The scheduling strategy of format radio is almost automatic."[68]

By the early 1980s, consultants were urging public radio programmers to form more contiguous programming blocks by reducing the "seams," or marked divisions, between programs. Concert and recital programs were often "stripped" into programs running five nights per week and placed in the context of larger classical music programs. In 1984, Tom Church's Radio Research Consortium advocated airing "seamless" blocks and boosting national programs while suggesting that low-drawing "specialty" programs be exiled outside of prime time, such as late at night.[69] As public radio stations began to compare themselves to commercial stations through ratings, consultants promoted narrowing audiences as common sense.

Yet formats serve neither public radio's traditional mission nor its new profit motive. David Kanzeg of WCPN in Cleveland described the hidden costs of reducing uncertainty through formats:

Financial pressures, among other things, have forced many of us to narrow our targets, to focus our resources and to limit our outlooks to compete with so-called real radio. By doing so, though, we have cut off options, sent talent fleeing in frustration, and undermined much of our original support base by becoming less diverse and less interesting.[70]

Stations are unwilling to take programming risks that might interfere with their pursuit of "core" audiences, which leaves new shows with few potential venues and thus reduces diversity.

However, the "stable" audiences produced by formats attract potential underwriters. David Giovannoni has noted that "businesses and other institutions have many reasons for underwriting programming. In all but the purest cases of altruistic philanthropy, the underwriters evaluate the *quid pro quo*—their return on their underwriting investment."[71] The ideology of audience "service" obscures the reality of target marketing; despite consultants' claims, formats serve underwriters, not the public. Public radio's practices increasingly are grounded in competition rather than public service. In 1998, NPR's Bob Edwards told *Current*, "You know, the suits see our competition as PRI. And I don't. I see our competition as Dr. Laura and Stern and Imus and Paul Harvey, [and] Rush [Limbaugh]." Consultants underscore this shift even more forcefully (though with less tact). During a debate with Larry Josephson at the 1996 Public Radio Conference, Giovannoni snarled, "If you think you're immune from the forces of competition, are you telling me it's your right to . . . get behind a mike and jerk off?"[72]

The basic assumption of commercial and public radio consultants is that listeners show allegiance to stations, not discrete programs. However, the rapid turnover and obsolescence of formats indicates that audience "churn" is high and station loyalty is limited. In 1989, Philip Marino, the publisher of the Los Angeles *Radio Guide*, claimed that "instead of formats, people are listening to programs." Conventional programming wisdom holds that "foreground listening" is rare, that requiring concentrated attention risks alienating listeners. A writer for the *New York Times* has noted, "Oddly, though, these same people who are said to listen without intention seem to care a great deal about their classical stations. Any change in format provides angry protests and letters to the editor."[73] Yet consultants argue that listeners must be kept at bay; their comments to stations stem from "uncontrolled" situations and may be orchestrated. Listeners who resist programming changes are referred to as "bossy aficionados" who are "atypical of your audience" and, most importantly, "even of your contributors."[74] Such remarks, designed to reassure station managers that their efforts at minimizing pluralism and public participation are completely logical, underscore the commercially derived view of the public radio audience as essentially passive and herdlike. Democracy, on the other hand, has never been noted for its "efficiency." Economics increasingly are equated with aesthetics: Citing the findings of *Audience '88*, David Giovannoni claimed that "opera lovers are not as well off financially as other persons in public radio's audience" and suggested that "programmers who must schedule opera programming must schedule it carefully.... [O]pera is a certain tuneout for most public radio listeners." However, Ray Nordstrand of Chicago's WFMT had found earlier that opera broadcasts actually increase average-quarter-hour figures for his station and drew highly responsive donors.[75]

In addition to narrowing audiences, many public radio stations are selecting music for accessibility and mood, eliminating anything unfamiliar. Much of the growing antipathy toward nontraditional classical music may be explained by station managers and consultants who are themselves unfamiliar with the genre and find it forbidding or intimidating. One consultant claimed that predictions of the death of classical music on public radio were becoming self-fulfilling prophecies; consultants "[lack] experience in the format, and are more attracted to other kinds of radio. They interpret audience data to say that classical music is dying, and that view has become a kind of dogma. Because people repeat this dogma to one another, they come to believe that it's true."[76] A 1990 article in *Current* described the changes in classical programming: "Opera is out. Organs are out. Harpsichords, early music and vocals are out. No atonal or 12-tone compositions. Very little 20th-century music. Little choral or vocal [music]." After extensively scrutinizing Arbitron reports, KNPR in Las Vegas retained its classical programming in 1990 but dropped jazz in favor of what program director John Stark termed "light, bright, lovely and feel-good music." Other decisions have been less objective: a former staff member at Minnesota Public Radio recalled a meeting in which William Kling urged MPR music director Michael Barone to play "more of those Handel symphonies." Consultants have suggested that station on-air personnel try to sound conversational rather than pedantic and talk about composers as "real people." The results are often smarmy and occasionally ludicrous. The general manager of WMRA in Harrisonburg, Virginia, once introduced a Rossini piece on the air by saying, "I played with Barbie dolls when I was 14, but when Rossini was that age, he wrote this symphony."[77]

A June 1993 article in *Music Notes*, describing the Denver Project's efforts at streamlining music airplay, cited the Project's goals as to "increase tune-ins, generate greater listener loyalty, improve appeal to defined target audience segments, create congruent affinity among news and music, and increase the value of service to the listening audience." As one observer noted, "The first four relate to some aspect of increasing a station's ratings, and exactly one makes a token mention of increasing 'the value of service,' without defining what is meant by that phrase."[78]

Part of the impetus for aggressively promoting music consulting is the rewards that stations can reap from selling data to other stations. In addition to Denver's KCFR, KPLU in Seattle-Tacoma sponsored music-testing sessions early in 1996 and began selling data to other stations later that year.[79] To ferret out "incompatible" music and assemble schedules, a growing number of stations are relying on music selection software. According to Rachel Goodman:

Consultants from a Cleveland, Ohio affiliate are hard-selling public radio stations a new, $8000 computer software package. The program spits out playlists each day based on key words that are designed to inspire people to tune in. For the morning, it chooses "uplifting, inspirational" classical pieces. The computer prints out popular selections which are composed in major keys, or if not, suggests omitting the movements in minor keys.[80]

Imitation and borrowing are important sources of new ideas in organizations (as shown by periodic format "crazes" in commercial radio), and business, trade, and professional organizations promote a common frame of reference. Reflecting the growing professionalization of public radio, several public radio program directors formed a "program director's task force" in 1985 to spread the gospel of consultants. This self-appointed task force was formalized into the Maryland-based Public Radio Program Directors Association, which held workshops on audience-building across the country in the mid 1980s. *The Public Radio Program Director's Handbook*, which originated in these workshops, is tantamount to an advertisement for formats and consultants. The *Handbook* summarily dismisses block programming as "inconsistent," in that it impedes the abilities for station "positioning"; it concludes with a comprehensive list of public radio consultants and services.[81] By 1991, the PRPD had 150 dues-paying members. It offers a variety of consulting services at extra charge and has played a major role in programming design, inasmuch as several program distributors and independent producers use the organization as a sounding board. However, as Eric Rothenbuhler notes, organizations like the PRPD "constitute a professional audience that is independent of listeners, who, in contrast, are thought of in only vague typifications."[82]

Many of NPR's recent efforts have strengthened the trend toward formatting public radio. In 1995, following several personnel layoffs, NPR decided to position itself to support the dominant formats of classical and jazz. The following February, to artificially prime the market for NPR's growing emphasis on news programming, the network offered stations a discount on audience research, to help them evaluate the probable outcomes of switching to all-news formats.[83] This application of research is hardly "neutral'; NPR gains from increasing economies of scale for its news programming while freezing out local production, and consultants stand to benefit financially from NPR's subsidies. By mid-1996, NPR could call itself a twenty-four-hour news/talk service. Daytimes featured *Morning Edition, The Diane Rehm Show, Fresh Air's* noon feed, *The Derek McGinty Show, Talk of the Nation,* and *All Things Considered.* NPR feeds *ATC* until 10 P.M. Eastern time, and daytime shows may be rolled over in the evenings. The future of NPR cultural efforts is indicated in programs like the *Talk of the Nation*, call-in talk shows that are highly derivative of commercial offerings, with a crucial demographic difference.

Format streamlining also is indicated by the fact that many major-market public radio stations are switching to all-news programming, relying heavily on NPR satellite feeds and augmenting them with syndicated news and talk programs. San Francisco's KQED went all-news in 1987, followed by WUWM in Milwaukee in 1988. WHYY in Philadelphia and KPBS in San Diego adopted all-news programming in 1991; by early 1996, more than twenty-five CPB-supported stations had classified themselves as strictly news/information stations.[84] Baltimore's WJHU, KJZZ in Phoenix, and KERA in Dallas replaced their midday music with news/talk programming in the early 1990s, and KXJZ in Sacramento and WUNC in Chapel Hill also extended their news programming. Public stations airing jazz programming are particularly prone to adopt all-news formats, since the audience for jazz programming is seen as small and likely to be drawn to "smooth jazz" commercial stations. This trend may well be reinforced by the recent lifting of radio ownership regulations, which will allow commercial stations to target small-niche audiences with highly researched, automated formats. Given its historically reactive stance, public radio undoubtedly will follow suit.

Consultants are advocating "multiversioning" NPR programming to slice and dice the public in the name of efficiency. For example, David Giovannoni suggests multiversioning NPR's *All Things Considered* into *ATC-35* (targeting thirty-five-year-olds), *ATC-45* (the current version, with a sharper demographic focus), and *ATC-55* (for classical music listeners). To Giovannoni, such programming "could offer tremendous economies for the network, as well as large pay-offs for public radio stations and the system in total." Michael Arnold of KWSU-FM in Pullman, Washington, has dryly noted that "Giovannoni's vision of the future is tremendously exciting. Every night at five, older listeners can tune in for in-depth interviews about estate planning and good deals on caskets on *ATC 65*. . . . The listeners will be getting just what they want—news that involves only them."[85]

Public radio strategies have long advocated a greater number of stations, each of which would cater to a discrete, demographically honed audience. The CPB's *Five Year Plan for Public Telecommunications*, issued in 1981, claimed that "multiple stations serving the same area substantially increase the diversity of programming available to the listener, because each station is able to build its programming around a different format." In 1992, a CPB-funded study conducted by consultants Giovannoni, Thomas, and Clifford suggested that 250 additional stations could be included in a CPB-supported, satellite-interconnected public radio system.[86] Such expansion would certainly produce economies of scale for programming, yet it ignores the barriers to entry in the narrow-spectrum space allocated to noncommercial broadcasters; the present system is saturated at 550 stations, and the noncommercial spectrum is nearly full in most metropolitan areas. Formats also have failed to diversify the audience of public radio. In 1994, Mark Feurst of WXPN noted that "many diversification efforts were, in reality, format breaks that splintered rather than expanded listenership. Thus, a decade of effort produced only a handful of programs or stations that effectively reached beyond the market segments public radio served in 1985."[87]

The unspoken premise behind public radio's urban expansion is that existing stations could skim off the cream and relegate less-popular "conscience" programming to smaller, low-power stations, effectively ghettoizing public radio. The history of Boston's WBUR provides a case in point. According to station manager Jane Christo, WBUR in the early 1970s "had just about everything—classical, jazz, alternative music, Latino. There was a woman's program, different types of minority programs, how-to programs." After Christo was promoted to general manager in 1979, the station switched from free-form to all-classical programming and then gradually developed an all-news format. At present, it has the fifth-largest public radio audience in the United States. WBUR's rise in listenership was matched by its success in fundraising. In 1997, the station raised $170,000 in hour-long pledge-drive sessions spread over three days; a Boston-area producer observed that "the sheer number of underwriting credits that you hear in a given hour of drive time can be overwhelming." Christo shrugged off suggestions that WBUR's focus on "seamless" programming had hampered diversity:

If you take a specific program, like a minority program, and put it on for an hour on Saturday afternoon, I've never been one that thought that was diversity. I think we do a better service and are more diverse by doing our best to cover everything that we possibly can, at a time when all these diverse members of the community are available to listen to radio.[88]

Yet it is arguable whether WBUR actually seeks to cater to "all these diverse members of the community." The "conscience" items have been relegated to the University of Massachusetts's tiny WUMB, which focuses on folk music and broadcasts at a fraction of WBUR's power. In addition, the CPB's institutionalization of average-quarter-hour ratings has further marginalized urban stations that serve diverse publics. If the commercial model is any guide, proposals that public stations purchase existing licensees are not likely to encourage diversity. To save on costs and encourage economies of scale, managers are apt to use syndicated programming that precludes public involvement and consideration of local issues.

Consultants define "value" in terms of listener donations, yet they recommend that station managers ignore listeners when their reactions interfere with organizational efficiency and control. They also disparage local programming, which is less popular with underwriters attracted to the "product image" of NPR news; they often advocate axing local news entirely. In 1992, the station manager of Tampa's WUSF commissioned George Bailey to examine the station's programming in light of declining membership income. At the time, the station aired a combination of classical, jazz, NPR news, and local news. Bailey suggested three possible new formats: all-classical, all-news, or classical/news. None of Bailey's recommendations made any provision for local news.[89] While the overall growth in public radio news programming appears to serve the needs of local communities, the cost of news production remains extremely high, because it is labor intensive. These costs are passed along to stations, who then are compelled to repeat and roll over NPR news and features to maximize their investments in programming. A survey of 568 public radio stations in the early 1990s found that one-fifth emphasized news and public affairs programming and two-fifths music programming; the remainder were characterized as "mixed format." The prognosis for local programming was grim. The study predicted that mixed classical, news, and jazz stations will specialize in one of the three, particularly syndicated classical and network news. Due to format focusing, " 'specialty' programs . . . will be the first to be displaced. The Saturday morning kid's show, the Saturday afternoon ball game, the Sunday morning church service, the Sunday night drama . . . most stations anticipate a declining role for these programs as well."[90]

This bottom-line obsession will surely increase as more station managers emerge from the ranks of development rather than programming. The ideology of the marketplace is reflected in David Giovannoni's comments that the "real" inefficiency in public radio occurs when public money sustains what he terms "boutique" programming and small stations with insignificant audiences. According to Giovannoni, "Acquired programming offers a gross return per hour of listening twice that of local programming."[91] Local "service" is used to justify the lack of localism; the use of syndicated news material is rationalized by managers like Dennis Kita of Baltimore's WJHU, who has declared, "I am not at all apologetic for airing nationally syndicated programs that have won the most prestigious awards in broadcasting. . . . It comes from a deep commitment all of us have to our communities.'"[92] The use of syndicated programs like *Talk of the Nation* reflects consultants' claims that localism has changed from a spatial grounding in geographically localized communities to a social orientation, in which "community" is defined in terms of shared interests, tastes, and values.[93] However, this formulation of community implicitly serves the interests of managers, since it is based on preferences for consumption rather than participation in civic discourse.

Public radio stations are public trusts, designed to serve their respective communities rather than merely pledging members. Instead of providing an arena for public debate, the industrial strategies adopted by National Public Radio and its affiliates divide the audience into taste cultures. The "public" NPR was chartered to serve remains a public in name only. By adopting the rigid and reductive programming practices of commercial format radio, public radio perpetuates the isolation and exclusion that are collectively the antithesis of "public" life.

In 1987, as NPR was in the midst of its efforts to double its audience within five years, independent producer Loni Ding told a Senate subcommittee that "the worst change for us is to see the steady march of public broadcasting away from its original mandate of public service, innovation, diversity, and toward proven formulas and market-driven programming that tends to safe uniformity."[94] The crisis of public broadcasting is not due to "quality"; instead, it is due to the inability to conceive of the public in terms other than those used by commercial broadcasters. This inability is triggered by an obsession with money, an obsession grounded in economic uncertainty and diffuse and contradictory goals and manifested in the system's embrace of ratings and formats. Former NPR president Douglas Bennet recalls:

One of the things I ran into when I got to NPR was derivative, commercial broadcast research that said, you've got these classical music listeners who never want anything else. You've got news listeners and they will never want anything else. The evidence was clearly the opposite. . . . Radio stations are homogeneously devoted to these formats, and it is just stupid. It is a failing business.[95]

In order to reduce uncertainty, National Public Radio and its affiliate stations have attempted to transform their operations into a consistent, marketable "product," justified by market research. Yet decision making ultimately remains nonrational. Philadelphia's WXPN was the creator of *World Cafe*, which received millions of dollars in CPB funding for research and design. In 1992, station manager Mark Fuerst admitted that "a lot of it is intuition. . . . People are going to get upset when they read this, but working with music is partly a fashion industry. Why things are the way they are is not always a matter of rational discussion."[96] The recent success of *This American Life* contradicts the scientism of consultants; host Ira Glass noted that the program's development was "stunningly unscientific."[97] Nevertheless, public radio continues to be seduced by what Max Weber has referred to as the "romance" of numbers. In the process, NPR, abetted by consultants, continues to abandon a varied mission in favor of a uniform "value." The rhetoric of value conceals the reality of commodification, which John McManus defines as "the creation of a monetary price and market for virtually every aspect of human experience."[98]

The mission of public radio has become exclusively focused on body counts rather than public discourse. NPR once dreamed of a *public*; the adoption of commercially derived audience research, the ascendance of station consultants, and the embrace of programming formats show that it has settled for an *audience*, or numerical symbols of people.[99] The institutional practices of National Public Radio and its affiliates effectively close it to the public; public radio fails to provide a valid public sphere. Instead, public broadcasters consider the public to be a market; something to be objectified and controlled for purposes of furthering their own positions in the political, social, and cultural hierarchy. The commercial ethos has all but eclipsed the glimmer of light that public radio once offered. As public broadcasting adopts "rational," goal-directed business practices and steeps itself in ersatz social science through the fetish of audience measurement, it surrenders all traces of rationality. In its efforts to survive and expand as an institution, National Public Radio has embraced the logic of the marketplace and relinquished the claims to public service that represent the reason for its existence.

NOTES

1. J. Peters, "Historical Tensions in the Concept of Public Opinion," in *Public Opinion and the Communication of Consent*, T. Glasser and C. Salmon, eds. (New York: Guilford Press, 1995), p. 20.

2. T. Thomas and T. Clifford, *The Public Radio Program Marketplace* (Washington, DC: CPB, 1985), pp. 14–15.

3. Cited in R. Avery, "Access and Ascertainment in Broadcasting: An Overview," *Western Journal of Speech Communication* 41 (3), Summer 1977, p. 139.

4. M. Heller, "Problems in Ascertainment Procedures," *Journal of Broadcasting* 21 (4), Fall 1977, p. 432.

5. E. Krasnow and J. Quale, "Ascertainment: The Quest for the Holy Grail," *Public Telecommunications Review*, June 1974, pp. 7–8.

6. Herman W. Land Associates, *The Hidden Medium: Educational Radio* (New York: National Educational Radio, National Association of Educational Broadcasters, 1967), p. 1–17.

7. Krasnow and Quale, "Ascertainment," p. 10.

8. W. Rowland, Jr., "Ascertainment and Research in Public Broadcasting," *Public Telecommunications Review,* November/December 1979, p. 39. Several groups representing minority students quickly filed a petition with the FCC to include public broadcasting in ascertainment procedures, as a result of the system's change in nomenclature from "educational" to "public," which implied wider mission and service. The National Black Media Council proposed the creation of citizen advisory boards and recommended that station managers "spend at least a day every three months in the black community" (Krasnow and Quale, "Ascertainment," pp. 9, 11).

9. A. Branscomb, "A Crisis of Identity: Public Broadcasting and the Law," *Public Telecommunications Review,* February 1975, p. 16.

10. Krasnow and Quale, "Ascertainment," p. 6.

11. T. McCain, C. Hofstetter, N. James, and J. Hawkins, "Method Dependent Opinion Leadership: Implications for Ascertainment of Black Community Needs for Public Television Stations," In *Six Experiments in Ascertainment Methodology,* Office of Communications Research, ed. (Washington, DC: CPB, 1977), p. 38.

12. R. Avery, P. Birdsall, and A. Rey, "Issues in Ascertaining the Different Needs of Urban and Rural Community Leaders," in *Six Experiments in Ascertainment Methodology,* Office of Communication Research, ed. (Washington, DC, CPB, 1977), p. 8.

13. Rowland, "Ascertainment and Research in Public Broadcasting," p. 40.

14. A. Yih, "FCC Deregulates Public Broadcasting," *Current,* July 17, 1984.

15. Rowland, "Ascertainment and Research in Public Broadcasting," p. 42.

16. A. Stavitsky, "Listening for Listeners: Educational Radio and Audience Research," *Journalism History* 19 (1), Spring 1993, p. 15. Much of the information on pre-1980 audience research presented here is taken from his account.

17. S. Holt, *The Public Radio Study* (Washington, DC: CPB, 1969), pp. 7, 116.

18. A. Stavitsky, " 'Guys in Suits with Charts': Audience Research in U.S. Public Radio," *Journal of Broadcasting and Electronic Media* 39 (2), Spring 1995, p. 181.

19. Ibid.

20. Ibid., p. 180; D. Giovannoni, "Taking Responsibility," *Current,* March 30, 1988, p. 20.

21. Stavitsky, " 'Guys in Suits with Charts,' " p. 181; B. Gladstone, "Public Radio Turns to Ratings," *Current,* March 30, 1981, p. 4.

22. G. Bailey and T. Church, "Public Radio and the Ratings," *Public Telecommunications Review,* November/December 1979, pp. 47, 48.

23. Ibid., p. 49.

24. B. Gladstone, "Public Radio Turns to Ratings," *Current,* March 30, 1981, p. 4.

25. Giovannoni, "Taking Responsibility," p. 20.

26. T. Looker, *The Sound and the Story: NPR and the Art of Radio* (New York: Houghton Mifflin, 1995), p. 123.

27. I. Molotsky, "Public Radio Tries 'Morning Edition,' " *New York Times,* November 25, 1979, p. 77; "Morning Edition Hits the Airwaves," *Broadcasting,* November 12, 1979, p. 81.

28. B. Gladstone, "NPR Tries for Mag on Sunday Afternoon," *Current,* September 28, 1981, p. 1.

29. Ibid.

30. "NPR Buys More Time for 'Sunday,' " *Current*, September 17, 1982, p. 1.

31. M. Collins, *National Public Radio: The Cast of Characters* (Washington, DC: Seven Locks Press, 1993). p. 62.

32. "NPR Considers Releasing Shows to Commercial Radio," *Current*, May 11, 1981, p. 4.

33. Stavitsky, " 'Guys in Suits with Charts,' " p. 185.

34. Ibid., p. 184.

35. D. Giovannoni, "Your Payback from Research Depends on What You Put into It," *Current*, December 14, 1992, p. 22.

36. R. Barbieri, "Public Radio Audience: Bigger is Better," *Current*, September 22, 1986, p. 13.

37. D. Kanzeg, "Where Public Radio's Audience-Doubling Report Errs," *Current*, October 20, 1986, p. 2; W. Siemering, "Audience Building: Some Cautionary Words," *Current*, September 22, 1986, p. 15; E. Frost, "Hype-Notizing Public Radio," *Current*, October 20, 1987, p. 2.

38. Stavitsky, " 'Guys in Suits with Charts,' " p. 182

39. D. Giovannoni, "The Economics of Programming," *Current*, November 3, 1987, p. 12.

40. T. Bush, "Looking at What Audience '88 Saw," *Current*, January 27, 1990, p. 19.

41. D. Giovannoni, "Appeal Revisited, Part Four," *Current*, September 20, 1993, p. 17.

42. D. Giovannoni, "A Measure of Program Value: Cents per Listener-Hour," *Current*, September 22, 1997, p. 19.

43. D. Giovannoni, posting on Pubradio listserv, October 17, 1997.

44. J. Robertiello, "What Do Programmers Want?" *Current*, March 1, 1989, p. 2; Stavitsky, " 'Guys in Suits with Charts,' " p. 183.

45. J. Conciatore, "Radio Sharpens Formats to Keep CPB Grants," *Current*, April 17, 1997, p. 9.

46. In 1975, the CPB commissioned the Roper Report to conduct a national survey of 2,007 adults aged eighteen and over to determine the characteristics of public television viewers. The report, published in February 1976, found that public TV audiences closely matched the overall demographic patterns for the U.S. population. This information was useful to PBS for debunking allegations that the service was elitist. However, Karen Farr, the director of research at WNET-TV in New York City, claimed that the report had been hampered by severe methodological problems and was of questionable value at best. The report failed to compare adequately public television viewers with the general population: "In fact, persons with only a grade school education are underrepresented among viewers by 40 percent" (K. Farr, "Ask a Silly Question . . ." *Public Telecommunications Review*, March/April 1976, p. 8). Response rates were poorly clarified (racial categories were limited to blacks and whites, and "white collar" occupations were subdivided while "blue collar" categories were undifferentiated), and "don't know" or "refused to answer" responses were not included. In addition, the Roper Report made no mention if household respondents had been asked about the viewing of members under eighteen.

47. See I. Ang, *Desperately Seeking the Audience* (New York: Routledge, 1991).

48. D. Leroy, "Who Watches Public Television," *Journal of Communication* 30 (3), Summer 1980, p. 162.

49. D. Giovannoni, "Your Payback from Research Depends on What You Put into It," p. 22.

50. A. Griswold, "A Consumer Guide to Radio Research Services," *Current*, August 9, 1993, p. 30.

51. J. Conciatore, "Researchers Invite Others to Use Audience 98 Data," *Current*, September 8, 1997, p. 1.

52. A. Bartholet, Jr., "Psychographics: More Than a Buzzword," *Current*, December 1, 1986, p. 8.

53. See National Public Radio, *The NPR Audience*, (Washington, DC: NPR, 1981).

54. Cited in D. Giovannoni, "The Importance of Being Important," *Current*, January 13, 1987, p. 4.

55. Cited in Giovannoni, "It Takes Time: Part Two," *Current*, December 21, 1988, p. 24.

56. Stavitsky, " 'Guys in Suits with Charts,' " p. 184.

57. H. Beville, Jr., *Audience Ratings: Radio, Television, Cable* (Hillsdale, NJ: Lawrence Erlbaum Associates, 1988), p. 137: H. Jassem, R. Desmond, and T. Glasser, "Pluralistic Programming and Radio Diversity: A Review and a Proposal," *Policy Science* 14 (3), August 1982, p. 355.

58. D. Giovannoni, "New Age and Your Jazz," *Current*, September 8, 1987, p. 8.

59. P. Elwood, "Denver Audience Study Completes First Phase," *Current*, March 1, 1989, p. 14; D. Giovannoni, "Music Research," *Current*, September 4, 1990, p. 13; J. Robertiello, "Pledging Tune-Up: Views from WKSU's Focus Groups," *Current*, October 7, 1991, p. 13.

60. R. Barbieri, "Radio 'Program Testing' Begins," *Current*, July 5, 1989, p. 1; R. Barbieri, "Radio Producers Get Test Results," *Current*, October 16, 1989, p. 3; Engelman, *Public Radio and Television in America*, p. 18.

61. D. Giovannoni and M. Wycisk, "A General Manager's Research Experience," *Current*, October 2, 1989, p. 10; K. Bedford, "Wooing Rockers with the Classics," *Current*, February 17, 1992, p. 8.

62. E. Katz, "Introduction: The State of the Art," in *Public Opinion and the Communication of Consent*, T. Glasser and C. Salmon, eds. (New York: Guilford Press, 1995), p. xxx; Ang, *Desperately Seeking the Audience*, p. 145; C. Keegan, "Qualitative Audience Research in Public Television," *Journal of Communication* 30 (3), Summer 1980.

63. J. Berky, "And on the Other Hand . . ." *Current*, September 8, 1987, p. 6; R. Mahler, "Using Research to Wake Up Public Radio's Sleepy Heads," *Current*, December 11, 1989, p. 18; G. Bailey, "The Next Format," *Current*, July 21, 1987, p. 13; D. Giovannoni, "News on Public Radio," *Current*, March 17, 1987, p. 4.

64. R. Engelman, *Public Radio and Television in America: A Political History* (Thousand Oaks, CA: Sage, 1996), p. 118.

65. See S. Katzman and N. Katzman, *Public Radio Programming by Category: Fiscal Year 1978* (Washington, DC: CPB, 1979).

66. D. Mullally, "Public Radio: Options in Programming," *Public Telecommu-*

nications Review, March/April 1978, p. 9; R. Goodman, "Why Public Radio Isn't (and What You Can Do about it)," *Whole Earth Review,* Winter 1992, p. 52; D. Giovannoni, "Under-Performance Today," *Current,* April 21, 1987, p. 16.

67. See D. McFarland, "Up from Middle America: The Rise of Top-40," in *American Broadcasting: A Source Book on the History of Radio and Television,* L. Lichty and M. Topping, eds. (New York: Hastings House, 1976).

68. D. Mullally, "Public Radio: Options in Programming," p. 9.

69. F. Werden, "NPR Programmers Hash Out Mission," *Current,* December 4, 1984, p. 4.

70. D. Kanzeg, "Competitive and Creative Radio for the '90s," *Current,* June 21, 1989, p. 23.

71. D. Giovannoni, "A Measure of Program Value: Cents per Listener-Hour," p. 20.

72. S. Behrens and J. Conciatore, "We've Got the Journalism Down—I've Got Problems with Our Radio," *Current,* May 25, 1998, p. A-8; " 'Picasso vs. Giovannoni': A Congenial Debate at the PRC," *Current,* July 17, 1996, p. 40.

73. D. Kanzeg, "Competitive and Creative Radio for the '90s," *Current,* June 21, 1989, p. 23; J. Conciatore, "Changing Skeds Usually Means Facing Anger," *Current,* September 11, 1995, p. 1; D. Schiff, "Classical Radio Plays Only to Sweet Tooths," *New York Times,* May 31, 1998, p. R1.

74. G. Bailey, "How to Research and Program Music," *Current,* August 4, 1987, p. 3; D. Giovannoni, "Why Do They Listen?" *Current,* March 12, 1990, p. 8.

75. D. Giovannoni, "Who Listens to Opera?" *Current,* February 3, 1987, p. 4; R. Nordstrand, "Audiences Are People Too," *Current,* November 17, 1986, p. 2.

76. B. Goldfarb, "No Need to Mourn 'Lost' Classical Music," *Current,* March 26, 1990, p. 31.

77. J. Robertiello, "Listening for the Audience," *Current,* January 29, 1990, p. 12; A. Platt, "Empire of the Airwaves," *Twin Cities Reader,* May 24, 1989, p. 11; K. Bedford, "Wooing Rockers with the Classics," p. 8.

78. D. Gawthrop, "The Emperor's New Research," *Current,* September 6, 1993, p. 28.

79. S. Behrens, "Jazzcasters Try Music Testing to Pick Cuts," *Current,* September 2, 1996, p. 1.

80. Goodman, "Why Public Radio Isn't (and What You Can Do about It)," p. 52.

81. Public Radio Program Directors Association, *The Public Radio Program Director's Handbook* (Olney, MD: PRPD, 1994), pp. 34–35.

82. E. Rothenbuhler, "Commercial Radio as Communication," *Journal of Communication,* Winter 1996, p. 126.

83. J. Conciatore, "Emphasizing Classical and Jazz, NPR Trims Music Offerings," *Current,* June 19, 1995, p. 16; S. Behrens, "Notes from the PRC," *Current,* May 27, 1996, p. 9.

84. J. Conciatore, "Stations Adopt News/Info Schedules in Midday," *Current,* February 12, 1996, p. 9.

85. D. Giovannoni, "Appeal Revisited, Part 5," *Current,* October 18, 1993, p. 15; M. Arnold, "Appealing Things Considered," *Current,* November 15, 1993, p. 22.

86. Corporation for Public Broadcasting, *Five Year Plan for Public Telecommunications* (Washington, DC: CPB, 1981), p. 10; D. Giovannoni, T. Thomas, and T. Clifford, *Public Radio Programming Strategies: A Report on the Programming Stations Broadcast and the People They Seek to Serve* (Washington, DC: CPB, 1992), p. 82.

87. M. Fuerst, "What Could Make Public Radio Alter Its Course?" *Current*, February 14, 1994, p. 17.

88. G. Collins, "Christo's Bet on New/Talk Paid Off for Boston's WBUR," *Current*, October 6, 1997, p. 23.

89. J. Conciatore, "Dispute over Research Sunders Tampa Staff," *Current*, June 20, 1994, p. 1.

90. Giovannoni, Thomas, and Clifford, *Public Radio Programming Strategies*, p. 40.

91. S. Behrens, "Local Talks, National Rules Aim to End Wasteful Overlap," *Current*, April 17, 1995, p. 16; D. Giovannoni, "A Measure of Program Value: Cents per Listener-Hour," p. 20.

92. J. Conciatore, "Stations Adopt News/Info Schedules in Midday," *Current*, February 12, 1996, p. 9.

93. See Stavitsky, "The Changing Conception of Localism in U.S. Public Radio."

94. "What They Said on Capitol Hill," *Current*, December 8, 1987, p. 17.

95. R. Ohmann, *Making and Selling Culture* (Hanover, NH: Wesleyan University Press, 1996), p. 170.

96. J. Wilner, "Triple-A Rescues Stranded Audience," *Current*, February 17, 1992, p. 9.

97. J. Conciatore, "From Chicago . . . If You Love This Show, You Really Love It," *Current*, June 2, 1997, p. 1.

98. J. McManus, *Market-Driven Journalism* (Thousand Oaks, CA: Sage, 1994), p. 199.

99. Thanks to John Peters for this formulation.

6

Epilogue

> Rather than broadcasting to people from some contrived and precarious
> eminence next to the White House, we shall, with a little bit of luck,
> hand over this incredibly powerful, immediate and comparatively cheap
> invention to millions of Jews, Whites, Catholics, Blacks, Baptists, Farm-
> ers, Mormons, and Texans . . . for them to use for once, instead of letting
> them be described, interviewed, sandwiched, packaged and oversold by
> professional peddlers and pedagogues.
> —Bernard Mayes, Chairman of the NPR Board of Directors,
> address to the National Public Radio Membership
> Orientation Meeting in Denver Colorado, October 8, 1970[1]

In a 1995 speech to the International Radio and Television Society, PBS
president Ervin Duggan likened the prospect of a commercialized PBS
to the prostitute of Thomas Hardy's "The Ruined Maid": if deprived of
noncommercial support, PBS would be "no longer pure and simple [but]
brazenly working the streets in her new commercial finery, doing whatever is necessary to survive."[2] This self-serving rhetoric belies the fact
that commercial broadcasting has equated "public" with "consumer" so
successfully as to taint the noncommercial broadcasting services. Although some public broadcasters cringe at the prospect of dirtying their
hands with commercialism, most already are buried in it. Public broadcasters work for increased subsidies (the "nonprofit" equivalent of
profit), not for public service. In their view, the public itself can only

interfere with this goal, unless it is shaped and segmented for purposes of fundraising or marketing. Rather than reflecting the diversity of public life, public broadcasting is focused primarily on its own institutional survival. Larry Josephson has claimed, "Public radio is boring. More and more, it is an unending drone of safe, bland 'services.' Much of the news programming now sounds like its network counterparts, highly professional but unexciting." In the *New York Times*, Greil Marcus has argued that NPR's Bob Edwards, like NPR's other news hosts, conveys "a distinct sense of disengagement with the subjects he is presenting. . . . [I]t's a distance that translates into a sense of superiority over what is being talked about." In response, Edwards sniffed, "Well, I'm not going to be terribly upset that I don't appeal to a guy who liked the Sex Pistols." Even public radio's preeminent show horse, Garrison Keillor, accused *All Things Considered* of being "a dreary melange of personal essays and whimsy and liberal piety and sheer tedium."[3]

These criticisms have been leveled at NPR since the early 1980s, when, in response to uncertain funding, it came to prefer disinterested professionalism to diversity or localism. In 1981, Josephson argued, "You never hear the raw anger of the people affected in the news [on *All Things Considered*]. Experience is always filtered through a host or interviewer. You hear about things in that *New Republic*, distanced, nicey-nice way."[4] A producer attending the 1997 Public Radio Conference offered a more telling critique:

Most of the sessions addressed issues of management and technology, and seemed pervaded by anxiety over who would successfully grab the future revenue streams when the technology (that never seemed to work at the sessions) got the bugs worked out. Creativity was given a perfunctory nod as "and this year's network-approved wunderkind is . . ." rather than being acknowledged as a vital part of a healthy system.[5]

Public broadcasting cannot present a real alternative to commercial media, because it consistently ignores questions of public participation and accountability. This neglect stems from the disparate goals and chronic warfare between programmers and development personnel, producers and station managers, large stations and small stations, stations and NPR, NPR and PRI, everybody and the CPB, and the CPB and Congress. Public broadcasting legislation is designed to appease various pressure groups that, while purporting to represent the public in one capacity or another, ultimately fragment the public in the pursuit of their individual interests. The "public sphere" represented by public radio is little more than a battleground for competing interests, the most vociferous of which set the public agenda. The tragedy of public broadcasting is its ceaseless factionalization; in this regard, it reflects the overall status of contemporary public life. The complexity of society requires bureaucracies like the CPB to manage a plurality of interests; the public itself, which is effectively shut out of participation, grows increasingly atomized, disinterested, and cynical.

PRINCIPAL PROBLEMS OF PUBLIC BROADCASTING

One can make the case that the establishment of direct federal funding for broadcasting was a historical anomaly, due in large part to the skyrocketing rate of domestic economic growth following World War II. Certainly, fiscal retrenchment, beginning in the late 1970s, has dramatically impacted public broadcasting. National Public Radio could be judged a success in that it has managed to draw increased funding and expand its operations while holding together a highly fractious coalition, in which key elements operate at direct cross-purposes. However, the increasing dominance of private funding within the system has led public broadcasting to devote itself to selling product concepts rather than meeting public needs. The more it ignores these needs, the more resources and efforts it must devote to promotion, which further detracts from service. Diverse funding sources have not insulated the system from pressure to sell itself. Because they measure success by the size of their budgets, public broadcasters will always want larger budgets. Public broadcasting's tradition of tentative funding has given public broadcasters an excuse to disengage the public from their operations, unless to tap it for financial support or harness it to suit their lobbying needs. Efforts to increase public radio's popularity have been based on practices adopted from commercial broadcasters: While continuing to invoke the public as a means to justify its existence, the practices of public radio actively undermine its possibility to serve as a public medium. Some public radio officials even call for abandoning the nomenclature of "public" broadcasting altogether. Lee O'Brien, the general manager for WSIU TV/FM in Carbondale, Illinois, suggests that

we would be better served by substituting the word *noncommercial* whenever we are tempted to describe ourselves as a *public* service. . . . If, in the minds of people on most other issues, "public" equals "poor," and "public" equals "low quality," how in the world can we sell the notion that "public" broadcasting is a high-quality and desirable alternative to the pricey and flashy stuff out there?[6]

Public broadcasting faces three particular problems. First, its practitioners frequently have abandoned the local in favor of the universal. They neglect the needs of their communities in favor of industrial strategies that minimize decision making, reduce uncertainty, and entrench their own professional status. The federalist model of public broadcasting is based upon national coordination and local variety, but this model has been problematic from the outset. "Public" broadcasting merely centralized programming production and control without addressing the issues of participation and accountability invoked by the term. National Public Radio's mission statement envisioned an "imagined community"; yet NPR, obsessed with Washington politics and elite culture, is, as one observer noted, "neither national in its appeal nor public in its reach." In contrast, some critics call for "counterpublics" based on issues of race, class, and gender.[7] While this strategy might allow for greater public input on the local level, such counterpublics readily perpetuate a balkanized public based on singular attributes and narrow interests—which ultimately serve the interests of elites within and across these groups, as well as external authorities who prefer to deal with separate, clearly defined, and co-optable client groups.

A second problem is that although the system professes to be "public," its organizational structure and practices have been largely determined by private organizations and individuals. Public representation has been skewed to meet the needs of the public broadcasting system. This also characterizes pluralistic public broadcasting systems, such as the "pillarization" model of the Netherlands, in which specific political and religious groups control broadcasting outlets, and the representation of these groups within the overall national broadcasting matrix reflects the balance of power in society. While ostensibly offering greater diversity, this system is still hampered by centralized bureaucratic control and tacit support for the political and cultural status quo. Such a system may avoid commercial pressures in theory, but as individual groups wane in popularity, their broadcasting operations may be prompted to emulate their commercial counterparts in the struggle for market share.[8] Inexpensive, grassroots-based "micromedia" such as pirate radio stations may provide dominated social groups with greater control of and access to mass media, yet the existence of these media does not in itself provide public empowerment. Such stations are frequently operated by private groups and individuals as means to achieve their own ends, not as ends in themselves. Domestic microbroadcasting may not depart significantly from existing commercial programming; conversely, it may provide an ongoing soapbox for endless conspiracy theories and racist harangues.[9]

Third, public goods often are intangible, and their benefits may be impossible to ascertain definitively. As a result, public broadcasting has measured success quantitatively, by size of subsidy or by audience share. Although this trend has been accelerated by the virus of target marketing, the public has appeared as a collection of numerical abstracts rather than discursive participants throughout its history. This pattern leads some critics to blame the victim: Karol Jakubowicz argues, "It has been demonstrated time and time again that the mass of the population fails to take advantage of opportunities for access to programming, whether offered by establishment media or alternate ones, specially dedicated to this goal. . . . Ordinarily, the urge to (mass) communicate simply is not there."[10] Public apathy is the product of the public sphere's atomized nature—the fact that our media systems are structured so that people are passive consumers rather than active producers. This atomization in turn results from the myth of consumer sovereignty, which, in the guise of freedom of (limited) choice, ultimately serves purposes of social control. Through processes of commodification, both commercial and public media provide us with an objectified view of ourselves, abstracted into an omnipresent spectacle of alienation. A fully formed and vigorous public, waiting to burst forth if the gates are lifted, does not exist. It awaits a considerable transformation of the material, educational, and affective structures of society.

WHAT IS TO BE DONE?

The need for public radio remains, despite the advent of new media delivery systems. Much has been made of the movement toward "tele-democracy," or electronic "town halls," in which the public has direct feedback to legislators. The idea of such a forum is ominous, for a variety of reasons. First, it has no guarantee of public representativeness and access. Second, criticism is reduced to a simple yes/no, binary response. Third, these technologies essentially isolate the public's members; they would supplant the public meetings and assemblies that focus individuals on the common good. While their proponents claim that new technologies would revitalize the public sphere, such a "democracy" inevitably would become the province of political elitists, single-issue partisans, and cranks with too much time on their hands. Information technologies are hailed as a means of engendering pluralism, yet they are equally suited for commodifying and controlling information for private gain. For every advantage, they extract an equal cost. These technologies are not a miraculous solution to the problems of public life. They are as likely to extend and deepen existing power relations as engender pluralism and public discourse. The "public" these technologies produce will undoubtedly be different, but it will not necessarily be more inclusive, better informed, or more effective.

A public sphere ideally should allow directly participating equals to form identities, deliberate issues, and contest interests. However, the challenges to the formation of such a sphere have proven formidable in a vast and diverse society. The *polis* of ancient Greece, Tocqueville's New England townships, and Habermas's 18th-century public sphere embraced small, homogenous populations, but a truly "public" sphere based on exclusion is a contradiction in terms. The public was never an

Table 6.1
Commercial, Noncommercial, and Public Radio Systems (the present "public" system is defined as noncommercial for purposes of differentiation)

	Commercial	**Noncommercial**	**Public**
Ownership	Stockholders	Nonprofit Institutions	Public
Control	Board of Directors	Board of Directors	Public
Public Input	None	Limited	Full
State Influence	Limited	High	None
Programming	Format	Block/Format	Eclectic
Motive	Profit	Subsidies	Public Involvement
Audience	Market	Taste Culture	Citizenry

active participant in public broadcasting, yet this also is true in just about every other place it is supposed to be active. While American public life is structured (theoretically) on democratic egalitarianism, the public is either constructed by the marketplace or reified through the machinery of polling. The ideology of equality is denied by the everyday experience of inequities of opportunity and power, and the result is a perpetual disappointment, anxiety, and alienation. The marginalization of the public in public broadcasting is emblematic of the general eclipse of the public in 20th-century democracy. The public is invoked by media and policy makers, but nowhere does it act as such. Even so, public broadcasting may be a powerful shaper of political work, by bringing "private" issues to public concern. As it severs the constraints of geography, class, nationality, and ethnicity, mass communication plays an increasingly central role in shaping institutions, culture, and everyday life. Mass communication traditionally has been viewed as an "indiscriminate mode of dissemination," as opposed to an "intimate mode of conversation."[11] Thus arises the paradox of community and mass communication: can personal bonds based on informal interaction be formed through an impersonal medium that relies on institutionalized, one-way address?

Raymond Williams believes that truly democratic media are necessarily abstract, with no concrete embodiments in the modern world: "The democratic system, in any full sense, we can only discuss and imagine."[12] Let us, then, imagine a truly "public" radio system, with the knowledge that few guides exist and no model will perfectly suit all situations (see Table 6.1).

First, a genuinely public system should be highly localized, not based on one channel linking private citizens to the state. A dispersed network of communication can more easily circumvent economic and political censorship, by providing many channels of communication between individuals and groups. More important, a return to the tradition of the commons would foster a sense of shared traditions and expectations for the future. John Keane echoes Tocqueville when he argues that the "decentralization of power is sometimes the most effective cure for an undue parochialism; that through involvement in local organizations, citizens overcome their localism."[13] A decentralized and readily accessible system would help citizens focus on particular problems of moral practice in everyday contexts and to counter received ideas about possibilities of human action that serve the ends of those in power. Such a system might be built from low-wattage stations affiliated with public libraries; the limited coverage of these stations (approximately three to five miles for five watts) would allow several to coexist in a single metropolitan area, like branch libraries, and they also might catalogue and distribute programming to other locations if desired. A city with one million residents could easily support five such stations, and the costs would be small. A radio transmitter can be constructed for as little as five hundred dollars, a complete broadcast unit for approximately $2,500.[14]

Second, a "public" medium should be owned by all members of the public rather than individuals, groups, or the state. Instead of serving as a conduit of individual and group views to society, a role in which the primary interaction between individual stations and their communities remains that of sender and audience, a public station should serve as a center for sharing information among community members.[15] It should provide a physical site for members to strengthen commonalities as well as air disagreements. Instead of operating according to a formal, hierarchical structure, with a professional staff employed as managers (and gatekeepers), each public station should be managed by volunteers, configured as a common carrier, and subsidized by voluntary donations or minimal access fees, which could be waived for contributions of time and labor. To discourage monopolization by a few individuals or groups, minimize factionalization, and encourage public participation, turnover should be institutionalized; individual or group participants would be limited to one or two hours per week for a maximum of six months per year. While somewhat draconian, this measure would lessen the fractiousness and territoriality that historically have plagued the Pacifica stations and other community broadcasters. Other rules should be minimal and informal, depending on the particular locality. Because the organizational requirements of such a system would be negligible, the division of labor (such as training and administration) might be accomplished through rotating roles, task sharing, and diffusing specialized knowledge through workshops.

Finally, a public system must place art on an equal footing with talk.

Political content has been the defining characteristic of state-oriented conceptions of the public sphere, which frown on mere "entertainment." Yet politics and culture are deeply interconnected; even the most seemingly apolitical creations are grounded in "ethical codes or expressive values that lie at the heart of political creeds."[16] More so than rhetoric, art cuts across class and cultural lines, and it celebrates commonality as well as difference. Commercial media package culture into commodities, and noncommercial media increasingly are following suit. In truly public broadcasting, diverse cultural programming would provide a way for us to appreciate the rich subjectivity of human life. In the process, it would promote understanding and tolerance. The most artless music may say as much as the most gifted politician, particularly when it articulates the hard-won truths and inchoate dreams of the individuals and communities from which it emerges.

In the 1960s, after conducting a door-to-door survey of minorities, Buffalo's WBFO established a public-access satellite station in a storefront, broadcasting twenty-five hours per week. William Siemering's experiment at WBFO was a model for what could have been public radio.[17] It may provide a model for public radio's future. Seismic changes in the packaging and delivery of national programming are forcing station managers to reconsider their commitment to local communities; as one observer suggests, "strong local content may be the safest refuge under a hail of satellite signals."[18] At the 1998 Public Radio Conference, the NPR board of directors discussed the possibility of bypassing stations through streams of multihour news and single-format programming delivered through the Internet and digital satellite services.[19] This delivery system would provide a cost-effective means for NPR to recycle programming, and it would also pave the way for a pay-per-use system, charging per download or "tollgating" for access. Despite the nettlesome fact that NPR is presently supported in large part through station fees, such an outcome is not especially far-fetched. It is the logical result of public radio's emphasis since the early 1980s on "seamless" programming. Given the development of diverse delivery systems (which do not guarantee diversity in themselves, as they target lucrative niche audiences), local stations will not be able to survive if they continue their present practices. Mark Starowicz of the Canadian Broadcasting Corporation told the 1998 Public Radio Conference that public broadcasters should "adopt yourself to the perishable real-time stream by intensely serving your neighborhood. . . . [I]t is time to return to the Town Square."[20]

Radio is uniquely suited to fill the role of a public medium. Its low cost and mobility afford a sense of immediacy and flexibility that make it "an ideal instrument for collective self-construction, for the enactment of a community's oral and musical history."[21] A highly localized public radio system would provide an independent, neutral arena for public discourse, not merely channel the "common sense" handed down through governing institutions. Through public ownership and active public participation, this system would lessen the material demands that have shaped the development of public broadcasting and detached it from its beneficiaries. Freed from the need to maintain streams of subsidies or paternalistically "educate" the public, the system would have no mission other than engendering discursive participation.

Ultimately, a public radio system would provide a site for *communitas*, or fellowship, outside the rigid structures of social hierarchy. Victor Turner finds this fellowship essential to society; he notes that *communitas* "is almost everywhere held to be sacred, or 'holy,' possibly because it transgresses or dissolves the norms that govern structured or institutional relationships and is accompanied by experiences of unprecedented potency."[22] The anarchy implicit in *communitas* also makes it powerful in mystical ways. It is an epiphany, a rite of reconciliation in which undefined states and inversions of social status, however brief, reinforce the human against the artificial. The transitory nature of radio broadcasting makes it uniquely suited to such activity. Instead of an arena in which discourses compete for ruling authority, a public radio system would provide a space for fellowship, a moment out of time, a medium in which people can communicate with each other.

In Greek and Latin alike, the concept of "public" has two distinct meanings: *social-political* (the *polis*, or body of the people) and *visual-intellectual* (fame, or open exhibition).[23] Public life is based on both theatrical spectacle or exhibition and political participation. To participate in public life involves the threat of shame as well as the potential for honor. The cost of an active public life is enduring personal exposure, potential abuse, and ridicule of cherished beliefs. A truly public radio system would not necessarily lead to a consistently enlightened level of discourse. It would not single-handedly heal the cultural, political, and economic cleavages in society. It would not completely or permanently redress imbalances of power or guarantee universal participation in public affairs. A public radio system would not provide a miraculous panacea for society's ills. The struggle is continuous, and there is no final solution. But a public radio system *would* at least afford possibilities for greater political and cultural pluralism. It would embody, in a highly decentralized and egalitarian manner, both aspects of public life that have endured for thousands of years—political debate and theatrical spectacle. The reciprocity intrinsic to a public radio system would not erase the alienation endemic to modern society. This reciprocity would, however, leaven the strict divisions of modern life. In the process, it would summon the better angels of our nature.

NOTES

1. *Educational Broadcasting Review*, December 1970, p. 52.

2. K. McAvoy, "Washington Watch," *Broadcasting and Cable*, April 24, 1995, p. 46.

3. L. Josephson, "We're Drunk on Numbers, Boring to Our Listeners," *Current*, April 27 1992, pp. 31, 34; G. Marcus, "Public Radio Hosts Drop In and Maybe Stay Too Long," *New York Times*, March 16, 1998, p, B2; S. Behrens and J. Conciatore, "We've Got the Journalism Down—I've Got Problems with Our Radio," *Current*, May 25, 1998, p. A-7; J. Conciatore, "Keillor Scorns Talk Radio, 'ATC,' and Pities G.M.'s," *Current*, October 27, 1997, p. 8. Of course, Keillor spared his distributor, PRI, from any such criticism; presumably, he believes that the likes of *Marketplace* make a greater contribution to public life than *All Things Considered*.

4. S. Behrens, "ATC: Caught in the Act of Thinking," *Current*, April 27, 1981, p. 4.

5. E. Wininger, "Where Were Program Concerns at the PRC This Year?" *Current*, June 23, 1997, p. 19.

6. L. O'Brien, "Is 'Public' a Positive First Name Anymore?" *Current*, February 3, 1992, p. 14.

7. See N. Fraser, "Rethinking the Public Sphere: A Contribution to the Critique of Actually Existing Democracy," in *Habermas and the Public Sphere*, C. Calhoun, ed. (Cambridge, MA: MIT Press, 1993).

8. See J. Curran, "Rethinking the Media as a Public Sphere," In *Communication and Citizenship*, P. Dahlgren and C. Sparks, eds. (London: Routledge, 1991).

9. See S. Jones, "Unlicensed Broadcasting: Content and Conformity," *Journalism Quarterly* 71 (2), Summer 1994; A. Yoder, *Pirate Radio: The Incredible Saga of America's Illegal, Underground Broadcasters* (Solona Beach, CA: HighText, 1996).

10. K. Jakubowicz, "Stuck in a Groove: Why the 1960's Approach to Communication Democratization Will No Longer Do," in *Communication and Democracy*, S. Splichal and J. Wasko, eds. (Norwood, NJ: Ablex Publishing, 1993), pp. 38, 42.

11. See J. Peters, "The Gaps of Which Communication Is Made," *Critical Studies in Mass Communication* 11 (2), June 1994.

12. R. Williams, *Communications* (Harmondsworth, UK: Penguin Books, 1976), p. 133.

13. J. Keane, *The Media and Democracy* (Cambridge, UK: Polity Press, 1991), p. 146.

14. K. Noble, "Defying Airwave Rules and Exporting the Way," *New York Times*, January 24, 1996, p. A7.

15. See J. Hochheimer, "Organizing Democratic Radio: Issues in Praxis," *Media, Culture and Society* 15 (3), July 1993.

16. Curran, "Rethinking the Media as a Public Sphere," p. 34.

17. R. Engelman, *Public Radio and Television in America: A Political History*. (Thousand Oaks, CA: Sage, 1996) p. 90.

18. S. Behrens, "Race for Digital Radio is Uphill from Here," *Current*, March 31, 1997, p. 14.

19. J. Conciatore, "Looking to Future, NPR Board Eyes Station Bypass Prospect," *Current*, June 8, 1998, p. 1.

20. M. Starowicz, "Will Radio Survive the Digital Revolution?" *Current*, July 27, 1998, p. 17.

21. J. Berland, "Radio Space and Industrial Time: The Case of Music Formats," in *Rock and Popular Music*, T. Bennett, S. Frith, L. Grossberg, J. Shepherd, and G. Turner, eds. (London: Routledge, 1993), pp. 106–107.

22. V. Turner, "Liminality and Community," in *Culture and Society: Contemporary Debates*, J. Alexander and S. Seidman, eds. (New York: Cambridge University Press, 1990), p. 153.

23. L. Holscher, *Offentlichkeit und Gehelmnis: Eine Begriffsgeschichtliche Untersuchung zur Entstehung der Offentlichkeit in der Frühen Neuzeit* [Publicity and secrecy: A conceptual-historical study of the genesis of the public sphere in the early modern period] (Stuttgart: Klett-Cotta, 1979), p. 37, cited in J. Peters, "Historical Tensions in the Concept of Public Opinion," in *Public Opinion and the Communication of Consent*, T. Glasser and C. Salmon, eds. (New York: Guilford Press, 1995).

Selected Bibliography

BOOKS

Anderson, B. *Imagined Communities*. New York: Verso, 1983.

Ang, I. *Desperately Seeking the Audience*. New York: Routledge, 1991.

Barnouw, E. *A History of Broadcasting in the United States, Vol. 1: A Tower in Babel: To 1933*. New York: Oxford University Press, 1966.

————. *The Sponsor: Notes on a Modern Potentate*. New York: Oxford University Press, 1978.

Bellah, R., R. Madsen, W. Sullivan, S. Swidler, and S. Tipton. *Habits of the Heart: Individualism and Commitment in American Life*. New York: Harper and Row, 1985.

Beville, H., Jr. *Audience Ratings: Radio, Television, Cable*. Hillsdale, NJ: Lawrence Erlbaum Associates, 1988.

Blakely, R. *To Serve the Public Interest; Educational Broadcasting in the U.S.* Syracuse, NY: Syracuse University Press, 1979.

Collins, M. *National Public Radio: The Cast of Characters*. Washington, DC: Seven Locks Press, 1993.

Czitrom, D. *Media and the American Mind: From Morse to McLuhan*. Chapel Hill: University of North Carolina Press, 1982.

Davis, M. *City of Quartz: Excavating the Future in Los Angeles*. New York: Verso, 1990.

Day, J. *The Vanishing Vision: The Inside Story of Public Television*. Berkeley: University of California Press, 1995.

Dewey, J. *The Public and Its Problems*. In *John Dewey: The Later Works, 1925–1953; Volume Two; 1925–1927*, J. A. Boydston, ed. Carbondale: Southern Illinois University Press, 1988 (1927).

Dizard, W., Jr. *The Coming Information Age: An Overview of Technology, Economics and Politics*, 3d ed. New York: Longman, 1989.

Douglas, S. *Inventing American Broadcasting*. Baltimore: Johns Hopkins Press, 1987.

Downing, J. *Radical Media: The Political Experience of Alternative Communication*. Boston: South End Press, 1984.

Engelman, R. *Public Radio and Television in America: A Political History*. Thousand Oaks, CA: Sage, 1996.

Fornatele, P., and J. Mills. *Radio in the Television Age*. Woodstock, NY: Overlook Press, 1980.

Garnham, N. *Structures of Television*. London: British Film Institute, 1978.

Gibson, G. *Public Broadcasting: The Role of the Federal Government, 1912–1976*. New York: Praeger, 1977.

Guimary, D. *Citizen's Groups and Broadcasting*. New York: Praeger, 1975.

Habermas, J. *The Structural Transformation of the Public Sphere: An Inquiry into a Category of Bourgeois Society*. Cambridge, MA: MIT Press, 1989 (1961).

Holscher, L. *Offentlichkeit und Geheimnis: Eine Begriffsgeschichtliche Untersuchung zur Entstehung der Offentlichkeit in der Frühen Neuzeit* [Publicity and secrecy: A conceptual-historical study of the genesis of the public sphere in the early modern period]. Stuttgart: Klett-Cotta, 1979.

Horwitz, R. *The Irony of Regulatory Reform: The Deregulation of American Telecommunications*. New York: Oxford University Press, 1989.

Hoynes, W. *Public Television for Sale*. Boulder, CO: Westview Press, 1994.

Keane, J. *The Media and Democracy*. Cambridge, UK: Polity Press, 1991.

Lashley, M. *Public Television: Panacea, Pork Barrel or Public Trust?* Westport, CT: Greenwood Press, 1992.

Ledbetter, J. *Made Possible by . . . The Death of Public Broadcasting in the United States*. New York: Verso, 1997.

Lewis, P., and J. Booth. *The Invisible Medium: Public, Commercial and Community Radio*. Washington, DC: Howard University Press, 1990.

Lind, M. *The Next American Nation: The New Nationalism and the Fourth American Revolution*. New York: Free Press, 1995.

Looker, T. *The Sound and the Story: NPR and the Art of Radio*. New York: Houghton Mifflin, 1995.

Macy, J. *To Irrigate a Wasteland: The Struggle to Shape a Public Television System in the United States*. Berkeley: University of California Press, 1974.

McChesney, R. *Telecommunications, Mass Media and Democracy: The Battle for the Control of U.S. Broadcasting, 1928–1935*. New York: Oxford University Press, 1993.

McManus, J. *Market-Driven Journalism*. Thousand Oaks, CA: Sage, 1994.

McQuail, D. *Media Performance: Mass Communication and the Public Interest*. London: Sage, 1992.

Neilsen, W. *The Big Foundations*. New York: Columbia University Press, 1972.

Ohmann, R. *Making and Selling Culture*. Hanover, NH: Wesleyan University Press, 1996.

Ostrower, F. *Why the Wealthy Give: The Culture of Elite Philanthropy*. Princeton, NJ: Princeton University Press, 1995.

Schiller, H. *Culture Inc: The Corporate Takeover of Public Expression*. New York: Oxford University Press, 1989.

Smith, S., and M. Lipsky. *Nonprofits for Hire: The Welfare State in the Age of Contracting*. Cambridge, MA: Harvard University Press, 1993.

Smulyan, S. *Selling Radio: The Commercialization of American Broadcasting 1920–1934*. Washington, DC: Smithsonian Institution Press, 1994.

Sola Pool, I. de. *Technologies of Freedom*. Cambridge, MA: Harvard University Press, 1983.

Streeter, T. *Selling the Air: A Critique of Commercial Broadcasting in the United States*. Chicago: University of Chicago Press, 1996.

Tocqueville, A. de. *Democracy in America*. New York: Vintage Books, 1990 (1835/1840).

Turow, J. *Media Industry Systems*. New York: Longman, 1992.

Williams, R. *Culture and Society 1780–1950*. New York: Columbia University Press, 1958.

———. *Television: Technology and Cultural Form*. New York: Schocken Books, 1975.

———. *Communications*. Harmondsworth: Penguin Books, 1976.

Witherspoon, J., and R. Kovitz. *The History of Public Broadcasting*. Washington, DC: Current, 1987.

Yoder, A. *Pirate Radio: The Incredible Saga of America's Illegal, Underground Broadcasters*. Solona Beach, CA: High Text, 1996.

BOOK CHAPTERS AND JOURNAL ARTICLES

Amos, D. "Producing Features." In *Telling the Story: The National Public Radio Guide to Radio Journalism*, L. Josephson, ed. Dubuque, IA: Kendall/Hunt, 1983.

Appadurai, A. "Disjuncture and Difference in the Global Cultural Economy." In *Global Culture*, M. Featherstone, ed. Newbury Park, CA: Sage, 1990.

Aufderheide, P. "Public Television and the Public Sphere." *Critical Studies in Mass Communication* 8 (2), June 1991.

Avery, R. "Access and Ascertainment in Broadcasting: An Overview." *Western Journal of Speech* Communication 41 (3), Summer 1977.

———. "Introduction." In *Public Service Broadcasting in a Multichannel Environment: The History and Survival of an Ideal*, R. Avery, ed. New York: Longman, 1993.

———. "Contemporary Public Telecommunications Research: Navigating the Sparsely Settled Terrain." *Journal of Broadcasting and Electronic Media* 40 (1), Winter 1996.

Avery, R., and R. Pepper. "An Institutional History of Public Broadcasting." *Journal of Communication* 30 (3), Summer 1980.

Baldwin, T, and S. Surlin. "A Study of Broadcast Station License Application Exhibits on Ascertainment of Community Needs." *Journal of Broadcasting* 14 (4), Spring 1970.

Barlow, W. "Community Radio in the US: The Struggle for a Democratic Medium." *Media, Culture and Society* 10 (1), January 1988.

Barnett, S., and D. Docherty. "Purity or Pragmatism: Principles and Practice of

Public Service Broadcasting." In *Broadcast Finance in Transition: A Comparative Handbook*, J. Blumler and T. J. Nossiter, eds. New York: Oxford University Press, 1991.

Berland, J. "Radio Space and Industrial Time: The Case of Music Formats." In *Rock and Popular Music*, T. Bennett, S. Frith, L. Grossberg, J. Shepherd, and G. Turner, eds. London: Routledge, 1993.

Blumler, J. "Television in the United States: Funding Sources and Programming Consequences." In *Broadcast Finance in Transition: A Comparative Handbook*, J. Blumler and T. J. Nossiter, eds. New York: Oxford University Press, 1991.

———. "Meshing Money with Mission: Purity versus Pragmatism in Public Broadcasting." *European Journal of Communication* 8 (4), December 1993.

Boyte, H. "Public Opinion as Public Judgment." In *Public Opinion and the Communication of Consent*, T. Glasser and C. Salmon, eds. New York: Guilford Press, 1995.

Buzenberg, W. "Growing NPR." In *Radio—The Forgotten Medium*, E. Pease and E. Dennis, eds. New Brunswick, NJ: Transaction Press, 1995.

Campbell, D., and J. Campbell. "Public Television as a Public Good." *Journal of Communication* 28 (1), Winter 1978.

Carey, James. "The Press, Public Opinion and Public Discourse." In *Public Opinion and the Communication of Consent*, T. Glasser and C. Salmon, eds. New York: Guilford Press, 1995.

Carey, John. "Public Broadcasting and Federal Policy." In *New Directions in Telecommunications Policy*, Vol. 1, P. Newberg, ed. Durham, NC: Duke University Press, 1989.

Crotts, G., and W. Rowland, Jr. "The Prospects for Public Broadcasting." In *Telecommunications in the U.S.: Trends and Policies*, L. Lewin, ed. Dedham, MA: Artech House, 1981.

Curran, J. "Rethinking the Media as a Public Sphere." In *Communication and Citizenship*, P. Dahlgren and C. Sparks, eds. London: Routledge, 1991.

Dietz, M. "Context Is All: Feminism and Theories of Citizenship." *Daedalus* 116 (4), Fall 1987.

DiMaggio, P. "Nonprofit Organizations in the Production and Distribution of Culture." In *The Nonprofit Sector: A Research Handbook*, W. Powell, ed. New Haven, CT: Yale University Press, 1987.

DiMaggio, P., and M. Useem. "Cultural Democracy in a Period of Cultural Expansion: The Social Composition of Arts Audiences in the United States." In *Art and Society: Readings in the Sociology of the Arts*, A. Foster and J. Blau, eds. Albany: State University Press of New York, 1989.

Elliott, P. "Media Organizations and Occupations: An Overview." In *Mass Communication and Society*, J. Curran, M. Gurevitch, and J. Woolacott, eds. Beverly Hills, CA: Sage, 1979.

Ermann, M. "The Operative Goals of Corporate Philanthropy: Contributions to the Public Broadcasting Service, 1972–1976." *Social Problems* 25, June 1978.

Ettema, J., and D. Whitney. "The Money Arrow: An Introduction to Audiencemaking." In *Audiencemaking: How the Media Create the Audience*, J. Ettema and D. Whitney, eds. Beverly Hills, CA: Sage, 1994.

Fowler, M, and D. Brenner. "A Marketplace Approach to Broadcast Regulation."

In *Mass Communication Review Yearbook 1983*, E. Wartella and D. Whitney, eds. Beverly Hills: Sage, 1983.

Fraser, N. "Rethinking the Public Sphere: A Contribution to the Critique of Actually Existing Democracy." In *Habermas and the Public Sphere*, C. Calhoun, ed. Cambridge, MA: MIT Press, 1993.

Friedland, L. "Public Television and the Crisis of Democracy: A Review Essay." *The Communication Review* 1 (1), 1995.

———. "Public Television as Public Sphere: The Case of the Wisconsin Collaborative Project." *Journal of Broadcasting and Electronic Media* 39 (2), Spring 1995.

Garnham, N. "Public Service Versus the Market." *Screen* 24 (1), January/February 1983.

———. "The Media and the Public Sphere." In *Habermas and the Public Sphere*, C. Calhoun, ed. Cambridge, MA: MIT Press, 1992.

Garnham, N., and G. Locksley. "The Economics of Broadcasting." In *Broadcast Finance in Transition: A Comparative Handbook*, J. Blumler and T. J. Nossiter, eds. New York. Oxford University Press: 1991.

Glasser, T. "Competition and Diversity among Radio Formats: Legal and Structural Issues." *Journal of Broadcasting* 28 (2), Spring 1984.

Haight, T., and S. Vedro. "Fighting the MGM Syndrome: Reform at the Station Level." In *Telecommunications Policy Handbook*, J. Schement, F. Gutierrez, and M. Sirbu, Jr., eds. New York: Praeger, 1982.

Hall, S. "The Rediscovery of 'Ideology': Return of the Repressed in Media Studies." In *Culture, Society and the Media*, M. Gurevitch, T. Bennett, J. Curran, and J. Woolacott, eds. New York: Methuen, 1982.

Heller, M. "Problems in Ascertainment Procedures." *Journal of Broadcasting and Electronic Media* 21 (4), Fall 1977.

———. "An Argument for Elimination of Ascertainment Requirements." *Journal of Broadcasting and Electronic Media* 25 (1), Winter 1981.

Herbst, S. "On the Disappearance of Groups: 19th and Early 20th-Century Conceptions of Public Opinion." In *Public Opinion and the Communication of Consent*, T. Glasser and C. Salmon, eds. New York: Guilford Press, 1995.

Hochheimer, J. "Organizing Democratic Radio: Issues in Praxis." *Media, Culture and Society* 15 (3), July 1993.

Jakubowicz, K. "Stuck in a Groove: Why the 1960's Approach to Communication Democratization Will No Longer Do." In *Communication and Democracy*, S. Splichal and J. Wasko, eds. Norwood, NJ: Ablex Publishing, 1993.

Jassem, H, R. Desmond, and T. Glasser. "Pluralistic Programming and Radio Diversity: A Review and a Proposal." *Policy Science* 14 (3), August 1982.

Jones, S. "Unlicensed Broadcasting: Content and Conformity." *Journalism Quarterly* 71 (2), Summer 1994.

Katz, E. "Introduction: The State of the Art." In *Public Opinion and the Communication of Consent*, T. Glasser and C. Salmon, eds. New York: Guilford Press, 1995.

Keegan, C. "Qualitative Audience Research in Public Television." *Journal of Communication* 30 (3), Summer 1980.

Kossof, A. "Public Radio—Americans Want More." In *Radio—The Forgotten Me-*

dium, E. Pease and E. Dennis, eds. New Brunswick, NJ: Transaction Press, 1995.

Lashner, M. "The Role of Foundations in Public Broadcasting, Part 1: Development and Trends." *Journal of Broadcasting* 20 (4), Fall 1976.

———. "The Role of Foundations in Public Broadcasting, Part 2: The Ford Foundation." *Journal of Broadcasting* 21 (2), Spring 1977.

Leroy, D. "Who Watches Public Television." *Journal of Communication* 30 (3), Summer 1980.

McCain, T., and G. Lowe. "Localism in Western European Broadcasting: Untangling the Wireless." *Journal of Communication* 40 (1), Winter 1990.

McChesney, R. "Public Broadcasting in the Age of Communication Revolution." *Monthly Review* 47 (7), December 1995.

McFarland, D. "Up from Middle America: The Rise of Top-40." In *American Broadcasting: A Source Book on the History of Radio and Television*, L. Lichty and M. Topping, eds. New York: Hastings House, 1976.

McLeod, J., Z. Pan, and D. Rucinski. "Levels of Analysis in Public Opinion Research." In *Public Opinion and the Communication of Consent*, T. Glasser and C. Salmon, eds. New York: Guilford Press, 1995.

Mullally, D. "Radio: The Other Public Medium." *Journal of Communication* 30 (3), Summer 1980.

Murdock, G. "Large Corporations and the Control of the Communications Industries." In *Culture, Society and the Media*, M. Gurevitch, T. Bennett, J. Curran, and J. Woolacott, eds. London: Metheun, 1982.

———. "Citizens, Consumers and Public Culture." In *Media Cultures: Reappraising Transnational Media*, M. Skovmand and K. C. Schroder, eds. New York: Routledge, 1992.

———. "Communications and the Constitution of Modernity." *Media Culture and Society* 15 (4), October 1993.

Pearce, J., and J. Rosener. "Advisory Board Performance: Managing Ambiguity and Limited Commitment in Public Television." *Journal of Voluntary Action Research* 14 (4), 1985.

Perrow, C. "The Analysis of Goals in Complex Organizations." *American Sociological Review* 26 (6), December 1961.

Peters, J. "Satan and Savior: Mass Communication in Progressive Thought." *Critical Studies in Mass Communication* 6 (3), September 1989.

———. "The Gaps of Which Communication Is Made." *Critical Studies in Mass Communication* 11 (2), June 1994.

———. "Historical Tensions in the Concept of Public Opinion." In *Public Opinion and the Communication of Consent*, ed. T. Glasser and C. Salmon. New York: Guliford Press, 1995.

———. "Publicity and Pain: Self-Abstraction in Adam Smith's *Theory of Moral Sentiments*," *Public Culture* 7 (3), Spring 1995.

Peterson, R. "Measured Markets and Unknown Audiences: Case Studies from the Production and Consumption of Music." In *Audiencemaking: How the Media Create the Audience*, J. Ettema and D. Whitney, eds. Beverly Hills, CA: Sage, 1994.

Powell, W., and R. Friedkin. "Political and Organizational Influences on Public

Television Programming." In *Mass Communication Review Yearbook 1983*, E. Wartella and D. Whitney, eds. Beverly Hills: Sage, 1983.

Reeves, M., and T. Hoffer. "The Safe, Cheap and Known: A Content Analysis of the First (1974) PBS Program Cooperative." *Journal of Broadcasting* 20 (4), Fall 1976.

Rothenbuhler, E. "Commercial Radio as Communication." *Journal of Communication* 46 (1), Winter 1996.

Rothenbuhler, E., and T. McCourt. "Commercial Radio and Popular Music: Processes of Selection and Factors of Influence." In *Popular Music and Communication*, 2nd ed., J. Lull, ed. Newbury Park, CA: Sage, 1992.

Rowland, W., Jr. "Public Involvement: The Anatomy of a Myth." In *The Future of Public Broadcasting*, D. Cater and M. Nyham, eds. New York: Praeger, 1976.

———. "The Federal Regulatory and Policymaking Process." *Journal of Communication* 30 (3), Summer 1980.

———. "The Illusion of Fulfillment: Problems in the Broadcast Reform Movement and Notes on the Progressive Past." *Journalism Monographs*, no. 79, 1982.

———. "The Struggle for Self-Determination: Public Broadcasting, Policy Problems and Reform." In *Telecommunications Policy Handbook*, J. Schement, F. Gutierrez, and M. Sirbu, Jr., eds. New York: Praeger, 1982.

———. "Continuing Crisis in Public Broadcasting: A History of Disenfranchisement." *Journal of Broadcasting and Electronic Media* 30 (3), Summer 1986.

———. "Public Service Broadcasting in the United States: Its Mandate, Institutions and Conflicts." In *Public Service Broadcasting in a Multichannel Environment: The History and Survival of an Ideal*, R. Avery, ed. New York: Longman, 1993.

Rowland, W., Jr., and M. Tracy. "Worldwide Challenges to Public Service Broadcasting." *Journal of Communication* 40 (2), Spring 1990.

Salmon, C., and T. Glasser. "The Politics of Polling and the Limits of Consent." In *Public Opinion and the Communication of Consent*, T. Glasser and C. Salmon, eds. New York: Guilford Press, 1995.

Scannell, P. "Public Service Broadcasting and Modern Public Life." *Media, Culture and Society* 11 (2), April 1989.

Stavitsky, A. "Listening for Listeners: Educational Radio and Audience Research." *Journalism History* 19 (1), Spring 1993.

———. "The Changing Conception of Localism in U.S. Public Radio." *Journal of Broadcasting and Electronic Media* 38 (1), Winter 1994.

———. " 'Guys in Suits with Charts': Audience Research in U.S. Public Radio." *Journal of Broadcasting and Electronic Media* 39 (2), Spring 1995.

Stavitsky, A., and T. Gleason. "Alternative Things Considered: A Comparison of National Public Radio and Pacifica Radio News Coverage." *Journalism Quarterly* 71 (4), Winter 1994.

Tracy, M. "Beyond Governance: The Triumph of Populism and Parochialism in the 21st Century." *Javnost—The Public* 3 (2), Summer 1996.

Turner, V. "Liminality and Community." In *Culture and Society: Contemporary Debates*, A. Alexander and S. Seidman, eds. New York: Cambridge University Press, 1990.

INDUSTRY REPORTS AND PUBLICATIONS

Avery, R., P. Birdsall, and A. Rey. "Issues in Ascertaining the Different Needs of Urban and Rural Community Leaders." In *Six Experiments in Ascertainment Methodology*, Office of Communication Research, ed. Washington, DC: CPB, 1977.

Carnegie Commission on Educational Television. *Public Television: A Program for Action.* New York: Bantam Books, 1967.

Carnegie Commission on the Future of Public Broadcasting. *A Public Trust: The Report of the Carnegie Commission on the Future of Public Broadcasting.* New York: Bantam Books, 1979.

Corporation for Public Broadcasting. *Public Participation in Public Broadcasting.* Washington, DC: CPB, 1978.

———. *The Public Radio Handbook: Starting and Operating a Public Radio Station.* Washington, DC: CPB, 1979.

———. *An Overview of Community Service Grants for Public Broadcasting.* Washington, DC: CPB, 1980.

———. *Five Year Plan for Public Telecommunications.* Washington, DC: CPB, 1981.

———. *From Wasteland to Oasis: A Quarter Century of Sterling Programming.* Washington, DC: CPB, 1992.

Frischknecht, L. *The Policy for Public Radio Assistance of the Corporation for Public Broadcasting, 1969–1978.* Washington, DC: CPB, 1978.

Giovannoni, D., T. Thomas, and T. Clifford. *Public Radio Programming Strategies: A Report on the Programming Stations Broadcast and the People They Seek to Serve.* Washington, DC: CPB, 1992.

Herman W. Land Associates. *The Hidden Medium: Educational Radio.* New York: National Educational Radio, National Association of Educational Broadcasters, 1967.

Holt, S. *The Public Radio Study.* Washington, DC: CPB, 1969.

———. *Islands in the Stream: Some Thoughts on Public Radio Programming.* Washington, DC: NPR, 1986.

Katzman, S., and N. Katzman. *Public Radio Programming by Category: Fiscal Year 1978.* Washington, DC: CPB, 1979.

McCain, T., C. Hofstetter, N. James, and J. Hawkins. "Method Dependent Opinion Leadership: Implications for Ascertainment of Black Community Needs for Public Television Stations." In *Six Experiments in Ascertainment Methodology*, Office of Communications Research, ed. Washington, DC: CPB, 1977.

National Public Radio. Annual Reports. Washington, DC: NPR, 1975–1998.

———. *The NPR Audience.* Washington, DC: NPR, 1981.

Public Radio Program Directors Association. *The Public Radio Program Director's Handbook.* Olney, MD: PRPD, 1994.

Shooshan, H., and L. Arnheim. *Public Broadcasting.* Washington, DC: Benton Foundation, 1989.

Siemering, W. *National Public Radio Purposes.* Washington, DC: National Public Radio, 1970.

Smith, A., P. Nester, and D. Pulford. "Volunteer Ascertainment Panels." In *Six*

Experiments in Ascertainment Methodology, Office of Communication Research, ed. Washington, DC: CPB, 1977.

Southern Educational Communications Association. *Editorial Integrity in Public Broadcasting: Proceedings of the Wingspread Conference*. Washington, DC: CPB, 1985.

Thomas, T., and T. Clifford. *The Public Radio Program Marketplace*. Washington, DC: CPB, 1985.

Twentieth Century Fund Task Force on Public Television. *Quality Time? The Report of the Twentieth Century Fund Task Force on Public Television*. New York: Twentieth Century Fund Press, 1993.

DISSERTATIONS

Garry, K. "The History of National Public Radio: 1974–1977." Dissertation, Carbondale: University of Southern Illinois at Carbondale, 1982.

Haney, J. "A History of the Merger of National Public Radio and the Association of Public Radio Stations." Dissertation, Iowa City: University of Iowa, 1981.

Kirkish, J. "A Descriptive History of America's First National Public Radio Network: National Public Radio, 1970 to 1974." Dissertation, Ann Arbor: University of Michigan, 1980.

McCauley, M. "From the Margins to the Mainstream: The History of National Public Radio." Dissertation, Madison: University of Wisconsin, 1997.

MANUSCRIPT COLLECTIONS

Lee Frischknecht Papers. National Public Broadcasting Archives, College Park, Maryland.

Samuel Holt Papers. National Public Broadcasting Archives, College Park, Maryland.

Frank Mankiewicz Papers. National Public Broadcasting Archives, College Park, Maryland.

National Public Radio Audience Research Papers. National Public Broadcasting Archives, College Park, Maryland.

Index

About the Author

TOM McCOURT is Assistant Professor of Communications at the University of Illinois at Springfield. His research interests include media history, communication technology, music, and cultural studies, with particular focus on the historical relationship of technology and the public sphere.

ISBN 0-275-96358-6

9 780275 963583

90000>

HARDCOVER BAR CODE